◆ HOW TO ROCK CLIMB SERIES ◆

Advanced Rock Climbing

◆ HOW TO ROCK CLIMB SERIES ◆

Advanced Rock Climbing

John Long
Craig Luebben

CHOCKSTONE PRESS, INC.
Conifer, Colorado

COVER PHOTO: Tommy Caldwell on a Wiggins route (12a), Indian Creek, Utah.
Craig Luebben photo.

BACK COVER PHOTO: Jo Whitford on Black Angel (11), Tuolumne Meadows, California.
Greg Epperson photo.

All other photographs by Craig Luebben unless otherwise credited.

ISBN 1-57540-075-8

PUBLISHED AND DISTRIBUTED BY
Chockstone Press, Inc.
Post Office Box 1269
Conifer, Colorado 80433

OTHER BOOKS IN THIS SERIES:
How to Rock Climb!
Climbing Anchors
Sport Climbing
Big Walls
Flash Training!
I Hate to Train Performance Guide for Climbers
Knots for Climbers
Nutrition for Climbers
Building Your Own Indoor Climbing Wall
Gym Climb
Clip and Go!
Self-Rescue
More Climbing Anchors
Top-Roping
How to Climb 5.12!

Acknowledgements

ADVANCED ROCK CLIMBING

JOHN LONG
CRAIG LUEBBEN

Special thanks to Steph Davis and Carol Adair, the ever-patient models; Gary Ryan, for reviewing the Face Climbing chapter; Alan Lester, who made valuable suggestions per crack climbing technique; Herm Feissner, who offered feedback on the Sport Climbing and Training chapters; Topher Donahue, who reviewed the Crack Climbing, Anchors, Belaying and Rappelling, and Adventure Climbing chapters, and added many useful comments; Mike and Tommy Caldwell, who contributed beneficial words of advice on training; Alain Comeau, who made many valuable additions and corrections to the Self- rescue chapter; Stuart Dietrich, Chuck Rosemond, Millard Jones, and Paul Beiser, my (C.L.) clever self-rescue course students who studied the Self-rescue chapter and pointed out the fuzz. I (C.L) also thank Kennan Harvey, who stepped in with his cameras and body for a marathon photo session in Little Cottonwood Canyon; Tom Kelley, Steve and Becky McCorkel, Jake Latendresse, Rob Poukas, David Vartanian and Mike Hickey, who I photographed at Horsetooth Reservoir; Craig DeMartino, who contributed some desert offwidth photos; The Mountain Shop of Fort Collins for providing gear to photograph, and Silvia DeVito, who kept me home long enough to finish this book.

And I (C.L.) personally thank John Long, aka Largo, for this, the third book I've worked on with him. My job on Advanced Rock Climbing was to forge out a rough draft, to be fleshed out and polished by Largo. Largo used the telephone like a whip, a prod and boot. I'd be off on climbing trips, "doing research," and return home to phone messages like: "Aye, carumba Luebben, where the hell are you this time?" "You're slower than a glacier" and "Craig Luebben? John Long. You're fired!" Three years after beginning, and two years past deadline, I'm happy to finish *Advanced Rock Climbing*, mostly so Largo will stop hounding me. Thanks, Largo, for hanging in there with me.

This book is dedicated to all rock climbers looking to pick up some new tricks.

I (J.L.) dedicate this book to Ms. Mona Miller, who has taught me vital lessons on how to become a human being.

WARNING: CLIMBING IS A SPORT WHERE YOU MAY BE SERIOUSLY INJURED OR DIE

READ THIS BEFORE YOU USE THIS BOOK.

This is an instruction book to rock climbing, a sport which is inherently dangerous. You should not depend solely on information gleaned from this book for your personal safety. Your climbing safety depends on your own judgment based on competent instruction, experience, and a realistic assessment of your climbing ability.

There is no substitute for personal instruction in rock climbing and climbing instruction is widely available. You should engage an instructor or guide to learn climbing safety techniques. If you misinterpret a concept expressed in this book, you may be killed or seriously injured as a result of the misunderstanding. Therefore, the information provided in this book should be used only to supplement competent personal instruction from a climbing instructor or guide. Even after you are proficient in climbing safely, occasional use of a climbing instructor is a safe way to raise your climbing standard and learn advanced techniques.

There are no warranties, either expressed or implied, that this instruction book contains accurate and reliable information. There are no warranties as to fitness for a particular purpose or that this book is merchantable. Your use of this book indicates your assumption of the risk of death or serious injury as a result of climbing's risks and is an acknowledgement of your own sole responsibility for your climbing safety.

*Ancient Arts,
Fisher Towers, Utah*

C O N T E N T S

ADVANCED ROCK CLIMBING

JOHN LONG
CRAIG LUEBBEN

Mia Axon working on Sphinx Crack (13b/c), South Platte, Colorado.

Introduction

Sticky boots, spring loaded camming devices, "working" a route—these things are now passé but were unheard of twenty years ago. And twenty years is a short time in the history of rock climbing, though ample for the sport to redefine itself. Yet for all the changes, certain ever-evolving techniques apply to all climbing at the expert level, techniques that help us climb harder, longer, faster, safer, and more efficiently—our focus in *Advanced Rock Climbing*.

This book was written for those who have completed, or are in the process of completing, the lengthy task of getting "dialed in," working through the grades, picking off prized test pieces and finally, establishing routes of your own. Looking back, I (J.L.) understand that my own journey into the upper grades could have gone much faster—to say nothing of avoiding a string of spectacular falls—if I wasn't half the time trying to reinvent the wheel. I had no access to the body of knowledge about advanced technique, procedures and equipment. Nor did anyone ever sit me down and say, for instance: take a day off when you're sore; if the fall is harmless, don't stop in the middle of a crux lieback and slot a nut—go for it; knowing how to rest is as important as the ability to yard on tweakers; use the heel and toe jam on offwidths instead of a godzilla arm bar; rack your nuts this way and your biners that way; take enough water; and all the rest. All told, crossing the threshold into the realm of higher numbers and wilder adventures was as tricky and demanding a task as getting up those first few climbs, when every move felt like I was trying to steal cheese from a set mousetrap. In light of this, we've skewed this book toward those crucial things that many climbers learn the hard way, through trial and error. While we can't know how many tricks a given climber understands, we trust that the experienced climber is fluent with all the fundamental techniques that this book builds upon.

Sport climbing, with its emphasis on short, relatively benign, technically demanding routes, dominates the climbing scene. While we've devoted considerable time to the particular demands of sport climbing, we have not limited ourselves to the narrow borders of "clip-and-go" routes. Recently, adventure climbing has enjoyed a revival, with many heading out to towering desert spires, into alpine areas, off to China, Indonesia and the Caribbean, where a perlon rope was never before seen. In light of this, we've tried to cover the climbing game at large. And this is a broad canvas. The playing field varies dramatically from route to route and area to area—from the radical gymnastic routes at Rifle or New River Gorge to 4,000-foot walls on the frosted ramparts of Nameless Tower in Pakistan. Each milieu requires special knowledge and abilities—the very stuff of *Advanced Rock Climbing*.

Tommy Caldwell, belayed by his father Mike, on Renaissance Wall (12b), Lumpy Ridge, Colorado.

Face Climbing

To climb well on real rock, you must log countless miles on real rock. Period. For any climber looking to jump into higher grades, a combination of bouldering and roped climbing builds the repertoire of moves crucial for reading the rock quickly and discovering a workable sequence for a given route. Gym climbing builds the strength and technique required for face climbing. However, on real rock the holds aren't blue, green, red, and so forth. Both the holds and the moves are more subtle.

As we "wire" a particular sort of move or sequence, our brain stores the pattern of nerve impulses that it transmits to the muscles. The next time we encounter similar moves, our brain replays the imprint—the gift of experience. When we're scared or pumped, however, our brain tenses and we stumble recalling the pattern. Lost is that liquid, "been there before" touch just when we need it most.

One thing cannot be overstated: Climbing with a relaxed mind and body is half the campaign. We've all thrashed up a route, then returned later and in no better shape, waltzed over it. How so? Our minds were "right" the second time. And "right" always means relaxed and confident. More on this later.

Power and technique are requirements for climbing at a top level. Deficiency in either results in an imbalance that will limit our success. Many of the strongest climbers I've seen were poor leaders owing to sloppy and impatient technique. Conversely, I've seen climbers who flowed like a Keats ode but lacked the might to bag strenuous routes. Abundant cranking power and endurance inspire confidence, allowing us to stay relaxed and keep the flow going. Along with vast amounts of climbing to hone technique, a dedicated strength-training program is crucial to achieve our potential. But everything begins and ends with technique; if we don't have it, we'll be paddling our feet like a mallard duck. And for face climbing, technique starts with our feet.

SPLENDID FEET

Apt footwork translates to efficiency. And without climbing efficiently, we'll have no chance on the desperate routes no matter how strong we are. Foot control is key—putting our foot precisely on a hold, weighting it, and keeping it steady while we move. While slabs are scorned in sport climbing circles, they remain the finest medium for developing and maintaining the foot control required for climbs of all angles. Most of us broke in on the slabs. The experienced climber periodically returns to the slabs to polish footwork. (A valuable practice is to end each day with some edging/friction work. No

Lizz Grenard "Throwin' the Tortuga" (11b),
Cayman Brac, British West Indies.

matter how blown our fingers and arms may be, we can always paddle up a moderate slab.)

On grim slabs we can't simply pull down and call it good because often there's squat to pull down on. We have to use our feet, and use them perfectly. Splendid footwork demands concentration and balance; focus on footwork and good foot-work will become instinctive. Practice keeps our instincts sharp.

For those marooned in areas that either have no slabs or no rock at all, apply the ideas of foot control to your gym workouts. We rarely have to place our foot precisely on plastic, but develop this habit anyway. Once it becomes instinct, once you start taking that extra millisecond to toe just the right place in just the right way, you'll in effect be practicing actual rock technique while pulling plastic.

Spotless Sole

It's amazing the kooky rituals climbers perform before trying a difficult redpoint; then they neglect to check the soles of their boots. We always clean the dirt off our shoes before stepping off the ground. Sticky rubber grabs dust, gravel and dirt, but it won't grab the rock well unless we scour the grime off the sole. I (J.L) remember taking a skidder off a route called "Science Friction." I was stumped why I'd pinged, for one second I felt glorious, and the next second, was off. I checked the soles of my shoes to find that the left sole was soiled with raisins and tuna oil and such crud picked up from a squashed lunch bag in my pack. A quick wash job with plain water, or spit, followed by drying the soles will greatly increase our boot's friction. (Some climbers spit on the soles and frantically rub them together until they've melted a veneer off the synthetic rubber, causing them to stick together. This does not make the boots stick better to the rock, but it's a thorough way to clean the soles.)

Once the boots are clean, many boulderers place a small carpet, or "sketch pad," on the ground at the base of the problem as a starting platform. Some pads, often hilariously customized, feature thick foam for cushioning bouldering falls. Sketch pads work equally well as launching pads for tough sport climbs, where a spotless sole is vital.

Concrete Foundation

In a general way, let's consider a typical face climbing sequence and examine the details. All of us have executed this sequence thousands of times. Sports specialists insist, however, that when we build an intellectual model of instinctive motions, and study it closely, we can often spot our weaknesses. So picture this: we have two reasonable footholds, our hands are well positioned, and it's time to move our feet up again.

PHASE 1: First we scan the rock for the best footholds. Position is often more important than size. To better support our weight, we utilize holds in line with our legs, rather than off to the side (unless stemming, liebacking, traversing, or

Ball edging

Toe edging

Front pointing

Back stepping

Smearing

Heel rest

Instep rest

drop kneeing). For ideal stability, we try and keep our feet about shoulder width apart, but we're not rigid with this notion. Adapting to available footholds is key. When matching feet on the same hold, we compensate balance, foot strength and Fred Astair dexterity. A series of shorter steps is usually better than a high-step, which requires extra strength and balance. And if the high-step blows off—as it sometimes will—we'll likely rasp the hell out of our shins and knees. The legs on some active climbers/boulderers look as though they've just crawled across Tioga Pass in swim trunks.

All this to describe simply moving a foot up to a hold and standing on it. And yet for such a basic movement we can go wrong in numerous ways because a climb is comprised of hundreds of moves, not just one; and we usually go wrong with the manner in which we integrate one move to the next. Key factors include spotting the hold before moving our foot, lest we'll be searching for footholds midstep—sort of like trying to find the deploy handle on a parachute after we've leaped from the plane. Not good. We can't simply pull down and hope for the best and expect to find it. Not on real rock. Ideally, we locate both the left and right footholds before moving either foot, so we can plan the moves and quickly execute them. This is the biggest mistake made by those who climb primarily on plastic and have become addicted to clasping and pulling down mindlessly. The more we plan and the quicker we adopt needed changes in our plan, the more efficiently we will climb.

When set to move a foot up, we shift our hips and get our weight over the other foot. To initiate motion with the least effort, we bounce slightly off the foot we're moving, and thrust our hips in the direction of movement (unless the footholds are minute).

PHASE 2: We zero in with laser precision and place our foot precisely on the best part of the hold. Whether we *edge* on the ball of our foot, the inside of our big toe, or the outside of our foot just behind the little toe (back-stepping) depends on the size and shape of the hold, the move we're setting up for, and our personal style. Occasionally we'll edge on the front of our shoe (frontpointing) when standing in small pockets or edging on overhanging faces. Here, we "toe poke" the holds, effectively keeping our feet on the rock while relieving some weight off our guns.

We may also choose to *smear* the edge. If our feet are screaming and we have a grand edge, we may stand on our heel or instep (either the outside edge or the inside edge, whichever feels more natural) to give our feet and calves a break. If there is no pronounced edge, we'll have to smear a rough patch of rock, low-angled divot, or other supporting feature, getting as much rubber as possible in contact with the rock to optimize friction. We'll keep our heels relatively low when smearing to maximize contact area and minimize calf fatigue. However we position our shoe, consciously pressing our toes into the rock will increase purchase on tenuous holds, especially with slippers or soft-soled shoes.

If no hold exists, we can gain some purchase and balance by smearing our shoe rand or toes into the wall. Hopefully, our other foothold is better. If our foot starts to butter off, we push our shoe more into the wall. This puts a bit more weight on our hands, but it also helps keep our foot in place so our mitts don't have to support the whole show. The holdless smear can't bear much weight, but it can help stabilize our position—say, when we're flagging a leg for balance.

We're barely into the second phase, have barely gotten our foot on the next hold and already it's clear that the process is anything but cut and dry. Every move must be done in a particular way that obtains the best purchase via the least energy, and sets us up for what's next.

For this review to be valuable, think back to some memorable falls you've taken. The secret is to envision exactly what your body position was when you popped. Visualize the falls in order and search for a pattern in your personal "fall record." For example, if your feet keep blowing off, why? You'll have to work through this yourself, but it's essential that you come up with some pattern to your falls and failures lest you won't be able to discover the weaknesses in your technique. The "phase" commentaries give us a reference point to ideal technique; studying our fall record divulges the specific manner of our form breaks.

Rand smear/flag

PHASE 3: Moving on: We smoothly shift weight onto the foothold and rock our hips back to center our weight over both feet. The hold and the angle of the rock will determine how much weight it can bear. If the foothold is decent and the rock is gently angled, we load our entire weight on the foothold, then move our other foot up. Often we'll move both feet up before repositioning our hands.

This is the phase we most often bungle—fiddle around trying to get our feet set, can't, burn our fingers and either a toe blows off or we pump out. This generally means that we're struggling to crack the sequence at this transition phase. Our flow dissipates and we get desperate. Then we're stuck and can only hold on for the inevitable wrencher. Think through your fall record and see if this is true for you. If so, you need to drop down a grade and get your flow back, or develop it if you've never had it at your top grade. Climbing over your head can provide breakthroughs, but it can also cause backsliding if you keep failing without ever getting the feeling of mastery and flow that comes with cruising pitches well within your comfort range. If you feel you're reading the sequences correctly, and still blow off at this stage, your footwork needs attention. Again, dropping down a grade, or spending time on slabs, are the fastest ways to hone footwork and break the pattern.

PHASE 4: Once set, we keep our foot absolutely steady on

The foot drop

Edge roll

the hold. As our body moves, we hinge our ankle to keep the foot motionless. On smaller holds, the slightest movement can send our foot sketching off. Unless absolutely necessary—as required for extreme reaches—we avoid extending off our toe while reaching for the next hold. Doing so causes our heel to raise and lever our toes off the hold as our weight rocks up on the edge.

So goes the standard progression for our feet.

Light Switch

If the footholds are meager, we "milk" them. Even the slightest wrinkle can make a difference. If few footholds exist, we'll often *match feet* (sharing a single hold with both feet), or *switch feet* (replacing one foot on a hold with the other). This is especially common on artificial walls, where the features are generally sparse. A couple of tricks work well here.

One is the "foot drop." Place one foot right above the other, then slide the lower foot off the hold and drop the upper one onto the hold. Miss the hold, drop into space.

Another method is when we're edging and the foothold is big. Rotate (slowly) the first foot onto its frontpoint to create space for the other foot. Frontpoint with the new foot on the newly created space, then slide or pop the first foot off the hold.

Lastly, rotate the new foot onto its inside edge. If neither of these techniques works, or seems likely, we might take the first foot off the hold and smear it, then quickly hop the new foot onto the hold. The last and least desired technique requires us to momentarily support our weight with our hands, and perform a short shuffle step, hopping one foot off the hold and booting the other foot onto it.

With all of these techniques, we're usually dealing with fractions of an inch, so precision and control are crucial. The slightest miscalculation and we're out of there.

How does all of this square with our personal fall records? We're starting to narrow the field, so if a pattern hasn't emerged, we're either bungling every single move, or we're speed-reading this. We already know how to climb. Probably damn well. This discussion will help us to the extent that we contrast it to our fall record and see where we have gone wrong, where we need work. It is not enough to say, "I got to the crux move and couldn't crank it." We must isolate the move, and determine the exact phase in which we blew off. In technical terms, to simply say we pitched off the crux is gibberish. If we couldn't pull hard enough on the holds, fair enough. We need to get stronger. But it's far more likely that we're having a technical problem with a specific kind of move. Until we recognize what move—or moves—throw us, we cannot practice it on the boulders and in the gym.

If you take the time to think through your fall record, perhaps take a few notes and scribble out a few diagrams, a pattern will invariably arise. This is slow going, but the dividends are well worth the time invested to discover your weaknesses.

We all have them, and they tend to show themselves during some particular phase in our movements. Spot the phase, and you can start correcting it not only on routes, but also in the gym and on the boulders.

Steppin' Through

Switching and matching on footholds can be a near-miss activity, especially when the holds are small. Often when traversing we can increase security and eliminate complex moves with a *step through*. We cross one foot past the other, either in front of or behind the leg (whichever feels most natural). This sets us up for the next sideways foot movement, which uncrosses our legs. When stepping through, the crossing foot often backsteps (using the outside edge of your boot). Occasionally we find it best to shuffle our feet to avoid "barber-pole" legs (crossed up legs). Balance, precision and agility are required, especially when stepping through on the outside edge. The tendency is to lean in. Don't. We must stay light on our feet, even if we have to yank a little harder on the holds.

In my (J.L.) own climbing I can look back and see that while I've negotiated most step-throughs okay, four or five times I've shredded my tips in the process. That means I chronically overgrip, which means I don't feel comfortable with this move and need to practice it and gain confidence enough to let my feet do the work, rather than yarding past. How are you with step throughs? How can you improve?

Sketchin'

We've all been there. We need to move a foot up, but we can't afford to lose its purchase. Hail, hail the foot sketch, where we hop our foot up in several short moves, briefly paddling or "sketching" our foot off the rock, trying to get that extra umph that will gain us the promised land. Used sparingly the foot sketch can get us past some demonic rock. Used regularly and we'll get strong as sin from using bad form— and still won't climb any harder.

Hooked

On steep terrain the *heel hook* allows us to use our leg as a third arm, thus relieving weight on our hands. While hanging from handholds, we reach our foot up and grab an overhead hold with our heel, trying to set the heel onto an edge, depression, knob, rugosity, hueco, flake, crater, chickenhead, bollard, slot, cranny,

Stepping through

gargoyle, hollow or horn, however wee or rounded. If possible, we torque our toes against an opposing feature to lock our heel in place. Draping our heel on the hold is not enough. We pull with our leg (hamstring) just as we pull with our arms on a hold. Security is gained by the continuous force applied

to the heel by the pulling leg.

Shoes with a tight and sturdy heel rand work best for hooking. With loose fitting boots, we heel hook at our own peril. Heel hooking with slippers is also dicey. At Red Rocks, I (J.L.) stripped the slipper clean off my foot trying to hook a spike, and ripped a vicious flapper in my heel.

Toe hooking also gives us an extra arm. Hooking the toes and pulling with the legs on slanting edges often keep us in balance when having to lean sideways on vertical to slightly overhanging rock. We can likewise toe hook overhead. Either way, a good toe hook can take weight off our arms, and negate the barndoor effect when gravity wants to spin us on the holds.

On precipitous turf, when encountering a pocket or crack slightly smaller than the length of our foot, a FOOT CAM can sometimes shift additional weight off our guns and onto our legs. Place the foot into the feature toes first, then pull up with the toes to cam the foot fast. Remember to pull with your leg to get full value from an overhead foot cam. A stiff shoe works best.

Foot hooking

HAPPY HOUR

Of all the bars in all the world, a *knee bar* is the best for hanging out on steep rock. Knee bars work in large pockets and those places where opposing planes exist (under roofs). To work a knee bar, we put our foot on the lower hold and slide our knee into the pocket. Pull back on the knee to cam it against the top of the pocket. If the gap between holds is too big, we extend our toes, thus increasing the length of our leg and allowing us to brace our knee against the upper feature. A charitable knee bar often bestows a no hands rest. If possible, we switch legs to milk the rest, but we understand that our

Foot cam

abs, thighs and calves will work fiendishly to suspend our torso; and whenever the abs sheathing our diaphragm are taut, it's hard to breathe and nearly impossible to fully recover. It is sometimes possible to secure a double knee bar, but it's often about as comfortable as sitting on a rhino horn. With a stout knee bar, the opposite leg often acts like a tail for balance and flagging.

A large, incut bucket can sometimes be hooked with the upper part of our calf, just below the knee, to get all the weight off our hands. This technique is usually painful, and is ludicrous if we're wearing shorts.

Knee bar

WHAT FOUR

A dynamic (or "dyno") is no longer the only alternative for spanning long stretches of featureless rock. A *figure four* might do the trick. Here, we hang from the hold and with our legendary abs in Tarzan mode, swing our opposite leg (left arm/right leg) over the arm, hooking our elbow with our knee. We twist our body into the rock, pull with one leg and drive with the other, making a controlled reach for the next hold. In extreme cases (anytime we use the figure four is an extreme case), the knee is wrapped over our wrist to gain greater reach. This technique is most common on plastic, where natural features are few between the bolt-on holds. World Cup ace Francoise Legrande once made four consecutive figure fours in an event he went on to win. Its merits are that it is static and very often reversible, much unlike the committing dyno. Oddly enough, this extreme maneuver can take the piss out of some of the most grievous dynos. It also puts withering stress on our finger tendons, so we experiment on a jug before trying to crank the figure four off a tweaker.

Have you performed all of these maneuvers flawlessly, every time? Have you ever fallen at all? If you answered yes and no, you don't need this book, or any book on climbing. If

Calf hook

Figure 4

Herm Feissner cranking thin holds on "Third Millenium" (13d/14a), The Monastery, Colorado.

you're like the rest of us, you can gain insight into your weaknesses by studying your fall record and determining where your problems lie. Oftentimes the best results come from simply practicing the maneuver that has thrown you in the past. The trick, of course, is to discover what particular techniques have given you trouble so you can concentrate on your weaknesses. Practicing our strengths is fun, but will not improve our climbing much, if any. Identifying our weaknesses and working on them is the least amount of fun, but a certain way to improve.

HANDHOLDS

On slabs, we need our hands mostly for balance, so the dinkiest edge can feel like a hitching post. As the angle steepens, handholds become critical, as does our contact strength. Whatever the angle, we always guard against overgripping, while striving to stay relaxed and light on our hands.

Overgripping is a quick and certain way to pump out. I (J.L.) know because I chronically overgrip, and have to consciously "think feet" during every move of every climb.

When selecting handholds, we plan ahead, trying to envision the best sequence. Ideally, we keep our hands above our shoulders, about shoulder width—or slightly more—apart. The further our hands move laterally, or below our shoulders, the more power needed. The exception is on slabs and when liebacking, where our hands are often positioned at, or below, our shoulders. On popular routes, spangled chalk marks show the way, so we can "climb by numbers." But understand that even worthless holds will be chalked. Beware of chalked "sucker holds".

We'll generally *cling* when grasping an edge, dancing our fingers along the hold to find the most positive grip. Sometimes we find a feature for our palm to sit on, adding security. Once we have the most positive grasp, we don't dink around—we pull down and move through. "Hesitation blues" leave us pumped, discouraged and hanging on the rope. Nonetheless they are difficult to overcome when pushing our limits and unsure of the sequence.

If the edge or pocket supports our fingers out to the second joint (or further), our hand lies flat against the wall, sparing our fingers from battling their own leverage. Here, we try and use a large *open grip*, since our thumb will be negligible unless we can use an oblique pinch. With the *open grip* our fingers follow the contours of the rock, rather than projecting out from it, and thus avoid the nuclear stress created by crimping. If the hold is rounded, slopey, or if it's a pocket, the open grip may be our only option. As the holds thin, we not only have less to hold onto, but the leverage on our fingers increases dramatically. This is thumb territory.

When *crimping* smaller holds, we nestle the fingers close together, and wrap our thumb over the index finger. Because the thumb lies flat against the wall—even on small edges—it weathers less leverage than the fingers. The thumb is also our strongest "finger," and adds might to the crimp. Too much crimping can smoke our finger joints and tendons, so many active climbers favor the open grip, and spend hours in the gym trying to master it. We avoid crimping in favor of the open grip whenever possible. For example, if training on finger or campus boards, we use only holds that we can open hand. Open hand training greatly improves our contact strength, and eventually enables us to open hand what we'd normally crimp. When cranking on tiny pockets or crimpy holds—the most likely terrain to hear the tragic tendon pop —it's wise to support the finger tendons by taping. To improve

Open grip

Crimp (thumbs!)

Tips hold, notice the high leverage on the fingers

Taping the fingers

Open grip

Vertical grip, grim

Fingernail cling, very grim

Various pinches

blood flow, remove the tape immediately after climbing.

The *vertical grip* is torturous and rarely used. It does minimize the leverage on our fingers when grasping a razor edge—the very edge that will carve our tips into weeping stubs of pemmican if we overuse this technique. This grip works well if we have a vertically oriented pocket or edge with a positive lip. We bend our fingers at both joints and pull straight down on the hold with the tips of our fingers. On sharp edges the effect resembles having knifeblades driven under our fingernails. Feel free to grimace.

For extremely bald slabs, the *fingernail cling*, with the fingers oriented in the *vertical grip* position, and the fingernails hooked on micro-edges or crystals—as abusive as it sounds—may be our ticket. Keep the fingernails short, or risk having them fold back on themselves—an event no less comforting than getting kicked in the balls. I've seen willowy little ladies use this grip effectively, but the vertical grip holds little promise for a corn-fed man.

A slight *pinch* with the thumb can add security to a tenuous grip, particularly if the hold depends more on skin friction than a positive edge. The thumb usually pinches in opposition to the fingers, but it may pinch into the side of the hold, ninety degrees or so from the direction the fingers are pulling. The pinch is invaluable when pulling out on the hold ("rock lobster"), a standard move to keep feet pressing into scant holds. Sometimes all we get is a nipple of rock, which we can pinch between our thumb and the side (normally at the second knuckle) of our index finger.

On sharp or blunt arêtes, or smaller mini-arêtes, we can gain some purchase by pinching our hand around the corner. Here, our fingers work in opposition with the palm of our hand, and the thumb may or may not be useful.

Palming works in a variety of situations: to gain opposition against our other hand and foot in a dihedral; to mantel down on a shelf; and to grab slopey holds above our head. Sloping, rounded holds, the scourge of face climbing, are hideously insecure, and if we sweat one single drop—*ping!*—we're off. Palm these holds, and look for features on the rock—something to hook our fingers or the meaty part of our palm on, or anything to pinch. Any wart or nubbin will improve security when palming. If the climbing is desperate, cool, dry condi-

Palming

tions can make the difference between breezing up the route and getting spanked.

Occasionally we can pull a *thumb wrap* with the thumb over a positive edge and the fingers stacked atop the thumb. Owing to the thumb's strength, this configuration can be very powerful. It also gives our fingers a break.

On large holds, we can ease strain on our forearms by wrapping our wrist so the heel of our hand hooks the hold. The *wrist wrap* works in limited circumstances, but when useful, we shift the weight from our forearms and onto our bones. The wrist wrap is most practical as a rest position; it's difficult to pull on to gain height. It's most often used on buckets. Rare, but also useful as a rest on huge holds is the *forearm wrap*, where you hook your forearm over the bucket.

On smaller, positive knobs we can sometimes rest our forearms by wrapping the pinky side of our hand over the hold. This technique works especially well on rounded holds.

When reviewing these techniques and movements that we know so well, what aspect gives you the most trouble? How does your fall record factor in? Where do you need work?

Thumb wrap

Forearm wrap

Wrist wrap

Pinky wrap

Pocket Rocket

Pockets

Pockets abound on limestone, dolomite and welded tuff, and also appear in granite and sandstone. Much of modern sport climbing involves pocket pulling. Pockets range from shallow, one-finger dents to mini-caves that we can wheedle inside and snatch a few Zzz's. It's nearly impossible to judge the caliber of a pocket until we grab it. Large pockets, (larger than our hand) are often called "huecos" (pronounced wacos)— Spanish for holes—and provide the name for the bouldering paradise at Hueco Tanks, Texas.

When clasping pockets, we feel around inside to find the deepest part. Some shoot off to the side or expand upwards and are best used as sidepulls and underclings. One-finger pockets ("monodoigts") offer the grimmest in pocket pulling. They'll also give us a detached tendon if we're not careful. If the mono is vertically teardropped, we might stack our middle finger on top of our index finger for added might. If the pocket accepts two fingers (a "bidoigt") using the middle and the ring fingers balances the load on the hand, though the shape of the pocket often dictates use of index and middle fingers. If the pocket is deep, positive and large enough for three or four fingers, we're in tall cotton. Bomber pockets often appear when most needed, and nothing—well, almost nothing—feels better. As we advance our hands, we remember where the pockets are for our feet, as it's difficult to see them from above.

Perfect Match

On bigger handholds, or when there are no other handholds, we'll often *match* hands on the same hold. If the hold is generous, matching is simple. We leave a spot open for the second hand. We'll sometimes want to cross hands when matching, to set up for a sideways reach. Smaller holds are tricky to match on, and small fingers are an advantage. We somehow must momentarily share the hold with both hands. Occasionally we might stack one set of fingers atop the other to share a small edge. If the hold is only big enough to accommodate one hand at a time, switching is often dicey and taxing. If we can put, say, two fingers of the supporting hand on the hold, we try and create some space for the fingers of the other hand. In dire straits we might "walk" the fingers of one hand off the hold, one at a time, while walking those of the

Matching hands

other hand on, shuffling one finger at a time in a centipede progression. With experience we will better read the sequence and go with "cross-through" moves that usually save the time and energy wasted on grueling matches.

Again, the value of reviewing moves that we all know by heart is to reflect back on our fall record—or anytime we've had problems—and figure out why. The review serves mainly as a trigger to summon up those memories of when we've thrashed, and perhaps give insight as to a

better way to climb. To get optimal benefit from this material, we can't just browse, we must continually refer to our own experience. The topics covered so far contain information common to all experienced climbers. What is not common and is particular to each climber is how well or how poorly you have consistently performed the techniques so far discussed. Only you can determine that. You must conduct your own investigation and carefully think through things for any of this to pay off.

Switching hands

BODY POSITION

Without correct body position, the best footwork won't take us far. As we climb, our posture should constantly shift to minimize the weight on our hands and keep it over our feet and to improve the direction of pull on the holds. Easy enough to say, not always easy to see. The tiny shift in a stance that turns a problem from impossible to doable is often a subtle one, tricky to discern. Awareness of our center of gravity will help us adopt the optimal body posture.

If the holds allow, we (normally) climb with both hands and feet about shoulder width apart, with the body forming a relaxed "X". This is the most natural and stable posture and taxes our muscles the least. However if all climbs presented a ladder of holds that allowed us to climb in an X, we'd grow bored with the whole shebang. The most interesting, as well as strenuous, moves are often those that force us out of the X position.

"X" body position

On slabs, we stay balanced with our center of gravity directly over our feet—like a tightrope walker. Only with an upright torso is our balance keen, do our feet make good purchase, and can we see the footholds. On small footholds, if we lean in too far (typically when we're reaching), our center of gravity shifts, our balance falters, our feet sketch and we skid off. Plus, we can't see the footholds when we're leaning in. If both holds are good, our weight should be equally distributed between them—unless one leg is straight and the other bent, in which case the straight leg should bear most of our weight to relieve the quad of our bent leg. We might have to lean in to make an otherwise hopeless reach. Here we clasp hard and keep pressing our feet into the wall to maintain contact.

As the slab steepens, our hips and shoulders move closer to the wall to keep our center over our feet. If we need to

Stand directly over your feet on slabs (left). Leaning in too much will send your feet sliding. (right)

Turnout

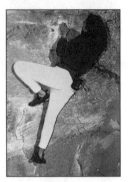

Suck in the hips

from left:

Straight arm: GOOD

Bent arm: BAD

Lock off with the hand close to the shoulder.

weight a poor smear, we drop our center behind our feet, to push them more into the wall. This also places more strain on our hands and worsens the direction of pull on the handholds. On a vertical face, we tuck our hips up close to the face using turnout or back stepping to keep our center line as near to our feet as possible. Here we must often position our body to maintain optimal direction of pull on the holds. When the going gets steep, we position our body to save strength, and so the holds best complement one another. Overhanging terrain forces our center out behind our feet as gravity pulls us out from the wall. Body tension and good body position keep our center inside the rough plane formed by the holds which allows us to pull sideways rather than outward on the holds, making them more positive. This is especially important when moving a hand or foot, when the other three holds (presuming we have three) define a plane. Unless we're heel hooking, foot camming, or knee barring, sucking our center into the plane with body tension often improves our cranking angle on scant handholds and maximizes weighting of the footholds. Oftentimes, as soon as our butt sags—moving our center outside the plane—we're off. On steep ground we try and feel the tension running through our legs and core.

Dem Bones

Whenever possible, we hang from straight arms and stand on straight (not rigid) legs. With the arm straight, our biceps and lats can relax somewhat, for much of the load-bearing is taken by the skeletal structure, by our bones. As soon as we bend the arm our bicep gets loaded and the lat muscles kick in. We can clearly feel this when hanging from a pullup bar. When we lock off on one arm, it's best to get our shoulder right up next to our hand to minimize the leverage on our muscles.

More than any other factor, body position determines style—the way our movements appear to other climbers. The difficulty in accessing our own style is that we can't see ourselves climb, and are at the graces of others to tell us. A shortcut in refining your style is to use a video camera. Virtually anyone can get their hands on one these days. Given a couple

hours of footage of yourself climbing, you can learn what might otherwise take years to understand: that you're posture is too stiff, your arms too bent, you're not weighting your feet enough, et al. Have a friend tape you climbing; study the tape and pick out your weaknesses; work on your weaknesses; tape yourself again and compare your performance.

To correct bad habits we often have to exaggerate things. If we climb too balled up, say, we must consciously try and climb "tall," keeping long lines. What feels like a ridiculous exaggeration is typically not so. We're simply going against our habits and the adjusted movement feels exaggerated. Again, the video camera is an invaluable tool here. Use it whenever possible. Most every other sport does.

Stemming

Stem Gem

When climbing a ninety-degree corner, or an obtuse one, STEMMING may be the only workable technique to surmount bald spots. It usually saves us energy as well. Here, it's not our forearms screaming, rather our calves, as each leg maintains counter-pressure against the other. Flexibility, balance and control are key. Even if the corner is overhanging, stemming gets our center of gravity out from the rock and over our feet. Often our hands will be palming rather than clinging, which further preserves our forearms but gasses our calves.

To varying degrees, all stemming requires us to assume a spring-loaded posture between two opposing footholds. The spring is held in place by the purchase at both ends and the tension between them. Moving the spring up is the tricky bit for the tension must go lax, if only momentarily. The secret is to maintain opposing pressure via some other body part— usually a hand—while jockeying the foot up. We continue alternating the bridge as we go—left foot opposed against right foot, then against the right hand as the right foot moves up; foot against foot again, then right foot against the left hand as the left foot moves up.

This is a gross simplification of the mechanics involved. How we ascend a stemming problem depends on the holds, the angle, and our style. Sometimes we'll stem one foot against the other hip and butt cheek, or against the hip and shoulder. The variations are endless. Many classic stemming problems have been tamed by sticky rubber shoes. Twenty years ago, routes like "Abstract Corner" and the "Bircheff/Williams" in Yosemite were impossibly insecure because both planes of the corner were steep and smooth. The old boots would not slowly butter off, they'd just sketch off. Should you ever want an exercise in humility, try climbing one of the old test piece corners in a pair of EBs. When no corner exists but the footholds face each other, we might "micro stem," pushing outward on the holds with our feet.

Stemming the foot against the hip.

Micro stemming

Like stemming in a corner, counter-pressure provides purchase. We must remain steady with our feet, and maintain even pressure between them to stay on the holds.

On vertical to overhanging face climbs it's physically impossible to keep our center of gravity directly over our feet, but we want to get it as close as possible. This requires keeping our hips sucked into the wall. There are three main ways to accomplish this: with "frog-style" turnout; by back-stepping; and by knee dropping.

"Riggit"

Frog position

For the frog move, we splay our hips wide—like a ballerina in the plié position—and keep them as close to the wall as flexibility allows. Ideally, while pressing our weight up, our hips will follow a straight line right next to the wall. If our turnout is poor, as mine (J.L.) is, our hips will be further from the wall, forcing more weight onto our hands and arms. A stretching regimen will enhance our turnout flexibility. Frenchman Patrick Edlinger was the master of this, even when cruising Indian Creek's cracks with legs splayed and pelvis tight to the wall.

An effective way to practice this and improve your turnout is to place your chest and hips against a wall and drop down, trying to keep the inside of your legs as close to the wall as possible. Start slowly, dropping only a couple inches. It takes time for your hip flexors and muscles to loosen up; if you pull one, recovery may take months.

Backstep

Backstepping

You can hardly find a climbing poster these days that doesn't show someone *backstepping*, reaching miles between dimples. It's no wonder, because when the rock is steep, especially if we must make long reaches, back-stepping reigns. This technique also works when the handholds are sidepulls or underclings. To back-step, we turn our torso sideways to the rock, facing the cranking hold, and stand on the outside edge of one foot and the inside edge of the other. The hip above the back-stepped foot is twisted into the rock to get weight on our feet, and the arm pulls tightly across the chest (or even abdomen if the reach is huge). Keeping the arm close to the body reduces leverage, and creates a *twist lock*, a stable position for making big reaches. When moving our left hand up, we'll normally back-step with our left foot. This provides stability between the left foot and the locked-off right hand, kills the barn door, maximizes our lockoff strength, especially on side pulls, and gives us maximum reach. After grabbing the left handhold, we rotate our backstep in the other direction, and reach up with the right hand. When there's a whole lotta' back-steppin' going on, the climber gyrates back and forth between the holds à la the King, Elvis himself, God bless his eternal soul. Mastering this gyrating sequence is required if we plan to bag the steep stuff.

Twist lock

King Tut

On steep rock, an extreme variation of the back-step is the *drop knee*—also called the "Egyptian." The drop knee pulls our center in, and creates complex opposition between our feet and hands, similar to stemming. Knee dropping is to the '90s what manteling was to the '70s. Sitting in a deep knee drop can provide a cush forearm rest, even on steep rock and may be the only way to reach between holds. As in back-stepping, with the left knee dropped we'll usually advance the left hand, and vice versa to maintain the stable diagonal orientation between the locked-off right hand and the back-stepped left foot.

Drop knee

The Patriot

If the handholds are all sidepulls and facing the same direction—say, to the right—we'll probably back-step or smear continuously with the left foot, and *flag* the right foot (for stability). This allows us to lean left, away from the holds, essentially liebacking to exploit otherwise unusable handholds. No footholds? Flag the right foot to stabilize the likely "barndoor effect" caused by the slanting holds. If the holds slant and we're not back-stepping, we must still lean away from the hold to use them with any heft.

Leaning holds

Sidepulls

Liebacking

One exception is the "Gaston," a technique named after legendary French alpinist Gaston Rebuffat. If we're to believe the photos, which I (J.L.) do not, Gaston scaled Europe's bleakest cracks not by jamming, rather by placing his hands, thumbs down, on the inside of the crack and heaving outward on them—like someone trying to pry open the doors on an elevator. A "Gaston" presently refers to grabbing a sideways hold, or the edge of a crack, thumb down and yanking sideways on it, whether with one hand or with both hands, work-

Double Gaston

Gaston

ing in opposition. Sometimes it helps to work the thumb in opposition to the fingers. The "Gaston" is most often used on sidepulls in front of or near a climber's face. Because we're not leaning away from the hold, a "Gaston" with the left hand must be opposed by the right hand and/or the right foot, and vice versa.

When the left handhold is directly above the left foothold, say, our body wants to "barn door" when we reach with the right hand. We can often cancel the "hinge job" by flagging our right leg behind the left leg, thus counter-balancing our torso. This is an instinctive move that makes sense once you try it. It's also strenuous as hell if the handhold is bunk.

Counter balance flagging

Flagging

Stemming, frog-stepping, back-stepping, the Egyptian and the Patriot all require repeated practice to master. And again, mileage on the rock is key. Video taping yourself can help you discover your form breaks and to start making adjustments. If you've thought through your fall record and know that drop kneeing gives you problems, video tape yourself drop knee-ing and keep taping yourself and comparing and making style adjustments until you move suave as a shadow.

Undercling

Underclinging will take us to hell in a heartbeat without good opposition between our hands and feet. Whenever possible, we bury our fingers in the undercling and pull straight out to create opposition against our feet. Often, the closer the footholds are to the handholds (to a point), the less strenuous the undercling—though if our feet are up by our hands, it's especially taxing. If the undercling is above our head, it may require Mr. Olympian strength to press our body up. The rarely climbed "Meathook" boulder problem at Horsetooth Reservoir is an extreme example. When first grasping the undercling holds from a nearby cheater boulder, the problem seems doable—until you try to step off the boulder and no sooner find yourself on your ass.

The trick in underclinging is to work your feet high enough so you can get your torso above the undercling. Otherwise it's Olympian pinching all the way. When reaching from an undercling, try and get the best extension by back-stepping. Of course, how hard we pull out on the undercling depends on the angle of the rock and the size and position of the holds.

Scrunch

The scrunch move is the curse of tall climbers—especially inflexible ones. Scrunch moves are required when the footholds are close to the handholds, such as on super low boulder problems, and when a roof or bulge prevents us from standing up. Often we're forced to scrunch when pulling over the lip of a roof. Tight scrunching requires good turnout, so we can get our rump in, and sit on one or both feet. Occasionally we can avoid scrunching by back-stepping or heel hooking, whereas we get our carcass laid out sideways, rather than scrunched. I've (C.L.) often been sandbagged in pukey little scrunch boulder problems conceived by a short climber who covets my reach.

Roofer

Even on bulbous holds, a relatively long ceiling climb is rarely easier than 5.11. Because gravity is pulling away, rather than toward, the wall, the techniques are radically changed. Good footwork is indispensable. If our feet come off, the rest of us follows. Body position is also critical. On extremely over-hanging ground, a minor miscalculation in body position drains our arms and everything else. So we keep our hips close to the wall whenever possible. And we never neglect the back-step. The drop knee is sometimes better still, given the footholds. All of these techniques work our hands against our feet to create a degree of opposition. Body tension is crucial in keeping the opposition tight; relaxing the tension is a quick way to fall off. Maintaining the tension is tortuous on abs and back muscles, as well as forearms, biceps, shoulders and legs. Often we must keep turning to best use the footholds. Heel hooks, foot cams and knee bars work great here for relieving our arms.

Sometimes the easiest way to quickly turn 180 degrees is to cut the feet loose, and swing our legs, flying Walendas-style, down and back up in the other direction, back toward the wall. We must know exactly where our feet are going before we kick them loose. If we can't stick at least one foot at the end of the swing, we'll trash our arms reestablishing our feet—or trying to.

Another move of the '90s is the "bicycle" step. This is restricted to very steep rock and ceilings, and is more common indoors than out. It works by using opposing pressure on a foothold, usually a large one. While toe hooking a hold in a roof to support some of the body's weight, push the other toe against the top of the same hold, pushing and pulling as if

Scrunch move

Robyn Erbesfield
Beth Wald photo

pedaling, or pinching the hold with your feet. This keeps a little of the body weight off the arms and allows greater extension under the roof. The bicycle step is usually better than dangling, which changes your alignment to the handholds, usually for the worse.

On roofs and steep faces, some moves are easier with our body dangling in the plumbline orangutan style, "campusing" the holds. This quickly blows our hands and forearms, so the holds best be good. We keep our arms straight whenever possible, but we may have to stay locked off to reach the next hold or thrust the hips to kip from hold to hold.

Think about how liebacking, stemming, drop kneeing, underclinging, back-stepping and so on all require opposition between the holds. The key is in using the holds to complement each other, and viewing the climb as the sum of the holds, rather than viewing the individual holds. Hard climbs often seem impossible if we view the single holds. But if we use the holds together, maintain adequate body tension, and possibly add some dynamics, we can often vanquish the impossible.

Every climber develops a personal style, a way of moving on the rock. For efficient movement, body and mind control are indispensable. Watching top climbers is instructive and motivating. They flow like water, never seeming to work hard, or at all. No wasted moves, no frantic movement. That's the goal—relaxation and control. The worse the way, the more necessary it becomes to let go of conscious thoughts and "let it flow." This is hot-tub wisdom, granted, but there's no easier way to state it. Move smoothly, making every move, clip and dip, as simple and effortless as possible. Let everything feel "on." Let your body flow smoothly upward with little premeditation, naturally adjusting to the most comfortable position. No distractions, just cool, crisp climbing. To climb with "the flow" is to experience perfection in motion; the event is an end in itself. You will probably find the flow on easier routes, so the trick is to transfer this skill to harder routes, where you need it the most.

Before starting a route, make sure that your body and mind are prepared. Some stretching, followed by one or two cruiser pitches will warm up muscles and joints and dial your focus in. Climbing hard routes without warming up invites injury and poor performance. A thorough warmup is a vital part of any strenuous sport.

Prior to casting off, scan the line to find the path of least resistance and to plan out the cruxes. Get your rack squared away. If you're not sure what to take, consult the guidebook or an honest climber who knows the route (more on this later). As you climb, continually look ahead for the best line and most probable sequence, always seeking rests. Avoid tunnel vision, thinking you must always go straight up, or this way or that. Stumped? Look around. Go right, left, even down if necessary. On popular routes, look for signs of previous passages—like chalk, rubber marks, fixed pro, or spots where grit and lichen have been worn off.

Settle into a comfortable pace, neither too fast, nor too slow. Relax, breathe and drift with the flow. In general, the steeper the rock, the faster the clock ticks, and the more important it is to pass the cruxes quickly and move on. Few climbers have the reserves to fiddle about on steep or overhanging faces; no one can do so for long. Keep an eye peeled for rests. When moving one part of the body, strive to make minimal demands on the rest. Maintain efficient body positions, make your reaches quickly, keep as much weight as possible on your feet, and use subtle dynamics to save energy.

Sequence

Many face climbing sequences unfold in four steps: 1) setup for the move by finding the best position and the best holds to crank from; 2) crank and step to raise your body, with most of the thrust coming from your legs; 3) lockoff in the most efficient position possible; 4) extend to reach the next set of holds. This accomplished, set up for the next move and repeat the process to the chains.

Holding a dumbbell out away from our torso takes energy, more so when moving it slowly against gravity. Likewise, it takes energy to hold our position, and usually more to move our mass against gravity. But once we get that dumbbell swinging, we can move it around with much less effort. Same goes for our body; and this is where the gymnastic side of climbing kicks in, and our primate side begins to shine.

During the crank and step phase we statically press our weight up as we move a foot up, though we can often save energy by bouncing off our foot as we move it up. The bounce can be subtle or exaggerated, depending on the move, our style, and the security of the hold. Sometimes we sink our weight down just before bouncing, and thrust our hips to get a better drive from our quads and gams. Other times it's no more than a little juke with the calf muscle. Depending on the terrain, this move should be used much of the time for efficient climbing. If we watch experts, we'll note that the subtle bounce makes them appear light on their feet. It takes some practice to do this move smooth and controlled, so we don't blow off the foothold. And don't get the wrong idea. The dynamic step is rarely, if ever, an explosive movement as though the climber were vaulting off the foothold to dunk a basketball.

On bleak slab routes, and other places requiring smooth weight transfers, a more static approach is required. Easier than pressing the body weight up on one leg at a time is the *frog step*, where we bring one foot up, then the other, while the torso and most of the body mass stays at the same level. After the second foot comes up we're in a scrunched, or "frog," position. At this point the legs work together to push our weight up. If both legs are needed to maintain the stability of the stance, we may need to move our feet quickly. If so, first

The Frog step

we swing our hips away from the foot we want to move up, momentarily transferring weight off that foot. Then we pop the foot up to the new hold and weight it. We'd best be precise with our foot placement or we'll pitch off when our weight settles back to the new hold. Now we sit on that foothold and pop the other foot up.

When the footholds are far apart, nothing saves us like a high-step. But nothing can hose us like an ill-conceived high-step, either. Our flexibility determines how high we can reach with our foot to grab the hold, while still keeping our hips close to the rock. For a high-step beyond our range of flexibility, we can often lean back off the handholds to get our foot up, then lean back in and rock onto the hold. To *rock on*, we use our foot like a hand to "pull" ourself up onto the hold. Before high-stepping, make sure to grab the highest practical handholds, to minimize the "scrunch factor" at the end of the move, and go from the highest possible footholds to tame the high-step. After we rock onto the foot we can sit on it, with our butt over our heel and the inside of our knee and thigh pressed against the wall. The other leg is probably dangling for balance, sometimes with the rand smeared to add stability. This position puts most of our weight on the rocked-on foot, so it's excellent for resting the arms. It's also a good way to blow out a knee, so go easy.

High step

Rock on

Harsh Lips

Moving out the underside of a roof is usually toilsome, but "pulling the lip" is most often the crux. The "rock on" is helpful, if not required. At the lip, we snag a heel hook if possible, then work our hands up as high as possible (with our torso still under the roof). Now, we switch from hooking to edging the foothold, and rock onto it. Sometimes we might roll the heel hook into a heel stance. The higher our hands, the easier to pull the lip. Once we get our hips over the lip, we balance through and get our other foot up. This often results in a scrunched body position, so turnout and high-stepping flexibility are welcome.

Pulling the lip

Reaching for Glory

The standard way to crank a long reach is to work the feet up to the highest usable holds, lock off one arm and reach with the other. We can often maximize a reach with our left hand by back-stepping the left foot and rotating our left shoulder toward the hold. To reach further when we're almost, but not quite, to the hold, we can sometimes pop our body a little higher at the end of the reach, or rock up on our highest foothold—a sort of slow motion powerglide. If the target hold is a sidepull or an undercling, we can reach nearly our entire arm span by working our feet up and, again, rotating our shoulders toward the hold. Performing this "iron cross" maneuver is often not as Herculean as it appears because our legs provide the thrust and our holding arm remains straight.

Reach through.

Cross to Bear

We set up for a long sideways move by crossing our hands through; this translates to fewer moves, saving time and stamina. Sometimes we'll match hands on the same hold, crossing our matched hands to set up for the next sideways reach. Cross hands only when it makes sense and feels natural, or risk getting corkscrewed.

If we're crossing to a distant hold, we may have to *reach through*. You've seen the pictures: legs fully back-stepped, right hand crimping powerfully behind the head, harsh focused gaze, left hand extending forward to the next hold. Every climber's mother has this photo of their son or daughter cranking this improbable looking move, and every mother shows it to her friends who all wonder why little Pepe or Ruthie is not going to summer school or mowing lawns.

PRESS IT

When the holds are well spaced between blank rock, a *mantel* —dreaded by most, relished by few—may be the answer. Because manteling is somewhat of a lost art, we'll take a look as though you have never heard of the word. Some haven't.

Manteling can take various forms, depending on the holds and the angle of the rock. Usually, but not always, the steeper the rock, the meaner the mantel. In its purest form, we start with handholds above our head. First, pull until the holds are at about shoulder level. Next we turn slightly sideways and reset the inside hand so we can push down on the hold with the heel of our palm. Next, we flip the elbow so it points straight up, directly above our manteling hand, with our armpit close to our hand. When we get the right position, we're able to lock off with little effort. Here, we may reposition our feet, then push through on the holds until they're at our waist. Now comes the balancey part: we reach up to the handhold with our outside foot and press through until we're standing up onto the hold. Sometimes we can cover seven or eight feet of ground with only one hold.

On steep mantels, there are several different sticking points. Sometimes it's grisly to get our elbow cocked on the hold, especially if the hold is so small or rounded that our movement is slow. A little dynamic thrust with either arms or legs, or both, usually provides enough upward momentum to get the arm cocked. On horrid mantels, the pullup and the arm cock must occur in one fluid, dynamic motion. Try and pause in the middle and we're buggered, and we'll never get our arm cocked. When we're cocked on a poor hold on steep terrain, the more bottomed out we are, the harder it is to initiate the press, or mantel. So when cocking the elbow, we try and keep our shoulder a little higher than the palm. While you're pressing down with all your might, don't forget to milk the available footholds. A rugged press requires brawny triceps—a muscle sport and gym climbing places few demands upon—so most climbers try and face climb around hard mantels whenever possible. One thing is for certain: a 5.13 face climber can get stopped cold by a 5.10 mantel if he or she has not encountered one before or practiced manteling on the boulders. (Cross-training, in the form of bar dips and mantels on a bar, are required drills to master manteling.) It's the one move that is virtually impossible to replicate in a climbing gym, and the very move that might spank you if you find a nasty one and don't have the technique to crank it. If a climb has a reputation for having a bleak mantel, count on having to crank it off. If you could face climb around it, the reputation wouldn't exist.

On low angle slabs, the mantel takes a different form because we can keep most of our weight on our feet and the holds are generally smaller. After we find the handholds, we walk our feet up until the holds are about waist level, then high-step with one foot to the handholds—hopefully we've left a space for our foot. Often we mantel off our fingertips, not the palm. Sometimes there's a foothold just below the handholds. Once we get the high foothold, we rock onto it and press through until we're standing up—although we might prefer the frog move, where we bring up both feet before standing. Either way, if the holds are small, this is delicate work. Sometimes we'll mantel on our thumb rather than our fingers.

Mike Auldridge dynos the mantel finish on "Pinch Overhang" (V6), Horsetooth Reservoir, Colorado.

Steep or slabby, mantels are performed more easily if we can discover a handhold above the mantelshelf to help balance through the step-up phase. There probably isn't much of a handhold above, however, or we wouldn't be manteling in the first instance. Even a small hold will help us to stand up. At what point we reach for the higher handhold depends on the move. After grabbing the higher hold (if there is one), we'll mantel on our lower hand while pulling down with the upper hand. Dozens of possible variations exist. Creativity will help find the best solution. Because mantels are relatively rare on roped routes—and are typically difficult—it's on the boulders that we build our repertoire of mantel moves.

Every problem on the infamous "Mental Block" at Horsetooth ends in a dicey mantel, with the ground an ankle-crushing distance below. Six-foot-five-inch Sam Nofsinger once pitched off a greasy "Mental Block" mantel (flying straight over five-foot-eight-inch spotter Jeff Elison) and landed on his head. Elison thought the unconscious Nofsinger was dead, until (according to Elison) he started mumbling in Farsi, a tongue the hulking Nofsinger had never studied. A stretcher carried Nofsinger to the waiting meat wagon.

Though the classic problems on the "Mental Block" were bagged over thirty years ago (by the original bouldering maestro, John Gill), many climbers still struggle with the exit mantels that were originally considered insignificant compared with the cranking to gain them.

FIRE OR RETIRE

Dynos, or lunges, were introduced to climbing in the early '60s by the father of modern bouldering, John Gill, questionably the first person to meld rock climbing and gymnastic techniques. In the ensuing 35 years, "dynos" have become a staple of bouldering, sport and gym

Full-blown dyno

climbing. While static movement promotes control—if you're trying to onsight a route you usually don't throw slapdash dynos—gently gliding or "popping" over obstacles is often less strenuous than slow, static movement. And certain long reaches require dynos. Dynamic movement runs the gamut from little foot hops to full blown double "'mos," where your entire body dislocates from the rock and you fly like Superman to the higher holds.

On extreme climbs, the holds are often so scrawny that we can't let go with either hand. Moving a hand up, then, may require a *deadpoint*. Or we may deadpoint to save energy on a move we could do statically. To deadpoint, we thrust our weight upward toward the hold. A quick pop with the hips and/or shoulders often helps. At the top of the thrust—the deadpoint—our body achieves minimum weight. At that instant, quickly and precisely we reach the hold above. Remembering that the hold might look like a bumper hitch but feel like a soap bar, we keep cranking with the lower hand. When deadpointing, we're not advancing our body mass much, rather we're setting it in motion so we can pop our hand up. Hand-eye coordination is critical for extreme deadpoints.

One step more dynamic than a deadpoint is the *powerglide*, where we throw our mass upward to snatch an out-of-reach hold. The driving leg provides most of the thrust, while our hands initiate the glide and hold our torso into the rock. If the driving foothold is in line with our body, it's easy to launch from. If the foot is out to the side, it's grim to generate upward thrust. Here, we get moving by yanking with our hands, popping our hips up (keep them in), and quickly extending on the foothold so our momentum carries us past the lockoff point to the higher handhold. Our driving foot must stay precisely on the hold throughout the powerglide. To control upward motion, the reaching hand stays on it's original hold until the last possible instant, when we release it and fire for the prize. Our hand must hit the hold exactly, preferably at the apex of our upward flight (the deadpoint). We must focus intently on sticking the hold, lest our fingers uncurl and we powerglide back down. If the target hold is to the right or left, a sideways pop may be the ticket.

If the next and only handhold is beyond our full extension, it's time to uncork a *full-blown dyno*, where we must generate enough momentum to carry our body to the target hold. We don't pump up and down before firing the move—a common mistake that wastes energy. Rather, at the inception of the lunge, we hang low, with arms straight and hips away from the wall. We eye the target hold, visualize grabbing it, then fire, cranking with the arms to initiate liftoff and control our trajectory, all while driving hard with our legs. If the footholds are near the handholds, we can initiate the lunge with our arms until our legs are straight enough to drive us home. From the start to the latch, we stay focused on the target hold. At the end of the lunge, our hips should be close to the wall, with our lower hand still grasping its hold (if possible). We reestablish our feet as soon as possible. Latching or "sticking" the hold is often the hardest part of any lunge, particularly if the hold is scant. If we can't stick the hold, we might try a figure four.

If the wall severely overhangs and the footholds are not positioned to drive a foot off, we can quickly snap our knees up and immediately kick them straight again. This kicking action often vaults us that few inches needed to latch the target hold.

For this to work, however, we must have the guns to chuck our entire mass skywards. The smaller the holds, the more power needed.

The most extreme of all dynamic moves is the Double Dyno, aka, the Double 'Mo. This high flying maneuver completely defies the archaic rule that we should move only one limb at a time. With the double 'mo, we launch like a moon shot for the higher set of handholds. At mid-flight, our body is entirely detached from the rock, much as a high bar gymnast is during a dislocate move. The double mo is performed similar to the full-blown dyno, except that we simultaneously shoot both hands to the higher hold(s). The key is getting enough momentum to carry us all the way to the hold, but not past it. Like other dynamic moves, we try and grab the target handhold(s) at the deadpoint of our trajectory. Since both feet have left their footholds, we must latch fiendishly to stick the move. Hopefully, we're shooting for a bucket. Otherwise, buen suerte. Rarely used on roped climbs, the double 'mo is most commonly performed on the boulders—a move sure to astonish your friends, and quite possibly rasp the hide off your hands.

As with gymnastics, a person doesn't jump up on the steel rings and start uncorking Olympic-caliber moves. The ability to tie difficult moves requires practice, often years of it. The same goes for dynamic climbing. I (J.L.) always fancied dynamics, and for the dozen or so years that I climbed 250 to 300 days a year, was always learning something new about the technique. Currently, many young climbers have become obsessed with pushing the limits of dynamic climbing. It will be interesting to see where they take it.

STRING OF PEARLS

Once you've acquired a repertoire of moves, stringing them together into fluid movement becomes the goal. In a single pitch you might use all of the techniques described in this chapter, and even some in the next chapter (crack climbing). If a move stumps you, try alternatives. Hopefully, you can hang out while decoding the sequence; if not, climb back down to regroup before trying again. Visualize yourself doing the move, then do it. Once you've committed to a move, have at it in earnest. Providing the fall is safe, you've got nothing to lose by going for it, even if you doubt success. It's better to fail trying, than to simply give up and drop off. Give yourself a chance, and don't be afraid to fail—you might crank it. Pacing is critical, especially on steep rock where the clock ticks fast, so try to keep moving upward. On a technical vertical face, the pace might be much slower.

Rest Stop

Shake out whenever possible. Always look for footholds to grab a moment's pause. Let your resting arm hang loosely, shake it and concentrate on relaxing it completely from shoulder to finger tips. When you're gassed, it's sometimes confusing whether to shake out or blow on through, especially if the "rest" hold is bunk. Much depends on your fitness and style. Regardless of both, a shake out will help relax you before a grisly crux. On fingery routes with prolonged crimping, a degree of relaxation can be had by briskly shaking your hand while reaching for the next hold. Top climbers need only one good handhold to recover almost as thoroughly as if they'd just stepped off the ground.

With experience, everyone develops ways to rest, and everyone comes to understand one crucial thing: he or she who best husbands strength usually climbs the highest.

Steph Davis enjoys
the only face hold on
the long, pumpy crack
"Quarter of a Man"
(12a), Indian Creek,
Utah.

Crack Climbin

Because this is an advanced book, we assume you know about crack climbing. However, we've geared the following crack discussion toward those of you who are talented face climbers. As far as difficult cracks go, face climbers have limited experience with anything but thin cracks (and thin ones are in many ways a form of face climbing). Off-hand cracks, fist cracks, offwidth cracks and especially squeezes, flares and chimneys are on few people's hit list these days, so it is unreasonable to think many have mastered them. It is likewise unrealistic to think that you *want* to master them. But one thing is for sure: if your sights are fixed on anything beyond quarries and bluffs, you'll have to be "crack fluent" or you won't get far. Historical big walls and free routes of any honest length invariably follow crack systems, so to climb them you must become crack fluent. Climbers who think otherwise are something to behold, trying all manner of kooky techniques to compensate for the crack skills they lack. I've (J.L.) seen champion plastic climbers trying to lieback the "Generator Crack" (a classic Yosemite 5.10 off-size crack, possibly 5.13 when liebacked), and have seen others use a 5.12 crimp rather than a 5.9 hand jam for lack of the most basic crack technique. It is interesting to note that throughout the '60s and early '70s, when American and British climbers were technically superior to all others, it was the gruesome cracks that humbled the surging European wannabes. However, in 1995 a lone German, Alex Huber, free climbed the stunning cracks of the Salathé Wall, showing that bleak cracks are no longer the private terrain of English-speaking climbers.

Sport climbing is not the only reason for today's lack of crack aficionados. Economics, time and convenience are also factors. Twenty years ago a climber could salt away a couple hundred dollars and spend the entire summer in Yosemite—or wherever—and live in style. Few climbers can presently take a three-month vacation, and those who can cannot squeak by on two hundred bucks. The result: gone are the days when a person could go to Yosemite or some other crack area and serve an apprenticeship that would often continue for three or four summers. Today's climber typically works a forty-hour week, pumps plastic two or three nights a week and goes cragging on weekends. Since cracks are difficult to replicate in a gym, the focus is on grim face routes. Unless a person lives at a crack climbing area, that person has the same chance of mastering cracks that a farmer living in Oklahoma has of mastering surfing. Time, money and convenience don't allow the climber or the farmer to do anything but what is at hand: face climb and till spuds.

Owing to incredible fitness, the modern sport climber is the ideal candidate to become a crack ace. But proficiency comes slowly and with difficulty. The old Yosemite adage was that a talented but inexperienced climber needed between one (rare) to four years to become an expert at climbing cracks of all sizes. From there, mastery required spending an entire season on one particular width—fist-and-hand cracks, thin cracks, off-size, flares and so forth. Mastering cracks of all sizes was rarely accomplished in less than four or five years. Contrast this to the incredible speed with which buck novices presently become excellent face climbers, and you'll start to understand the difference.

A fit climber can quickly acquire a feel for jamming, but advanced crack climbing techniques do not come naturally to most people. It is an esoteric art whose moves are not nearly so natural as those in face climbing. Many talented sport climbers don't believe much of this, and some expect to pump out severe cracks after a few weeks' work. And they might frig their way up a few liebacks; but once the size starts changing, especially when a bombay flare and a greasy offwidth are thrown in, the business can make the hardest gym climb feel like beachcombing.

No place on God's earth has crack climbing like the western United States. Yosemite, Devil's Tower, Indian Creek, Vedauwoo and Joshua Tree are among the cream of the world's crack climbing areas. Another dozen areas are nearly as good. While crack fluency is no longer an end in itself, crack techniques can aid on some sport routes. For instance, the veteran all-around climber will find hand-and-finger jam rests in limestone slots, where the uninitiated who have never seen a crack must rocket on through.

The majority of difficult crack climbs were bagged over fifteen years ago (except for the few thousand still waiting in southern Utah). The numbers are not spectacular, but the climbs are demanding nonetheless. A genuine 5.12 crack climb is a rarity at most areas, and is always a desperate piece of work. And the true crack master—one who gracefully and proficiently ascends all sizes of cracks—is a rare bird indeed. Given this skill, plus a modern grasp of face climbing, what could stop such a climber? Not much.

In reflecting back on the cracks you have climbed, understand that routes that once seemed dreadful will, after a few seasons, become reasonable, possibly even fun. I remember a crack at Joshua Tree that whipped me so ruthlessly on my first attempt that I quit climbing (for a week). A few seasons later I was climbing that crack without a rope. With practice, everyone can master moderate to difficult crack techniques and start upping the ante as prowess, endurance and confidence improve. Reading this chapter should provide some insight into the mechanics, but you must pump miles of cracks—of all sizes—if you hope to master the many techniques.

Topher Donahue going from thin hands to finger stacks on "Broken Brain" (12). Indian Creek, Utah.

Progress comes quickest by visiting a crack climbing area where you won't be distracted by high-numbered sport routes, where if you want to climb, it's a crack or nothing. Aspiring crack masters are well-served by heading to Joshua Tree, Yosemite, or perhaps best yet, onto Southern Utah's Wingate sandstone, like that found in Indian Creek. The thousands of uniform cracks of all sizes allow you to perfect each size in turn (and the surreal milieu feeds the soul). Most climbers first dial in the more manageable sizes (finger-and-hand cracks), only later moving on to the more technical fingertip, off-finger "rattlers," wide hand, fist and offwidth cracks.

If your crack limit is anything less than about 5.12c, avoid working routes too difficult for you. Find your comfort zone (usually a full grade below your limit) and start pumping them out, a dozen a day if you can. Proficiency comes from mileage covered. Squander a day on ten feet of impossible crack and you'll shred your hands and won't learn anything. Unlike extreme face routes, a climber in decent shape can pump out many crack pitches a day. Notch the difficulty up slowly. Keep your emphasis on mileage covered; flash ascents are the goal. And whatever size gives you the most trouble, work on that size the most.

During the crack era in Yosemite (early to mid '70s), I remember leading a crack, then dropping down with a toprope and working out on it, sometimes climbing it a dozen times to get the burn and polish technique. Once with Ron Kauk and John Bachar, we climbed "Butterballs" so many times that I couldn't clench my fist for half an hour afterwards. I was just out of school and wasn't in particularly good shape, a condition that didn't last long because I kept making laps on whatever climb we did. Nothing can substitute for mileage on the rock.

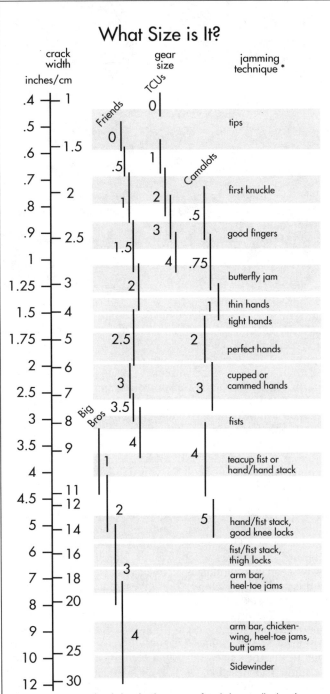

What Size is It?

crack width inches/cm		Friends	gear size TCUs	Camalots	Big Bros	jamming technique *
.4	1		0			
.5		0				tips
.6	1.5	.5	1			
.7	2		2			first knuckle
.8		1		.5		
.9	2.5		3			good fingers
1		1.5	4	.75		
1.25	3	2				butterfly jam
1.5	4			1		thin hands / tight hands
1.75	5	2.5		2		perfect hands
2	6					cupped or cammed hands
2.5	7	3		3		
3	8	3.5				fists
3.5	9		4	4		teacup fist or hand/hand stack
4					1	
4.5	11 / 12					
5	14		2	5		hand/fist stack, good knee locks
6	16					fist/fist stack, thigh locks
7	18		3			arm bar, heel-toe jams
8	20					
9			4			arm bar, chicken-wing, heel-toe jams, butt jams
10	25					Sidewinder
12	30					

* For average-sized male hands. The average female has smaller hands and should slide the given jamming technique up one row, so tips corresponds to 0 TCU rather than 0 Friend. Those with big hands will need to slide the scale down.

WHAT SIZE IS THAT CRACK?

The chart relates crack size, gear size (for Friends, TCUs, Camalots and Bigbros), and corresponding jamming techniques for an average-sized male climber. Understand that knowing the precise crack size is less crucial than immediately sinking the right jam and knowing what gear to place based on the type of jam. Sewn slings on camming devices are color-coded so we can relate a gear color to the type of jam: e.g., good finger cracks mean yellow #1 Friends. This system allows us to quickly identify the required gear and fire it in. Whatever our coding system, knowing it at a glance will save precious seconds when we need to slam in pro and pump on through.

Per the chart: climbers with small fingers and hands move up one row, while those with sausage fingers move down a row. A butterfly jam with average mitts provides thin hand jams for those with small hands, and finger jams for those with big hands. Tall or short, thin or stout, everyone has good and bad sizes, so learn to climb them all. At some time you'll have to. Some of the most enjoyable yet demanding cracks are those that pass through many sizes. When the crack rapidly and frequently changes width, it's difficult to maintain rhythm because at some time we'll encounter awkward and insecure sizes relative to our body type. Skill at climbing all crack sizes, patience working through the moves, an eye for helpful face holds and judicious liebacking will ease the transitions.

BIG PICTURE

Difficult cracks require an even mix of applied technique and physical endurance. Every climber has different measures of both. Charles Atlas endurance will get you up many hard cracks, but not as many as polished technique. Pure crack climbing is more regimented and mechanical than gymnastic face climbing, but at the top end, the nuances are many and inobvious. A master crack climber often resembles a human locomotive rolling steadily up the crack, always following a rhythmic sequence: right hand, left foot, left hand, right foot, and so on. Ever alert to changes in the rock, the crack ace continually alters his rhythm, pace, body position, and jams to secure the best purchase and save strength. Always searching for face holds that offer repose, but leery of those that interrupt the flow, the crack climber ferrets out stances for resting and firing in gear.

Like in face climbing, we strive to keep our center of gravity over our feet, consciously weighting them to conserve our arms. We balance this with leaning from side to side to most efficiently use the jams. On low-angle cracks, we climb with our hips and torso away from the rock. As the angle steepens to vertical and overhanging, we move our hips closer to the rock. On steep splitters, we move our knees out and suck our hips in. And we always try to stay relaxed and avoid over-jamming. Crafty selection of jams translates to efficiency. We try to slot our fingers or hands above bottlenecks so the jam is maintained with the least amount of strength. Barring constrictions, we look for other variations in the crack that add security to the jams. Many inexperienced crack climbers hastily stuff their fingers and hands into the fissure. If they don't pump out and pop off, they'll take their wounds to the grave. Slapdash jamming will crucify our mitts, and deep crack abrasions heal slowly. Instead, we remain calm—or try to—jam precisely and rest when possible. Releasing our jams smoothly is also important to avoid "gobies." Patience will be rewarded; haste will bear bad fruit every time. We ease the load on our forearms by using clever footwork and body position, keeping our arms straight when we can, and shaking out our hands when we're getting pumped.

Get Pro

Protecting strenuous cracks is often the most difficult part of "climbing" them. The ability to quickly arrange adequate pro becomes crucial the more we push our limits. Thankfully, if we have the skill and the gas to hang on in some confounded positions, good pro is usually available. We always look for a decent jam or stance where we can relax when placing pro. Develop an eye for the placements, and keep your rack organized by size. It cannot be overstated: slotting the right pro straightaway is as important as hitting the right jamming sequence, and can make the difference between flashing the pitch and yelling "Take!"

If the rock is steep and the fall clean, we'll sometimes set several bomber pieces from a restful jam, then run it out through the crux above. Don't run it out too far, though. Sound pro calms an anxious mind, and long falls on steep turf put high loads on the gear. I (J.L.) climbed with many of the world's foremost crack climbers, and none of them made a habit of needlessly running the rope on desperate cracks. (Jim Bridwell taught me the rule which Frank Sacherer had taught him: never pass an obvious place to set pro.)

On unrelenting cracks we may set pro with one hand, jam that hand higher, clip with the other hand and move it up. Shuffling the jams like this shortens time spent hanging off one arm, and sustains a little upward momentum. At any rate, play it safe. Fire in sound gear and pump on. If the crack's width is uniform, carry several pieces of the same size. Alan Lester used fifteen #1 Friends on "Tricks are for Kids" in Indian Creek, Utah. Borrowing the gear was harder for big Al than firing the route.

Be careful not to dump the whole rack in the first half of the pitch. Sometimes it's easier and safer to place our gear slightly above or below eye level—easier both to place and to clip. Other times we'll set gear as high as possible, especially when moving off a ledge; but we're always careful not to hose a shorter second by placing gear so high that he or she must hang by the mankiest of jams to clean it. It's also hateful to follow someone who habitually places nuts that are stubborn to clean. Experience teaches us to place pro that is both bomber and easy to remove.

SPLITTERS, CORNERS AND LEANING CRACKS

Is the crack a splitter, which cleaves an open face, or is it a corner crack? Does the crack lean or head straight up? Both factors determine how we climb a given crack. On splitters or corner cracks, if the jams are sound and we're going for big moves, we'll consider reaching through, each hand jamming progressively above the other. On corner cracks and leaning splitters, reaching through often crosses our arms up and feels awkward. Shuffling our jams, where one hand leads and the other follows, is usually the favored technique. On splitter finger cracks, we'll usually jam with both hands thumbs down, which gives us good jamming leverage on the crack. When a long reach is necessary, thumbs up may be the ticket. Hand jamming usually flows best with both thumbs up. We eventually develop our own preference, and adapt to the route at hand; but regardless of our style, utilizing an assortment of thumbs up and thumbs down jams can reduce the strain on isolated forearm muscles.

TO TAPE OR NOT TO TAPE

Athletic tape protects our hands and fingers on extended sections of jamming, and adds confidence by allowing us to jam more aggressively without pain or the risk of Desert Storm-type "gobis" (abrasions). Tape is especially helpful on coarse-grained rock, like quartz monzonite (Joshua Tree) or conglomerate stone (many places). Tape also fattens our hand profile, which makes thin hand jams all the harder to pull. For grim finger cracks, only tape your finger knuckles. For hand jams, cover the entire back of your hand. If you expect hard fist jamming, don't miss the sides of your fist, especially the meaty part below the web formed by your thumb and index finger. Some climbers rarely use tape, instead substituting flawless jamming technique.

LAYAWAY

Liebacking and stemming are required on most corner cracks. On steep ground, liebacking is fast but exhausting. Whenever liebacking, we move quickly but controlled, and never bypass an easy place to slot pro. We move one limb at a time, and try to keep our arms straight. Pulling our chest in

Mia Axon firing in protection on "Sphinx Crack" (13b/c), South Platte, Colorado.

to the rock will torch our arms quickly, more so when the rock is steep or overhanging. The crucial decision is whether to shuffle our hands—which uses less power—or to cross our hands to move faster via longer moves.

It's often precarious and pumpy to stop and place gear when liebacking. A good jam can help immensely, but if none exists we must either lean into the crack so we can see, or place the gear blind, a sketchy job for sure. "Hangdog Flyer" in Yosemite is a perfect example of this. I remember a time (before camming devices) when four of us were making an early ascent of this severely overhanging/leaning test piece. We led in turns, each leader hanging for his life with his feet up by his nose, trying to blindly wiggle a taper into the crack while a "spotter" below yelled up at him to move the nut higher or lower (since he couldn't begin to see what he was doing). Grisly work. If you do have to place blind gear, try and get a peek at it before committing your all. Or get ready for the other side. You fire off an overhanging lieback like an arrow fires off a bowstring, pulling your gear outward.

Finding the right pace, and avoiding tensing up, are decisive factors on long, sustained liebacks. Half the battle is won once you know how little power is needed to hang on, and how much gas you have in your tank. And before you can know this and have confidence that you're right, you need to pump off a stack of long liebacks. An instructive exercise is to lead a lieback, then drop down on a toprope and climb it again, this time climbing slowly and carefully and trying to use the least possible energy on each move. You may be surprised to find that the slower pace (certainly not dallying, but not racing) uses less energy than tearing for the belay. Harried liebacking eats more energy, leads to overgripping and an avoidable flash pump. A more even pace begets more positive moves, less boot slippage (the bane of liebacking) and more fluid climbing. And beware of those climbs that start with robust liebacks straight off the deck. All liebacking is strenuous, so you need to be good and warmed up to avoid a flash pump.

liebacking

STEM IT

Stemming gives your arms a precious break by getting your center of gravity out over your feet. But as mentioned, fierce stemming can obliterate your calves. Head to Devil's Tower if you doubt it. For beta on stemming, check the previous chapter on face climbing.

GENERAL THOUGHTS ON FINGER CRACKS

A long finger crack bisecting a steep, smooth wall is a striking climbing prospect. In many ways a thin, razor cut splitter is the most improbable, and intimidating, thing you'll ever tackle. Difficulty is determined by the jams, the steepness and the presence or absence of face holds. If the jams are poor, but the climb is low angled and face holds abound, the

climb more resembles a face climb than a crack project, requiring delicate weight transfers and marginal jams. If the jams are poor, the angle steep and the wall smooth, you're staring at a test piece.

Here, we set our fingers like tapers, wedging them in a constriction, or camming them across a parallel section. Because we can rarely get our toes into the crack, our feet will face climb—working every edge and smear—as our fingers milk available jams. We'll often go outside the crack not only for footholds, but for supplemental handholds as well. When no footholds exist, we might try dropping our heels and smearing the rand of our boot against the crack. With pointy shoes we may get marginal toe jams, particularly if the crack flares or is offset. If the finger jams are good and the foot jams are bad, pullout on the fingers to press the feet into the edges of the crack. Often we'll move both hands up, then both feet, setting each hand and foot with royal care. If the crack is offset, with the right crack wall projecting beyond the left wall, jamming our right fingers may be tricky, though the left fingers should jam nicely (thumb down). Since the crack offsets, we have some footholds to lieback if the jamming gets too dicey, or when we need to crank past a thin section.

Extended finger jamming can gnarl our knuckles horribly, especially on sharp rock. Tape your knuckles if you plan to climb another thin crack in the next two weeks. The torquing action of extreme jamming can also torture finger tendons, so mindful jamming is a must to avoid injury.

Micro Finger Jams

"Petit" does not apply to my (J.L) fingers. Many times I have watched other climbers slide their digits into a scanty seam only to later discover my own units were too large to jam the same section. And yet, I was almost always able to thieve my way past these ultra-thin areas by liebacking the edge of the crack or crimping face holds. So while fat fingers are a disadvantage on truly slender cracks, there is usually an alternative that will work. But not always. On several climbs—like the"Pirate" at Suicide Rock—I was shit out of luck and had to like it.

Our best hope is that the crack offsets a bit so we can use the edge of the offset as a sidepull or lieback. As the crack widens to barely accept finger tips, the pinky jam comes into play. For pinky jams, we keep our hand thumbs up, and bury our pinky and ring fingers as deep in the crack as possible. We might have to shimmy our fingers to find purchase. This is ghastly on the cuticles, and if the angle is steep, pinky locking cannot be sustained for long without footholds. Scan for features, however small, to augment the minimal jams. We can often lean slightly to one side and reap a little lieback action off pinky locks. With all thin cracks, shrewd footwork is no less important than the jamming, probably more so. Extreme thin cracks are very technical and require a creative and taxing blend of crack and face climbing techniques.

Pinky jams

Finger Jams

As the crack widens, we can sink more fingers in, and deeper too. Ideally, we insert our fingers with the thumb down and outside the crack. Look for any constriction and wedge the knuckles of the index finger above it like a stopper. Be careful of razor-edged slots that could slice your fingers if a foot slips. If the crack does not pinch, we torque the fingers sideways to set them like a Tri-cam. We maintain consistent pressure on the jam, and keep our wrists low and elbows in as we pull past so our fingers don't rip from the crack. The protection of choice for most thin cracks are medium to large tapers and small camming devices (especially TCUs).

On Yosemite-type thin cracks that may soar for hundreds of feet with precious few footholds, it's not so much a matter of making individual moves, though thin cruxes would seem as arduous as boulder problems. The biggest challenge, and one requirement, is to stay relaxed, placing the least demand on our muscles, pulling the best jams right off and sinking pro at appropriate places. Tough, thin cracks are so continuous that no one can go with power over technique without quickly burning out. And if we make the wrong move, get crossed up, etc., we'll have to make a series of moves far harder than if we'd hit the sequence correctly, and probably won't be able to click back into the sequence for at least a body length. And all grim finger cracks are sequential.

It's essential to quickly find the most relaxed body position relative to the jams. There's a lot of locking off to reach past constrictions or for the better, higher jam, and the locked off position should be held as briefly as possible. Sometimes backstepping is helpful. Pace is also critical. Every aspect is crucial, and putting it all together to where you can start flashing infamous thin cracks is a challenge of the first order. As with difficult clip-and-go routes, reading the correct sequence is not important, it is everything.

The tricky part with thin cracks is that because everyone's fingers vary in size, someone else's perfect sequence might be wrong, if not impossible, for you. There was a six-year period when I did most of my climbing with Lynn Hill, whose fingers are only slightly plumper than a shoe lace. Had I tried to use the jams she did, I'd be writing this from a nuthouse.

Finger Stacks and Butterfly Jams

Next to the satanic offwidth, most climbers find *off fingers* the most insecure size crack—too big to accept finger jams, yet too small for thin hands. To make matters worse, we can barely get our toes in the crack (and only then if we're wearing slippers). Harder than climbing off-finger cracks is stopping to set protection; stay on the lookout for rest stances or better jams. It's no mystery which size to place: #1.5 Friends fit the size crack that skunks most climbers.

When we can't lieback past off-finger sections, we need off-finger technique. Tight off-finger cracks (barely larger than fingers) are especially dreary because we can't pull a butterfly

Thin jams (first joint)

jam (explained shortly). Here, we keep our hand thumbs down, stack the index, middle and ring fingers against one another, and lever down with our forearm. Vigorously twisting our fingers holds them in the crack—we hope—and also devours gallons of gas.

When the crack is just the right size, the butterfly jam often works best. Place the thumb against one side of the crack and stack the fingers on top of it. Pulling down on the fingers pins them against the thumb like a door on a door stop (and also cuts circulation to our thumb). Levering down with our forearm further secures the jam and tortures our thumb. With practice, this is a reasonable, if painful, jam. It is also one of the most inobvious, and at first, most insecure techniques in all of climbing. Most of the hardest one-and-a-quarter-inch cracks were climbed using this technique.

Another option, especially in flared cracks, is to stuff our hand in thumbs up and fight to wrangle a phony hand jam. The counter-pressure between our fingertips and the back of our fingers/hand affords a strenuous, marginal jam (and in sharp-edged cracks, feels as though we might splinter our bones). This may be our best bet when liebacking a rounded, off-fingers corner. I've been told that it's possible to wedge the fleshy part of the hand beneath the pinky, and to use this "pork stopper" as a perilous jam. The only time I tried this I (J.L.) pitched off. However, Luebben reports that "I use the pork stopper all the time in Vedauwoo's flared monstrosities."

Stacked finger cams

Butterfly jams

HAND CRACKS

No jug, no lip, no fulsome hueco beats a bomber hand jam. Crack climbers dream of beautiful, sweeping hand cracks. Once we get hand jamming down, it's amazing how easily we can cruise even overhanging hand cracks.

Thin Hands

Thin hand cracks are a tease because they allow us to almost, but not quite, sink a good hand jam. Thin hand jams (aka "rattlers") generally go best thumbs up, squeezing the fingers into the crack to create opposing pressure against the back of the hand, and forcing the thumb into our palm to increase the vigor of the wedge. Some climbers prefer to stuff the meaty part of the thumb into the crack and jam with the palm muscles. On super-thin hand cracks we may do best going thumbs down, with fingers angling slightly down into the crack, torquing each jam tight by cranking our arm down. We avoid taping our hands if we anticipate a section of thin hand jams, or else we keep the tape job thin. And we motor. Stalling on thin hand cracks will almost certainly foil us.

Much of the task with thin hand cracks is getting a feel for what works and what does not. Marginal, thin hand cracks will initially feel so insecure that we're certain to overjam, not understanding that like all crack climbing, it's much more a matter of finesse than raw power. Once we have pumped out

Thin hands

Topher Donahue finally sinking thin hand jams after the long crux section of "Lovelace" (IV 12d), Zion Canyon, Utah.

a couple hundred miles of thin ones, we'll know how to pull the best jams, how much tension is required for each one, and we'll learn to use and trust our feet in questionable positions. Watching someone who is dialed into thin hands cracks is deceiving. The jams appear solid—no problem, judging from the climber's fluid movement and seeming security. Then we go to second the same pitch and the rattler jams feel about as secure as a felon on bail. Experience…

Hand Jams

Nothing beats a good hand jam, especially one slotted above a constriction. If no constriction exists, we create opposing pressure by squeezing our fingers and the heel of our hand into the crack while also squeezing our thumb into the palm so it wedges like a door stop. This way we can jam with minimal strength instead of brute force. In flared cracks we must squeeze harder to set the jams, making them extra strenuous.

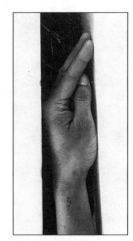

Good hands

On straight up splitters we can move out by crossing through, with both hands thumbs up. Two techniques work well, depending on the crack and our style—lock off between moves, or "windmill." To lock off, we bring our feet up, jam them well, drive our weight up with our legs, and lock the jam off near our shoulder to minimize leverage on our biceps. Reach up high, take the next jam, and quickly transfer weight to the higher, straight-armed jam. Now pull up and lock off the high jam, and reach through with the lower hand.

Making long reaches between hand jams helps reach past poor jams to good ones. To get full extension off the lower jam, we may need to reset it with the fingers pointing down and into the crack, and crank hard off our foot jams or holds.

The "windmill" is all about big moves, covering ground. We jam thumbs up, keeping our arms straight like the blades on a windmill, driving with the legs and sweeping from jam to jam. The windmill works well for moving fast and saving our guns. We might slot our hand closer to a 90-degree angle relative to the wall, hinging our wrist as we move up on the jam, so our jam doesn't pivot, rasping the hide off our hands. One of the drawbacks of taping for cracks is that, because we can avoid wounds from sloppy or improper jamming, polished technique is longer in coming.

Cupped hands

When locking off or windmilling, a sequence of right hand, left foot, left hand, right foot provides good stability and flow, though sometimes it's best to move both feet, then both hands. Often we'll switch up our sequence to accommodate face holds and changes in crack size.

Cupped or Cammed Hands

Beyond tight hand jams we must vigorously expand our hands to get purchase. These jams become more strenuous and less secure the more the crack widens, with the hardest size coming just before fist jams. For these wide sizes, we *cup* our hand by pushing the fingers forward into the crack, and hooking the thumb over the back of the index finger to empower the jam; or else we *cam* the hand by torquing it sideways between the two faces of the crack. Sometimes a combination of cupping and camming works best. Careful here, or our hands will look like our Saviors' after the crucifixion. So little surface area contacts the rock that the slightest pivoting will rip our hands up. Some of the nastiest jamming wounds I've ever gotten—or have seen other climbers get—have come from wide hand cracks. The saving grace is that this size crack has foot jams you could camp on. Tape is

Cammed hands

Rand smear, when you can't get your toe in

Toe jamming

Foot jam

extra helpful for this size crack.

After my (J.L.) first three seasons in Yosemite, I rarely taped my hands and never got the ghastly wounds I did during my earlier years. What I learned was to always try to slot my hands at a 90-degree angle relative to the edge of the crack. Before, when reaching for a hand jam, I'd slot my hand with my fingers pointed slightly up. When I'd pull past the jam, my hand would rotate in the crack resulting in mean flash wounds. Never let your hand move inside the crack; hinge at the wrist instead, unless you're deliberately resetting it for a long reach.

Foot Jams

For thin hand cracks, we turn our foot sideways and slot the toe into the crack, then torque sideways to lock the foot. Shoes with a narrow toe profile are preferred. Hand cracks offer bomber foot jams. We place our feet carefully, never punting them into the crack. Feet can get very stuck in hand cracks. It's terrifying and dangerous when our foot gets stuck in earnest. Ask Rob Allen, who took a lead fall with his foot stuck in the crack, and powdered his ankle. In wide hand, fist, or flared cracks, we can often set our feet comfortably across the edge of the crack without twisting our ankles, or we can bury them in the crack for maximum purchase.

Wide foot jam

FIST CRACKS

Fist jams are often solid, especially if the crack constricts; likewise, they can be rattley if the crack is a hair too large. When we squeeze our fist closed, it expands to create pressure on the sides of the crack. While hand jams provide a wide range of expansion, fists expand little, so they work through a narrow range of sizes. For straight-in, plumbline fist cracks, jamming with the palms facing out sometimes provides the most efficient movement, especially for the lower fist (imagine doing pullups with the palms facing toward you, versus away from you). Some climbers and some jams feel more comfort-

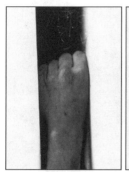 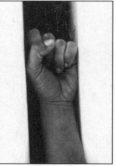  

Fist jams. "Teacup" fist jam. Finger bridge.

able with the palms facing into the crack. The best solution is usually to do what feels most natural.

There are three variations of the fist jam to accommodate slight changes in crack size. In the tightest fist cracks, we tuck our thumb into our palm and twist our hand from a wide hand jam into a fist. These are harsh to set but usually secure once obtained. They are also painful unless we're taped, including the thumb. We'll usually go with the standard fist jam, holding our fists like the Marquis of Queensberry, with our thumb wrapped over our index and middle fingers. If the crack is a bit large, we might try the "teacup" fist jam, with the thumb placed alongside the hand to widen the fist (trashes an untaped thumb), or the "finger bridge," with the tips of the fingers bridged against one side of the crack and the back of the hand against the other. We can't get much power from either of these, but driving hard on our foot jams might save the day.

Whenever the crack is a shade too wide, beware. Much less hide is contacting the rock and bearing the weight, and this is typically when we get battle scars.

Fist cracks generally provide excellent foot jams. Twist them laterally for bomber purchase. The trick is to work our feet so well that we don't have to jam hard. The best sequence will vary depending on the crack and the climber, but often it will be right hand, left foot, left hand, right foot, each limb crossing through. If the crack leans, is in a corner, or overhangs severely, the best sequence usually entails jamming with the top hand palm down, and the bottom fist palm up. This is a very powerful position that kicks all the big muscles into play, and we can pump off some major footage once we get comfortable with the technique.

OFFWIDTH CRACKS

Of all the cracks in the land, the most feared, despised and avoided crack is the offwidth. Too big for fist jams, too small to crawl inside, offwidths spew climbers fast and often. Without experience, offwidth cracks are about as much fun as the Ebola virus. But offwidths need not be desperate. With

patience and technique, most offwidth climbs are manageable. The key is experience. Offwidth technique is elusive to most climbers because they get discouraged or disgusted after the first couple of wide cracks, becoming so cowed by the necessity of working through the obligatory wrestling stage that they avoid offwidths altogether. Sorry, but it's impossible to acquire judicious offwidth technique without some initial thrashing. And you'll have to acquire at least basic offwidth proficiency if you want to climb big walls, because the bulk of them have mandatory offwidth climbing.

Offwidth work is a baffling game of body camming and wedging. It is possible to waste enormous amounts of energy doing precisely the wrong things, and it's probably by doing things incorrectly that you will most quickly learn how to do them right.

My (J.L.) first offwidth crack was the "Left Side of Reed's Pinnacle" in Yosemite. Jim Bridwell led the crux second pitch in about two minutes. By the time I'd followed the pitch, Haley's Comet had come and gone and I looked as though I'd fallen off a motorcycle on the freeway. And so started a season-long process of getting dialed into offwidth technique. Mastery of this most difficult size comes slowly and laboriously. Many offwidths rated 5.10a are, to the uninitiated, far harder than a 5.12 sport climb. Today's climber has one big advantage: protection.

Until the late '80s, most offwidths were poorly protected. The rule on routes like "Twilight Zone," "Left Side of the Hourglass," "Leverage" and countless others was that the leader must not fall. The numbers are not particularly high on these routes, but since no method existed to suitably protect them, there was no room for error. At all. In an era when boldness was revered, the more dangerous routes enjoyed a wide reputation, and to lead one gave a climber bragging rights. But while everyone wanted to go to heaven, nobody wanted to die—and nobody did simply because back then, only experts ever tried marginally protected offwidth climbs. I remember leading the "Left Side of Absolutely Free" in Yosemite, and all the way up this ghastly flare I felt myself fading toward a better land, on account of the two debatable nuts I'd arranged forty and ninety feet off the belay. Now, with the advent of mammoth Camalots, Big Dudes and Bigbros, most offwidths can be ascended safely.

Two standard techniques exist for offwidthing: Leavittation (hand stacking and knee locking) is often preferred in the smaller sizes, while arm barring and heel-toeing are key in the bigger ones. Personally, I (C.L.) prefer the technical trickery and subtleties of Leavittation to the brutish duty of standard offwidth technique. I'm often amazed how easily a ghastly looking section of wide crack is surmounted using a couple hand stacks. However, when the crack is larger than double fist, the standard arm bars and heel-toe jams are a must.

opposite:
The second ascent of the huge squeeze chimney roof "Lucille" (12d). Vedauwoo, Wyoming.
David Vartanian photo

Hand Stacks and Arm Holds

With some practice we can arrange hand stacks quickly and securely. Hand stacks are usually more powerful and stable when our arms are crossed (when the right hand is pinned against the left side of the crack, and vice versa). Other times it's more straightforward to go with straight arms, especially if we're only stacking for a move or two. The crack size determines the type of stack we'll use. A *hand/hand* stack works best with our arms crossed so both palms face the crack walls. It is quite sound, but because a knee jam won't fit in this size crack, our chances of advancing are about the same as picking a Brink's safe with a toothpick.

Hand/hand stack Hand/nestled fist Hand/fist Fist/nestled fist Fist/fist stack

The next size crack takes a *hand/nestled fist*. Set a nestled fist (a fist jam turned sideways with the fingers against the crack wall), then jam the other hand on top of it, with the backs of both hands pressed together.

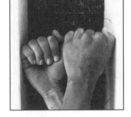

Stacked teacups

Bigger still is the *hand/fist*. With arms crossed, stack a hand jam against a fist jam. Sometimes we'll set this one with the arms straight, allowing us to set the large knuckle of our index finger into the center of the fist jam, which adds stability.

Now try a *fist/nestled fist*. Pin a nestled fist jam in the crack with a standard fist jam. Less secure, the *fist/fist* works in cracks twice the width of a fist crack. Cross the arms, jam one fist against the other and pray the Rosary. Biggest of all, and least secure, are *stacked teacups*, with the thumbs adding width to both fists. A forearm jam might help us rest during desperate hand stacks, though it's impractical to move on. To secure a forearm jam, we bury the elbow into the crack and fold the hand down to expand our forearm into the crack. Big guns are a plus.

Arm Bar

Arm bars are used when the crack is too wide or awkward to hand stack. We assume the classic offwidth position, with one side of our body in the crack. We reach the inside arm horizontally and slightly down into the crack, pressing against the front face of the crack with the palm, and the back of the crack with the tricep and shoulder. Arm bars work on cracks from just beyond fist to squeeze chimneys.

Wing It

The *chicken wing* is the mainstay arm lock for most difficult flares and tight chimneys. Trusting it takes time, for it initially feels like it won't possibly hold, or if it does, it will rupture sinew and splinter every bone in our arm. Just how and where to place it may confound us. In fact, we can pull a chicken wing between almost any two crack walls eight to twelve inches apart. The model chicken wing has the elbow pointing up and into the crack, with the tricep on the rear crack wall camming against the palm on the front wall. When the chicken wing is tight, it may best be set horizontally into the crack. In some situations, an inverted chicken wing works well, with the arm at or below the climber's torso, the elbow pointing down and into the crack. The chicken wing is extremely secure, but we have to work at this technique to master it. Some climbers use the chicken wing frequently for moving; others prefer it only for resting. A good chicken wing can cop us a rest in a desperate offwidth. A sage practice is to find a climb where the chicken wing works well for you, and repeat this climb numerous times. The confidence and polish you acquire on this climb will carry over to other routes. The forty-foot roof "Lucille," at Vedauwoo, is a masterpiece of chicken winging, supplemented by crimps for the outside hand.

John Govi arm barring his way up "Crack of Fear" (11a), Lumpy Ridge, Colorado.

Chicken wing   Inverted chicken wing

Kennan Harvey photos

Footwork

Offwidth foot jams are generally good if we set and use them correctly. Don't miss key face holds that can allow bigger moves and save effort.

Foot cams: if the crack is slightly larger than the width of our foot, we torque our foot diagonally, jamming our toe against one side of the crack and our heel against the other side. Wear ankle high shoes, or at least socks if you prefer skin over gaping holes in your ankles. I (C.L.) often tape my ankles if wearing low cut shoes.

Foot cam

Heel-toe jams: in wide offwidth cracks and squeeze chimneys, we bridge our foot across the crack by pushing our toes against one side and our heel against the other. Decrease the size of the heel-toe by steepening the angle of the foot. Lock the jam by pressing the heel down and pulling the toes up.

Inverted Heel-toe jam: on wide roof cracks we can often get heroic footholds by camming our feet overhead in the crack, similar to the foot cam described for face climbing. With our abs ready to blow, we suspend our weight from our feet—bat style—to advance our hands, or to rest. The "Owl Roof" in Yosemite is an example of where this technique is required.

Heel-toe jam

Calf lock: this agonizing leg lock is sometimes used when we're Leavittating a crack too tight for our knee. We cam our higher foot inside the crack (about waist level in a vertical crack) and lever our calf off the edge of the crack to hold our body in place. Our lower foot cams below and drives our body upward as our beleaguered abs suspend our torso.

Foot stack: if the crack is slightly too wide for a heel-toe jam, it may be possible to stack your feet. Set one foot along the crack wall, with toes pointing into the crack. Now heel-toe with the other foot jamming between the original foot and the opposite wall, sot he feet make a T. I've (C.L.) never gotten much mileage from this one, though some swear by it.

Inverted heel-toe jam

Knee jam: in cracks from about four to five inches wide, the knee jam is quite frank, but extended sections of knee jamming are excruciating. Wear pants or thin knee pads. For desperate stretches of knee jamming, taping the knee can help. No matter what, we keep the knee padding thin if we're expecting a snug fit. To set a knee jam, we ease it into the crack, fold it tightly back, and hook our foot on the outside edge of the crack. Knee jams work splendidly for resting, placing pro, and allowing us to advance hand stacks. We never force our knee in. If we drive our knee home, move up, then try to remove it, the knee may get stuck. If this happens, relax, try to set pro, move back down and work your knee out. Be gentle—you don't want to inflame your knee or you'll never get it out, you'll be fixed there and your skeleton will shortly have slings festooned from it. "Poor fellah," they will say as they chug past your bones. "He panicked, and now look at him." If our knee doesn't fit or feel right, foot cams also work in this size crack.

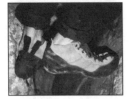

Stacked feet

Thigh jam: when the crack gets too big for knee jams, we

stuff our whole leg in the crack and fold it back
to get a thigh jam. Heel-toe jams for both feet
complement the jammed thigh, and allow us to
drive our body upward with the lower leg.

Butt jam: beyond the thigh jam we'll have to
work the heel-toe jams hard, and move steadily
through. Once the crack widens a little we can
get our hip inside. A butt jam is secured by flex-
ing our arse cheek inside the crack, at the same
time jamming our hip forward against the crack
wall. Even on overhanging routes the butt jam
often provides a welcome rest. On sharp-edged
cracks a protective cup (as worn by baseball
catchers) is an option.

Scissor leg lock: we can sometimes get a rest
in tight squeeze chimneys by folding our legs
across each other and pinning them into the
crack. (Marvin the Magician used to do this in

Knee jam
Kennan Harvey photo.

Resting on a thigh jam
after brutal climbing on
"The Mayor" (12a),
Long Canyon, Utah.
Craig DeMartino photo

Butt jam   Craig DeMartino photo   *Splayed knee bars*

a steel box, but he died.) We'll probably slide down just a touch before the scissors truly lock, so it may be three inches forward, two inches back if we overuse the scissors.

Knee bar: climbers are always discouraged from using their knees, but in chimneys the knee bar is our best friend. We set our foot against the back wall and our knee against the front wall. Weighting the knee cams it against the foot. Larger knee bars are the easiest to use—we can point our knees straight into the chimney wall, sit securely on the knee bars and scream our guts out if we're not wearing knee pads. As the crack tightens, knee bars become less secure, and we have to splay our knees out to fit the knee bars. Knee pads will keep the pain tolerable on long chimney pitches.

Everything from the foot cam to the knee bar shares one distinction that all climbers must come to grips with: they all slip or simply blow out if not properly placed and held firmly. It takes dozens of climbs before your feet will naturally assume an ideal, or even suitable configuration. Footwork is a matter of feel since our feet are inside the crack and we generally can't see how pitifully they are positioned. It's a little like assembling a rifle with a blindfold on. We'll fumble around and drop things and blunder through the process until we develop a feel for the various components and how they fit together. Eventually, everything will fall into place as though by instinct. But not at first. We'll wonder what dipshit coated the crack with pomade. Our feet will swim wildly as our torso flops around like a gaffed tarpon. And when we do manage a heel-and-toe jam or stacked feet or whatever, the jams will feel impossibly insecure and we'll most likely writhe by with Frankenstein arm barring anyhow. Rote is the only way to tighten up offwidth form.

Leavittation

While hand stacks have been around for awhile, it took the creativity of Tony Yaniro and Randy Leavitt to put all the pieces together—in a parking garage of all places. Out of such humble surroundings came Leavittation, a technique for ascending off size cracks via the exclusive use of hand stacks and knee jams. Leavittation is the technique of choice for moving efficiently through tight offwidths. Once you get the hang of it, hand stacking is a fun way to cruise an otherwise desperate offwidth. And it may be the only way to manage an offwidth roof short of wearing welder's gloves. Hand stacks perform well on cracks in the 3½ to 6½ inch range, regardless of the angle or difficulty. The tricky part is suspending our weight, or "leavittating," while moving both hands up.

Leavittating on the first ascent of "Ralph" (12b), Long Canyon, Utah.

Kennan Harvey photo

To Leavittate, we set a solid hand stack as high as we can comfortably reach. Next we lean out off the stack and set a knee jam high into the crack. The other leg may dangle, flag, stem, or work the crack with a funky "toe down" heel-toe jam; but most of our weight should remain on the knee jam. After locking the legs, we move the stack up, and repeat. If our knee won't fit in the crack, we're buggered. Maybe a foot cam, calf hook, thigh jam or weird stem will help out, because we need to lock our body in to move our hands up. It may be possible to maintain side pressure on the crack from each hand while we move the other up. We won't get much support here, but maybe enough to quickly reset our hands.

If nothing else works, try the ever powerful *high foot/low foot*. The high foot cams inside the crack slightly above waist level; the low foot cams across the crack directly below as our abs crank like hell to suspend our torso while we fire our hand stack up.

Aside from double dynamic moves, Leavittation is perhaps the most technical maneuver in all of climbing, and takes some doing to understand, let alone to perform efficiently. Most everyone I (J.L.) know who has mastered this technique did so by toproping a practice offwidth, wiring each aspect of the technique via repeated ascents over a period of weeks, sometimes months. The

Highfoot/low foot

Kennan Harvey photo

desert climber rarely has the option of toproping, since the cracks are often found on larger formations and must be led. An option here is to make laps on the route after you've led it, just to dial in the fine points, though most will be content with a single lap. Suave offwidth technique is all about efficiency, which comes from rote.

Traditional Offwidth Technique

When the crack gets too wide for fist stacks, or when Leavittation doesn't work, we still have good old-fashioned, blue collar "roll your sleeves up and grunt it out" offwidth technique. Arm bars, chicken wings, and heel-toe jams are the meat and potatoes of traditional offwidth crack climbing. Unexpected face holds are the dessert.

Trad offwidth technique is a process where a lot of effort often gains little ground. Offwidth cracks are the only articles where I have seen a climber heave halfway up a lead. As mentioned, before we get accustomed to the assorted arm barring and foot configurations, we'll find ourself slipping and cursing and swimming—and compensating with extra gusto to maintain security. Once we can set the locks well, the natural leverage provided by our cammed arms and legs replaces brute strength. The limbs quit slipping, the oaths tail off and we can climb the wide stuff efficiently. If we ever see a climber who has mastered this technique, watch closely. There is no thrashing or flailing involved, no downsliding at all. It's rather discouraging to someone who hasn't graduated from the writhe and wretch stage, whose technique has all the subtlety of a jack-hammer. The first time I saw Mark Klemens lead "Chopper Flake," I wanted to shoot him. But after a couple seasons I (J.L.) got a feel for the work, and found it easier and faster to chug out most offwidth cracks via arm bars and heel-toe jams than fiddling about setting fancy hand stacks.

The idea is to get a rhythm going and use the outer foot and leg to propel our body upward, while the inside leg and arms stabilize the body. We first set our arms—not too high or we'll have to work overtime. The inside arm performs an arm bar or chicken wing, while the outside arm palms or pulls at the front edge of the crack (usually at shoulder level), or grabs face holds. Next we bring our outside foot up into a foot cam or heel-toe jam, or stem it off a good hold outside the crack. We set the foot well and drive our body up with the outside leg. Understand this or you'll forever suffer on offwidth climbs: the driving leg propels us upward, hence the necessity that our feet are locked well.

If the crack is steep we often can't see our driving foot. Using good foot control and feeling our way into the foot cams is key. Now we slide our inside foot up and reset it at the top of the move. Sometimes we'll have our inside leg deep in the crack, other times nearer to the edge.

With our newly set legs, we lock our body in the crack and move our arms up again, one at a time. If the foot jams are especially good, we can relax our arms so they slide up while

Traditional offwidth climbing on "Texas Finger Crack" (11a), Escalante Canyon, Colorado.
Randy Joseph photo

our outside foot drives our body higher. If the crack opens enough to insert our hip, we can get a secure butt jam. Patience is a virtue here. It's important to conserve energy: keep our body securely wedged between moves (not so tight that we can't move), rest as much as we need to, and steadily work our way through the moves. Settle into a rhythm. With some practice you'll be able to comfortably wedge your body in some pretty creative positions. Creative resting is virtuous on wide cracks. Wide cracks usually offer many opportunities for resting. Good thing, too, because they're so brutal. You can camp for days on a good knee jam, knee bar, or butt jam. Often a small edge outside, or inside, the crack can feel like a bivy ledge. With practice, you'll cop rests in places you never dreamed of. Creative resting transfers to all types of free climbing.

The trick to offwidth climbing is to master the basic resting cams, stacks and locks, know how to execute them with the least amount of energy, and gain enough confidence that you can work on the outside of the crack, as opposed to trying to crawl inside it—which is everyone's first instinct and leads directly to hating God and all the Saints. Another crucial thing is to always keep your eyes peeled for helpful face holds both inside and outside the crack. Judicious use of available face holds can save tons of energy, and make the climbing more fun.

Pick a Side

Before beginning any wide crack we perform the offwidth ritual—determining which side goes into the crack. Study the crack. If it's a left-facing corner, if the crack leans left, or if the crack is offset with the right side projecting furthest, we'll usually go right side in so we can work our left foot off the face. If it's a vertical splitter, we can take our pick. If one side of the crack has more face holds, face that way. Once we've determined what side we want in, we put the rack on the other side and have at it. Often we'll retreat back to the ground, switch the rack to the other side, and have another go. Then we'll realize that we had it right the first time, switch back the rack, and send the offwidth.

Beware of the heinous "offwidth pod." Usually bulging above and below, in a matter of a few feet the pod can go from hands (or some other reasonable size) to six or more inches. The problem is that the feet below often don't support the offwidth moves into the pod. If possible, lieback around the whole mess and high step or knee jam into the pod. Otherwise you'll have to set your upper body high as possible and try and suck your legs up into the pod.

Protecting Offwidths

When it comes to wide crack protection you have two good choices: big cams and Bigbros. One system that works well on off-widths near your limit is to set Bigbros every twenty feet or so, and walk a giant cam up the crack. It's a little more pure, and committing, to "pro and go", setting your gear and climbing above it, rather than "toproping" your way up the crack by walking a cam as you climb.

FLARE UP

Wide flared cracks require a mixture of crack techniques and are some of the most technical, and malicious, and gripping, and insecure, and scary of all offwidth projects. Yosemite classics like "Edge of Night," "Right Side of the Hourglass," and "Left Side of the Slack" are all in the 5.10 range and yet are rarely led by anyone but specialists.

With many flares, we can pull hand or fist jams in the back of the crack. If the jams are deep it's nearly impossible to jam straight in, so we need to pick a side to put into the crack. Straight-in flares are rare. Most flares are formed by exfoliating flakes or dihedrals scoured by eons of rain runoff. With corner flares, we almost always are better off with our back against the main wall, with our outer hand palming or grasping the lip of the crack.

Resist the temptation to dive deep into the crack, which only makes movement all the more awkward and punishing. Only get deep enough for purchase so you don't box yourself in. The better you get with flares, the more on the outside you will work—to a degree.

On flares with a hand and/or fist crack in the depths, the inside arm and leg will jam, while the outside arm and leg perform offwidth technique, palming the edge of the crack and heel-toeing or knee barring. The deeper we must reach into the crack, and the more it leans, the more dastardly the effort. It feels as though you're reaching through the bars of a jail for the keys, laying on the ground just out of reach. If the jams are too buried, arm barring on the outside is usually a better way to go.

Because I (J.L.) am bigger than most climbers, I rarely "fit" flares very well and typically have to work far on the outside. With most flares, the farther outside you are, the more the bastard flares and the more insecure the business becomes. On some flares I had to stay so far on the outside that I could not climb them in the usual manner—with my back to the main wall, arm barring and pulling various foot stacks. Instead I'd often have to face the main wall and turn the climb into a chimney project, pulling the scantiest chicken wings with my inside arm and doing bizarre foot stacks with my feet. Unorthodox, but it worked. And I'm not alone here. Peter Hahn was also a big climber, and he specialized on flares and off-sized cracks. The point is, on all but the thinnest cracks, body size is hardly ever a valid excuse for failing.

SQUEEZE

We can wedge our body nicely inside most squeezers. Beyond the standard arm and leg jams, we can cam our hips,

Topher Donahue
squeeze chimneying on
the first ascent of
"Generations" (10),
Long Canyon, Utah.

wedge our shoulders, or scissor lock our legs to get a rest.
Moving up is nearly impossible, but so is falling out.

Tight squeezers are best ascended following the offwidth
technique already described: arm bar or chicken wing with
our arms, heel-toe with our feet, using the outside leg to propel our body upward. The butt jam is handy for locking the
body in place. Once the crack width exceeds the length of our
heel-toe jam, it's harder to move up in a vertical orientation.

"Sidewinder" in Long Canyon, Utah, is one striking corner
of Windgate sandstone. It protects with three Friends and
twelve Bigbros. On the first ascent, I (C.L.) was suffering
through an interminable stretch of tight squeeze chimney,
too wide for heel-toe jams, but too tight for decent knee bars.
After some heavy scratching for little vertical gain, I turned
horizontal and slithered up the suffocating chimney, dubbing
the technique and the route "Sidewinder."

To perform the Sidewinder, get your body horizontal, or nearly horizontal, jam your arms, hip, butt and legs across the crack, then slither up like a snake. Set the upper arm with a chicken wing and the lower arm with an inverted chicken wing; cam the lower hip off the front wall against the upper butt cheek on the back wall; and get shallow knee-heel bars with your legs. To move, rotate your torso upward and reset both chicken wings as high as possible. Next bring the hip/butt jam up and reset it. Last, move up the leg bars, then repeat. The skin on the lower triceps of your leading arm gets a buff job, so go with a long-sleeve shirt. You can also switch leading sides, and baffle your partners as they first see only your head sticking horizontally out of the crack, then your feet. Several variations to this main theme exist.

Knee-heel

As the crack widens, sidewinding becomes sketchy. Try the "wriggle worm" to motor through. Your legs will have shallow knee bars, while your arms enjoy inverted chicken wings. We lock off the left side of our body, and ratchet our right arm and leg up concurrently. Next we lock the right side and ratchet up the left side, and so on. This technique works favorably until the crack gets too wide for inverted chicken wings. If we can't move both the arm and leg simultaneously, try moving them separately. I (CL) learned this technique from desert master Earl Wiggins, who followed in ten minutes what I had just led in one hour.

Another trick that works marginally when you're desperate is the "head inch-worm" maneuver. When we need both our arms and legs to hold our body in place, we press the back of our noggin against the wall behind and slide our back up. Relock the limbs higher and repeat until you gain the belay or a migraine puts a merciful end to the whole business. Another similar trick is to extend the back and "reach" our shoulder blades up as high as possible. Next we scrunch our back so we can bring our rump up. Lock again and advance the shoulders. Both of these techniques are slow, and are rarely used except on short stretches when the going is dead grim and we have no other options. As with most offwidth climbing, creativity will get us everywhere, thrashing will get us skin grafts.

CHIMNEYS

Once we get a solid knee bar wedged across the crack, we're usually in cruise city. Several variations of standard chimney technique exist for difficult routes; each option depends on the width of the chimney. If we have sincere knee bars with each leg, we can press our feet and butt against the back wall. Taking one foot out of the knee bar, we smear it on the front face of the chimney. We palm our hands on the wall behind and slide our butt up. Reset the knee bar, smear the other foot against the front wall, palm hands behind us and again move our butt up. So goes the standard way; other variations to this sequence can also work. One of the most important aspects of all knee barring is to set your knees carefully with each move, as opposed to dragging them along. If you thought rug burns were bad, consider that you move each knee perhaps two- or three-hundred times during a pitch of chimneying, and that the surface is heartless stone. Without prudent technique, your knees are dust. Knee pads can be life-saving on long stretches of chimneying.

When the crack is too big for knee bars, we rest our butt against the back wall and support it by pushing our feet into the front wall. To move, we push one of our feet against the back wall so we can unweight our butt and move it up, then return the foot to the front wall. We push our other foot off the back wall, slide our butt up again, and return to the starting position. Look for footholds that will make the going easier. We can also move up with both feet in front, pushing the wall behind alternately with the hands and butt. When the crack widens still, we'll start stemming our legs across the chimney.

ALL OUT

The *full body stem* is one of the wildest maneuvers performed. Once the chimney is too wide to stem, span the gap with hands on one side and feet on the other. Now walk your hands and feet up their respective sides of the crack. Moving up is tricky and terrifying, but getting out of this position is even worse. "The Priest," in Utah, has a chimney that forces you to stem wider and wider until the only option is a full body stem, all the while staring 200 feet down into the black bowels of the maw. At the top of the chimney you grab an eroding sand-stone bucket and cut your feet loose, promising the Good Lord that if He only sees you through this nightmare you'll dedicate the rest of your life to helping orphans and saving the rain forest. As you continue free climbing a rotten bolt ladder your piety swells—till you gain a ledge and just want to get drunk. The first time I (C.L.) climbed this wild pitch, at the place where you swing over onto the rotten bucket, my second broke into tears, befouled her pants and became a dead weight on the rope.

The full body stem is, thankfully, a very rare maneuver.

ROOF DUTY

Jamming out the underside of a roof is one the most thrilling drills in all of climbing, and one of the few instances where the deed surpasses the photograph. Those first few roofs fill our trousers as we hunker beneath them and try to picture ourself jamming out horizontally. But after a few roofs, our body goes back to the early days swinging around the jungle

Chimneying on "Texas Finger Crack."

Randy Joseph photo

gym and a roof crack becomes just another climbing problem—almost. We never get fully accustomed to jamming upside down, and that's the beauty of it. There are plenty of moderate roofs out there, and they're all treats.

On all roofs we must milk the jams and work them in unison with our feet. Our body will move like an accordion as we first move our hands out, then our feet. (Avoid getting too compressed, however, for this makes breathing difficult and movement awkward.) It's amazing how much weight we can get off our hands and onto our feet in hand- to offwidth-size roof cracks. Many roofs are no more than a body length long, and it's possible to keep our feet on the main wall all the way out until our hands are at the lip. But the fun rarely starts until both our hands and feet are plugged into the roof crack and we're jamming horizontally. That's the Real Deal.

We will almost always lead with our hands, moving out the roof head first; but if the only good foot jams are in front of us, we might *kick through* and lead with our feet. This sounds insane, and is, but it works surprisingly well, especially when the roof crack slants down beyond 90 degrees (that means, when we're jamming out the roof, we're actually loosing altitude, jamming downhill). The first time I (J.L) tried this exercise was in 1973, on a cruel fist and offwidth problem at Suicide Rock called "Paisano Overhang." The crack jagged down to the lip perhaps a dozen feet away. It seemed more natural to lead with my feet, rather than trying to jam with my head lower than my boots. So I kicked my feet out and plugged them into the down-slanting part of the roof, and was able to sort of pull myself toward the lip because the foot jams were better than the rattling fist jams. A heel hook at the lip was arranged, and in turn I managed to pivot around head first and transition into a harsh arm bar sequence. Strenuous, but it worked. And lucky thing it did, for I cleaned the pro (two 4" steel bongs) with single hammer blows.

On some roof cracks you must reach elbow deep into the crack to pull decent jams. In any roof where we work to secure adequate jams, stout foot jams are imperative. We don't just kick our feet up into the roof crack, rather we pick our spot and place each foot as carefully as we do our hands. We might have to keep our knees sucked up toward our waist, because we must vigorously twist our foot jams to keep them firm. To increase the torque on our foot jams we may have to move our knee out away from the crack.

Other roof cracks are flared, bottomed, peppered with jugs. Every roof presents special problems that must be tackled on the spot, but several things hold true on all roofs. We strive to get our feet jammed as well as possible; we avoid getting balled up; we milk the jams; and we can count on needing bulletproof abs to stay suspended under the ceiling.

Turning the Lip

What we previously mentioned about turning roofs during face climbing holds true with cracks as well. But now we're using jams instead of face holds. Getting our *feet* over the lip is virtually always the crux, and how we manage this depends on the value of the jams and face holds just over the lip. Whenever possible, we reach as high as we can above the lip and try to pull a good jam. If the jams are poor above the lip, we're into grim duty. In any case, we'll eventually have to move a foot from the underside of the roof and either slot it back in the crack just over the brink, or paste it on a hold. Doing so, we're mindful to keep the foot beneath the lip well jammed. Even if there are no decent footholds at the lip, if the jams allow, it's generally easier to reach high for a jam, paste a foot over the lip, and then bring the lower foot up and jam it over the lip, moving quickly and aggressively. Quickly hauling our lower body up and over is typically less strenuous than walking our feet up by way of foot jams. Other times it might be easier to transition into a lieback and heave ourself over past the lip in a couple quick moves. In any case, we'll usually find ourself balled up at some point, so pulling the best available jams is crucial.

The lip of a roof crack is no place to cock around. Whatever sequence you go with, keep moving. Most climbers tape for roof cracks.

Vicious upside-down offwidthing on "Trench Warfare" (12d).

Kennan Harvey photo

Gearing up for a first ascent
in Long Canyon, Utah.

Equipment

The following gear talk excludes the business of basic usage because this is not a basic book. The focus here is this: what does an advanced climber need to know about gear, and what are the fundamentals that even world-class climbers need to constantly remind themselves of? In many cases, an advanced climber doesn't need to know much more than what he or she already knows—namely, all the fundamentals. If you are lacking these basics, refer to other manuals in the *How To Rock Climb* series.

SHOES

With more than fifty models of rock shoes presently available, how do we pick the "right" one? Two considerations make sense: fit, and the appropriateness of the shoe to your climbing. Choose a poor fit or the wrong shoe—either one can spank you. In decades past, one had to force one's dogs into ill-shaped shoes, always a torturous routine. Modern shoes fit better and don't have to be sized so grievously tight. Nonetheless, most climbers fit shoes snugly and wear them without socks (foot powder is virtuous).

Beginning to intermediate climbers might get by with one pair of shoes; advanced climbers need more: slippers for bouldering, sport climbing, gym climbing, and thin cracks; tight, semi-stiff lace up shoes for edging; and comfortable (but not sloppy), semi-stiff clunkers for big cracks and long routes. Whatever shoe you buy, lace it up and do a few moves on the practice wall, or wherever—to insure you're not blowing your paycheck (climbing shoes priced under $100 are rare) on something that doesn't fit perfectly. Quality control is good with most makes, but since the boots are worn snug as tattoos, even slightly irregular interior stitching means it's blister city. Walk around the store and make certain of how much pain you want to bear. Too tight a fit will numb toes and decrease your performance, but remember, all shoes will stretch in time.

Life Cycle

Cycle through your shoes, using the older, cozy ones for most climbing and training, saving the newer and snugger articles for hard routes or competitions. Worn shoes can be resoled, provided they haven't been ridden too hard. If the upper is worn through (from crack climbing) it's not worth resoling. The preferred rubber for resoling is Stealth.

Foot powder helps control stitch rot and trench foot. Always air out shoes—until they're totally dry—before storing them in a pack. Never leave them loose and exposed in the back of your car, where sunlight will age the leather and delaminate the soles and rands.

What Shoe?

Countless magazine articles, store employees and plain common knowledge tells us what model is suitable for what conditions. That still leaves us with thirty options. How to choose? Most climbing stores have rental programs, but the typical rental shoe is a low-performance hightop that will give you corns and hammertoes. Trade shows and bouldering/climbing competitions often have reps on hand who have demo boots to try. Other than that, magazines periodically run shoe reviews. The last resort is to go with the most popular model, which most likely gained its favor from high performance.

HARNESSES

The competition is so great in the harness business that only good ones are widely available. Crucial features include: a bomber sewn belay loop; sufficient but not excessive padding; gear racking loops; and a simple, fool-proof buckle. For sport climbing, go with an ultra-light harness; for longer routes, especially if you expect hanging belays, the harness needs more padding and a solid haul loop on the back. Like boots, a harness is a very personal item that must fit perfectly.

ROPES

The Cardinal Rules: lead only on UIAA-certified dynamic ropes; avoid loading your rope over sharp edges; never step on the rope; minimize exposure to the sun; and avoid contact with chemicals. To this end, keep your ropes in a cool, shaded and dry place, ideally inside a rope bag. Track your rope's history, and never loan it out.

Size

With advancements in climbing and rope technology, the standard rope has been getting longer and thinner. In the '70s, the free climbing standard was 45m x 11mm. Then it was a 50m x 10.5mm (most modern routes were engineered with this standard). Double ropes were in for awhile. Now, depending on the usage, many climbers favor 9.8 to 10.2mm ropes, 55 to 60 meters long. Longer ropes allow you to stretch out the pitches, make longer rappels, lower off longer pitches or higher on a pitch; and if you have to cut an end off, you still have a usable line. Another advantage of the longer cords is that you can use the lead rope to rig belay anchors without causing the leader to come up short on the next lead. For long alpine routes and ice climbs, a 100m x 8.8 to 9mm rope allows double rope technique or super long pitches, and there's no knot to hang up on rappels. A longer rope allows longer pitches and rappels; the drawback is that you must coil, carry and manage the extra line.

This rope was diced by a sharp edge under body weight.

Double, Twin and Fat Ropes

Ropes of 8.8 and 9mm, as well as some 8.5mm ropes are designated as double ropes. A double rope system works well on many traditional routes because you can clip the ropes into separate pieces of pro to control rope drag, and you always have two ropes for rappelling. And two ropes are less likely than one to be cut in a fall. Clipping both ropes into the same piece increases the force of a fall compared to clipping one rope, so only double clip bomber pieces, and use separate carabiners if possible. Otherwise, clip alternately whenever possible so you're not relying fully on just one of the ropes, and to shorten the potential fall if you blow the clip.

The smallest diameter ropes (7.8, 8.0 and some 8.5mm) are twin ropes. Both ropes must be clipped into all the lead protection. Unless you're concerned about shaving grams, double ropes make more sense than half ropes because you can single clip them. If you won't be single clipping, twins can save you a pound or two, but know that the thinner the lines, the more they're prone to tangle, especially if they get wet.

Piano Wire

The temptation to use lighter and lighter ropes is strong. Before you get on too skinny a thread, though, consider the application. Big walls, working sport routes, and portly climbers merit a thicker, more durable rope, while speed ascents, alpine routes and redpoint ticks justify a slender line. A fat rope improves your safety margin—it has more ability to withstand multiple falls and resist cutting. Fat ropes are heavy, though, so when you need to go light, a slender line is preferred (it's marvelous at the end of a long pitch not to be dragging a fire hose). However, it is madness (and possibly deadly) to lead on a rope designated less than a single rope. A sharp edge can dice a skinny rope in a heartbeat. Double ropes can hold only one or two severe falls. Beyond that, adios.

Science

According to Luebben (who apparently wants the world to understand the science), during a lead fall you gain kinetic energy as gravity accelerates your body toward Earth. At the end of the fall, the rope stretches to absorb the energy, limiting the impact force on the leader, the belayer and the anchors. Energy is also absorbed by the tie-in knot (which during a long whistler can cinch down to the size of a pea), and by friction in the system and movement of the belayer. After a hard fall, a rope needs a few minutes to recover (you could probably use the rest too).

After you fall off a route, clip off or lower and let the rope rest for a few minutes before clawing back onto the rock to ping off again. Those couple minutes will give the rope (and your heated tendons) time to recover some of its capacity to stretch and absorb force. Because the tie-in knot likewise absorbs energy when it cinches tight, each time you lower to the deck, make it a habit to untie, rest up, and tie back in; or better yet, switch to the fresh end of the rope.

Every leader should understand the fall factor, because it, along with your weight and the rope's elasticity, determines the force created in a lead fall. The fall factor is the length of a fall divided by the amount of rope out. Two falls with the same fall factor, the same falling mass and the same rope will theoretically create the same force, regardless of the length of the fall (obviously the longer fall is more dangerous in other ways). A factor 2 fall, with no intermediate pro between the leader and belayer, creates the greatest possible force. The leader impacts directly onto the belayer and belay anchors, and dangerously tests the limits of our gear. Suicide Rock regulars used to call such falls "wrenchers." With insufficient rope out to get a good stretch on the line, the leader felt as though he or she was falling on a steel cable. It's essential to set solid pro directly off the belay. Think of those first few pieces as backups to the belay anchors, because they are.

As you climb above the belay and set good pro, you have more rope out to absorb the energy of a fall, so the potential fall factor, and the force involved, decreases. A factor 1 fall (a ten foot fall with ten feet of rope out, for example) generates about 70% the force of a factor 2 fall, and a factor 0.5 fall (a ten-foot fall with twenty feet of rope out) generates around half the force. A marginal piece that would rip early in the pitch may hold at the end of the pitch—but don't bet on it.

Spaghetti

Ropes kink with use, as the core strands relax and the sheath shifts. To minimize kinking, avoid using figure eight rappel devices, Munter hitches and the mountaineer's coil. "Roll" new ropes off their original coil to avoid introducing kinks into the rope. To remove kinks, work them out through the end of the rope, or hang the rope down a cliff and let the kinks twist out. Coil your rope only with the backpack coil (see *How to Rock Climb* or *Knots for Climbers*), or stack it in a rope bag or tarp.

Retirement Plan

Retire your rope when: A) a hole wears through the sheath; B) after the rope holds an extremely harsh fall; C) whenever flat spots appear in the line. Periodically inspect the rope by working along every inch of it, pinching it between your fingers. If the sheath looks fine, if the rope has weathered no monstrous falls and has no soft or flat spots but is three or four years old, retire it anyway. Some climbers have taken a cavalier attitude toward ropes, thinking "ropes don't break." But they do in the UIAA tests, so retire your rope if there's any question. A good indicator is that once the sheath becomes stiff to the touch, it's finished. It might still be strong enough for regular use, but the handling properties (the "hand") are greatly lessened, and the rope will kink incessantly no matter how you coil it.

Rope Care

At minimum, clean your rope every six months—more often if you frequent desert areas where grit and loam work into the line. A rope washer that attaches to your garden hose works best. Otherwise a large bucket or barrel or bathtub will do. Leave the rope submerged (in clean water) for an hour, then swirl around until the water turns brown. Repeat the process until the water runs clear. Avoid detergents which often contain chemicals that can weaken the line. To dry, flake out the rope on a clean, shady floor—or better yet, drape it over a chair—and let the water evaporate. Do not use a dryer. Heat and nylon spell disaster.

Rope Bags and Tarps

Rope bags protect your line from sunlight, sharp objects, dirt and other betrayers of nylon. Some bags are designed so you stack the rope directly into the bag (rather than coiling it), whereas the rope can later be fed straight out of the bag—like pulling yarn from a spool. This works particularly well at hanging belays, though a lap coil is probably quicker.

Rope tarps protect your rope in storage and transit, and provide a clean space for the rope at the dusty base of a climb. Plus you never have to coil your rope—simply roll it up in the tarp. They're especially useful for sport climbing, when you're moving from route to route. In a pinch, a rope tarp also makes a reasonable—if dowdy—emergency wind/rain poncho.

Fixed Lines

For line fixing, static ropes are superior because they stretch little, which prevents the rope from sawing over edges (a frequent and sometimes fatal occurrence with dynamic ropes). Static cords are also far more durable than dynamic perlon lead ropes. Still, pad the sharp edges (and never lead on a static line).

CARABINERS

Dozens of carabiners are currently available in three basic shapes: oval, D, and asymmetrical D. Ovals are handy for racking, but the asymmetrical D shape gives the most strength for its weight. Bent gates allow you to fire the rope

in quickly, but they also allow the rope to unclip more easily (if the rope travels across the gate). Bent gates should be used only on the rope side of a quickdraw, and never for clipping the bolts. Locking biners are essential for your belay device, and are likewise reassuring when clipping off anchors and critical bolts (and pro) close to the ground or a ledge. A locked carabiner allows no opportunity for a rope or sling to unclip.

Generally, a locking biner is used as insurance in critical applications where if the rope somehow came unclipped death, broken bones or great inconvenience (say, in the case of a day pack coming unclipped) would occur.

Since most UIAA-approved biners are well made, selecting a biner is mostly a matter of personal preference and expected use. Look for a carabiner with a high gate-open strength (9 or 10 kN as marked on the carabiner). Some biners are specifically suited for sport climbing, others for all-around use. Learning and keeping abreast of the biner market is an ongoing job. Read. Keep your eyes open. Listen to feedback from friends and enemies and learn from experience what works best and when. As with all gear, once you've reached the advanced level, the decision about what specific gear to use is all yours, as it should be.

BELAY DEVICES

Long gone are the days of catching a long whistler and suffering a wicked rope burn across your ass. Belay devices make a climber's life easier, but they only work if used correctly. For advanced use, consider the four different styles: flat plates, cones, figure eights and self-locking devices.

Flat plates and conical tubes are light, versatile and easy to use. They work superbly for belaying and rappelling. If the device jams when rappelling or when quickly feeding rope, use two carabiners rather than one which also adds a little friction to the system. Figure eight devices work well for rappelling and belaying a toproped climber. When belaying a leader, though, the only acceptable method is to pass a bight of rope through the small hole in the figure eight and clip it into a locking carabiner (in the manner you rig a flat plate device). The exception is with the new Belay 8, which has a V-slot that jams the rope so the belayer can easily catch a lead fall. Like any figure eight, the Belay 8 is heavier than other devices, and a stopper knot (at the end of a rappel line) can pass right through the device.

Le GriGri

The latest generation of belay devices automatically lock the rope when weighted. Presently, the Petzl GriGri is the best of the lot. The GriGri especially shines in sport climbing: you can hold your partner effortlessly while he works the moves. If he pings, the GriGri locks the rope, every time, guaranteed, which is more than you can say for a standard device manned by an inattentive belayer. The GriGri is especially useful for guiding (in the event that the client struggles), and for descending a single rope, during which you can let go of the rope at will.

A GriGri gives piece of mind when you're big and your belayer is not. But the GriGri is not fool-proof. It must be rigged properly, and the cam must be unobstructed. Otherwise it will not engage if the climber falls.

Those unfamiliar with the GriGri may have difficulty feeding rope out smoothly for clipping or lowering, especially with fatter ropes. With practice, feeding rope is simple. Hold the cam open with the heel of your brake hand while you rifle rope through the GriGri with your guide hand. Release the cam if the climber falls.

The trick for lowering smoothly is to bend the rope around the edge of the GriGri, creating more friction and providing better control with the brake hand. Be careful never to open up the lowering lever quickly, lest you drop your partner quicker than he can say "Mon Dieu!"

Munter

A Munter hitch pinches for a belay device, so it's crucial to know in case you drop or forget your device—which everyone does at some time. Munter hitches work best with pear-shaped locking carabiners. Every time you change directions from feeding out to taking in (or vice versa), the hitch must invert; if the interior of the biner is too small, the hitch will bind so hatefully that it'll feel as though you're pulling a tractor through a keyhole—or trying to. And always run the load strand of the rope along the spine of the carabiner, otherwise you substantially reduce the strength of the biner. Whatever biner you use, the Munter hitch will kink your rope if the line is pulled rather than feathered through the device. Also, be careful that the rope sliding across the gate does not unscrew your locking biner. This is possible, though unlikely when belaying; however, if you should ever rappel using a Munter hitch, the continuous downward movement can result in friction on the locking gate, and can unscrew it loose in a matter of feet.

HELMETS

We would be negligent not to recommend helmets, especially on loose rock, alpine routes, ice climbs, rescues, big walls, and any other time you value your brain. The day of the dork in the helmet is dead. Smart people wear helmets in many situations because unexpected rockfall can happen to anyone, anytime, on any cliff. Gear comes falling out of the sky too, and ice in the alpine zone. And the worst injuries most climbers get in a lead fall are head injuries, which could often be prevented or lessened if a helmet was in use. A helmet is no magic shield of armor, though. Wearing a helmet is a personal choice, and many times, the hassle, weight, and stigma of the helmet results in it being left in the closet. Recently I (C.L.) was jamming a large sandstone flake at Lake Powell when it broke. I fell, then watched in horror as the rock dropped toward my partner, Silvia DeVito. It grazed off her head and leg, resulting in a $7,000 helicopter ride. Seven stitches later she was fine, luckily. All this because she forgot her helmet on the boat. A couple of inches difference in the trajectory of the 200-pound rock could have caused her to go home in a body bag, helmet or no helmet.

A Note on Belayers

The most important thing you can bring to the crags is a good belayer/partner. Partners hold our lives in their hands, so make sure they know what's up. Beware of climbers—and guides—who believe their own hooey, which makes them hazardous to themselves and others. Avoid loud-mouths, know-it-alls and whiners. Their minds are on other things. Never blindly trust partners fleeced from the base of the crags, no matter how righteous they talk or tooled out they appear. Talking a good game and looking the part doesn't necessarily translate to someone who knows what they're doing. They may let you down—and fast.

Anchors

This book assumes your sound understanding of anchors and anchor systems. The following information deals with considerations specific to the advanced climber, and is not a stand-alone treatise on anchors or related subjects. For more comprehensive analysis, see *Climbing Anchors*, and *More Climbing Anchors,* also in the *How to Rock Climb* series.

THE RACK

Every leader develops his or her own gear preferences. The so-called "standard" rack varies from area to area, and does not include those special and quirky items of gear most climbers come to trust. The rack prescribed below is generic, versatile, reasonable to carry and works for most climbers on "standard" advanced routes. On the other hand, there is no such thing as a standard hard route (save bolt-protected sport climbs and Yosemite-style cracks); nonetheless the rack listed below is a workable starting point for many leads.

If you sew up your leads, or if the pitch is long, you'll likely need more gear. This rack is a bit large for some routes, but often you're not sure what to expect, and you may need extra gear for the belays. A standard rack typically includes:

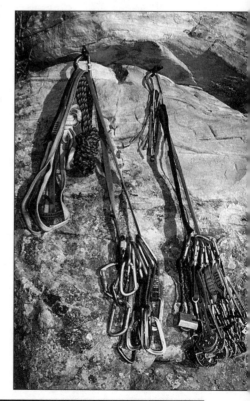

- A set of 10 spring-loaded camming devices (SLCDs), ranging from ⅜ inch to 3½ inches, each with a color-coded sling and racked on it's own biner.
- 5 or 6 brass or steel nuts, and 1½ sets of wired nuts to ¾ inch in width, racked on 2 or 3 biners.
- 2 or 3 small tri-cams, racked together on a biner, and 2 or 3 medium to large hexes on another biner doubles up the pro without adding excessive weight or bulk. On some routes it would be preferable to shore up the rack with extra SLCDs instead.
- 8-10 quickdraws
- 8 free biners and 2 or 3 locking biners
- 6 shoulder-length slings
- 1 nut tool with a keeper cord

Light is fast, though, so as your experience increases you might pare the rack down, depending on the route. If you expect no fist-size cracks, leave the bigger SLCDs in the pack and hope you won't need them—they're heavy.

Bomber taper.

Good for downward but not outward pull.

Good Hexcentric in a minor constriction.

Good Tri-cam, with the point sitting on a tiny ledge for stability.

Tri-cam in a parallel crack.

Maybe you can ditch a couple of quickdraws, some biners and the tri-cams and hexes. Now you're down to fighting weight. In Colorado it's called the "Eldo" rack, because it will get you up most Eldorado routes. You may have to run it out occasionally to get by on this rack. Husband the precious larger pieces.

Routes often have special gear needs: a thin, parallel crack that takes spring-loaded opposing wedges; a continuous crack that requires many SLCDs the same size; or an offwidth that requires wide protection. Do your research so you don't find yourself fifty feet out on a bombay flare with only two wires left. If the guidebook lists no suggested rack, and no one is around to milk for the beta, eyeball the route and take more than what you think is necessary. Keep in mind that cracks are generally wider than they appear from the deck, especially so in the desert rock. It's common that a leader will be short on big gear at mid-pitch. Pulling up gear on the haul line has saved many asses, but it's usually a poor and awkward way to do business.

Passive Chocks

Most present-day tapers are curved. Always orient them to best fit the crack with maximal surface contact. If you have a choice in sizes, go with the bigger taper, providing it wedges securely. Set tapers with a tug if there's a chance they might fall out, but don't over-jam your pieces. Use quickdraws or slings to connect wired nuts to the lead rope, so the rope can't wiggle them out.

Micronuts can afford a reasonable anchor—but only in the ideal situation. Regardless of what catalogs tell us, we know at a glance that a drop of brass or steel at the end of a piano wire is, at best, a stopgap device, a last resort when the rock affords nothing else. The limitations of micronuts are matters of strength—the strength of the cable, the actual nut and the rock surrounding the micro. Anything but a match fit, where most all of the nut's surface area is flush to the rock, should be considered marginal. The smallest ones have breaking strengths well below the force generated by an honest lead fall. If you urgently need pro, set two or three and equalize them. And don't fall. Clean stuck micronuts with a tap from the nut tool rather than yanking on the wire, which can damage the thin cable.

Hexentrics, Tom Frost's heroic innovation, work well in larger constricting cracks. They're simple, relatively light and in wavy cracks are often superior to cams. Particularly on adventure climbs, experienced hands will often carry a selection of three or four hexes on their rack.

Tri-cams bridge the gap between wedges and cams—they are both, and find purchase above bottlenecks. They cam in parallel-sided cracks and wedge into pockets. Climbers either love or hate them. These finicky devices often appear funky (especially the larger units), but they are versatile. Sizes # ½ through #2 are the most useful, especially in pocketed rock.

iend with offset ms–BAD.

Friend with cams open too wide–BAD.

Cams more than 50% closed–GOOD.

The next bigger size improves stability–BEST.

SPRING LOADED CAMMING DEVICES (SLCDs)

Ray Jardine revolutionized climbing when he introduced his Friends in the late seventies. Suddenly, long, parallel cracks could be protected with ease. Climbers—long terrified of hanging off slippery jams and trying to wiggle a bunk hex into a parallel-sided crack—suddenly scaled hard routes; great climbers climbed even harder. SLCDs are easy to use and very adaptable to various conditions. SLCDs are no miracle, however. They shine only when correctly placed in decent to excellent rock. The great majority of SLCD placements are sound and straightforward to set; for crafty placements, it is essential that you know the limitations of the devices which can be learned only through experience. Simple aid climbing is a good place to experiment.

When setting SLCDs, seek a uniformly parallel section of the crack, and set the largest piece that will fit. Beware not to overstuff the cams. You'll strand yourself at the belay while your second battles to clean the stuck—and very pricey—unit. Ideally, the cams should be halfway or more closed, with the stem pointing in the expected direction of loading. Camming units will often swivel toward the direction of pull once weighted, but don't count on it. They may swivel clean out of the crack. If the cams open more than halfway, try the next bigger size. Smaller camming units have limited expansion range and offer much less room for error. Make placements with the same precision as with a tricky taper placement.

Always visually inspect the cams before trusting an SLCD placement. Several configurations can spell danger, or at least trouble. If the cams are offset, tipped or inverted, the placement is worthless. These problems are common when the piece is too small for the placement, if the crack wavers in size, or if the piece walks. Rope drag/wiggle can cause the unit to walk after the leader has climbed above it, thinking he has sound gear below. A quickdraw or sling can help prevent this, though in straight up cracks you can usually clip them directly (provided they are slung). The key is to keep the rope running straight.

A Loweball in a tiny parallel crack.

Avoid setting a solid-stemmed SLCD in a horizontal crack with the stem protruding from the crack. A fall can bend or break the stem.

If you've fallen on a cam, always check the placement before trusting it again. A fall can rotate the cams into a bad position, especially if it's a swinging fall.

Everyone has their favorite units. My (C.L.) favorites are Friends and Camalots, though Metolius cams, Wired Bliss cams, Aliens, and HB Quadcams are also excellent.

Opposing Wedges

Opposing wedges, aka "slider nuts," evolved from "stacking" hexentrics, tapers and pins. As the name implies, two spring-loaded wedges oppose one another, pushing outward against the crack walls when loaded. These devices are not as bomber as bigger wired nuts, so if you must count on one, try to set two and equalize them, or clip in with a Yates Screamer. Because of limited expansion range, sizing is critical. Like SLCDs, opposing wedges should be placed in the smaller half of their size range, with maximum contact area between the wedges and the rock. If the crack is too large, a fall can force the wedges past one another.

The ingenious Lowe Ball fits more placement configurations than other designs. Its ball rotates to match any flare angle, maximizing stability and strength when the crack is not perfectly parallel. The #1 Lowe Ball is the smallest piece available for parallel placements, sizing down to ⅙ of an inch.

The problem with many slider nut placements is removing them. The key is to set them well but never yank too hard on them, which wedges them extra fast, forcing you to jostle the cable hard—often bending it—to clean them. A slider nut that has been fallen on is always a bearcat to clean.

Expandable Tubes

Bigbro expandable tubes protect offwidth cracks and squeeze chimneys from 3.2 to 12 inches (the name comes from "Big Brother" in Orwell's classic novel *1984*, the same year Bigbros were invented). Bigbros are smaller, lighter and less expensive than SLCDs in their size range, and the #3 and #4 units are the only gear available for cracks bigger than 6½ inches. Set in parallel placement, with both tube ends fully contacting the rock and the collar tightly secured, Bigbros hold a pull in any direction, so they make bomber belay anchors. On longer routes with short, wide sections, a Bigbro or two will give you pro while keeping the overall weight and bulk of the rack to a minimum. On the down side, Bigbros take more time and energy to place than spring-loaded cams; with practice most climbers can become proficient at placing Bigbros, although some never seem to master them. If the crack flares, SLCDs are preferred.

To set a Bigbro, place the unit in a parallel section of the crack and push the trigger button. Let the tube expand slowly to the width of the crack. Seek a place where both tube ends

Bigbro in a parallel crack.

fully contact the rock. The spring will hold the tube in place while tightening the collar. Now tug the sling in all possible directions of pull to test the placement. If you must place a Bigbro in a flare, search for a spot where the crack walls are most parallel, or look for a concavity to set the tube in or a crystal to fix the tube around. If no such possibilities exist, a Bigbro can work in mild flares by setting the chock with its slung end fully contacting the rock and the opposite end touching the rock in one point, similar to a Tri-cam. This is marginal territory, for sure. Careful not to kick the piece loose as you pass.

NATURAL ANCHORS

Slinging chockstones, flakes, blocks, trees, chickenheads and holes is often quicker than setting pro, saves your chocks for later use and often provides a multi-directional anchor. Be creative but realistic with natural protection, and don't waste time trying to thread a tight hole when you can fire in a wire and move on.

Natural anchors.

LEAD PROTECTION

Most advanced climbers feel that how often they set pro depends on the following factors: the availability of cracks, technical difficulty, quality of the rock, confidence and experience of the leader, presence of bone-breaking obstacles in the landing zone, quality of protection below, anticipation of good or bad protection above, selection of gear available and urgency of the situation. Is that all, you might ask? No. There are other factors, but these are the most crucial. Advanced climbing is not for fools, and if you want to stay healthy, you must know the game well enough to foresee problems and act accordingly.

Though there is no set rule on how often to place pro, I've (J.L.) climbed with some of the world's greatest and few of them needlessly ran the rope out. A mark of the ace leader is the ability to climb safely and quickly set pro even when it seems unnecessary. Few leaders feel comfortable going more than ten feet between placements, unless the climbing is casual. In practice, pro isn't always available every ten feet, so sometimes you must be prepared to run it out, or bail out. The frequency of placing pro is strictly a personal affair, but know that the best never make a practice of needlessly running the rope out. What's the point?

OK sling over a horn. A more defined lip would increase the sling's security.

Reminders

Some reminders for when the difficulty soars: constantly look for protection opportunities. Protect early and often on the pitch, particularly when the placements are quick and easy. Always place a good piece of pro immediately after leaving the belay to protect the belay anchors from a high-impact fall and shore up the anchors. Ideally, this first piece should be

Don't expect miracles.

You can help keep the sling in place by hanging some gear from it.

Standard fare in Dresden, the knot jam works in a pinch.

Silvia De Vito sews it up on "Fat City Crack" (10c), Lumpy Ridge, Colorado.

multi-directional to prevent the upper pieces from being pulled out. The highest force falls come early in the pitch, so the first pieces are critical. Again, careful not to burn the whole rack before the end of the pitch.

When looking for placements, avoid tunnel vision—don't scratch around trying to set a shaky piece when a good placement exists two feet higher. Experiment.

Don't bet your life on a single piece of pro. But if you must, consider clipping the bomber piece with two quickdraws or a locking carabiner. Redundancy is key. Create a system of protection to keep you off the ground or a ledge below. A long fall on a steep, clean face is often harmless, but a short fall onto a ledge can, and often does, leave bones showing. You might set two or more pieces at one stance, especially if the pieces look marginal, if the climbing above appears runout, or if you want to blast through a short crux without stopping in the middle to place gear. Avoid hanging out on difficult terrain—pro and go. To dick crux sections, climb smart but aggressively. Careful not to plug your best finger and hand jams with protection, though sometimes the pro is more vital than the hold.

Traversing

Whenever a route moves sideways or diagonally upward, place protection at the beginning of the traverse, and after any difficult moves—to keep the second safe from a dangerous pendulum fall. If the party consists of three or more climbers, make sure both ropes get clipped through the protection on traverses.

GOOD: ⅜" bolt.

BAD: ¼" buttonhead bolt. Don't expect much from these relics.

BAD: a ¼" threaded bolt.

Clipping off a bolt that is missing its hanger.

FIXED GEAR

Fixed gear can be a blessing or a curse. Quarter-inch bolts, rusty fixed pins, and tattered slings may hold a fall. The key word here is "may." Remember, nothing is guaranteed, even with perfect placements. Back up fixed gear whenever possible. Clipping shiny, ⅜" (or larger) bolts is a different story—usually, they're good. But it's still your ass and your responsibility to inspect the gear and decide if you want to trust your life to it. Is the bolt rusty, beaten with a hammer, or loose in its hole? Is the hanger a standard, trusty design, or some homemade crap? Once you deem the bolt good, clip it and move out.

Sometimes it's safest, and often quickest, to clip with your waist near the protection, so you don't have to pull a loop of slack into the rope, which adds distance to a fall. To minimize the possibility of the rope unclipping, always run the rope up and out through the biner, and face both biner gates (on the quickdraw) away from the anticipated direction of travel.

BAD: this pin isn't
very well supported.

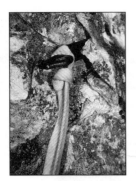

BAD: but at least it's
tied off now.

BAD: a fixed
knifeblade. Don't
count on it much.

BAD: way too much
leverage on this
piton.

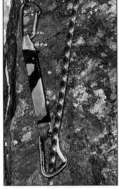

You can improve the
security of marginal
protection somewhat
by clipping to it with
a Screamer.

If you fall, the stitches
on the Screamer rip to
absorb energy and limit
the force developed on
your protection.

Never back clip a quickdraw. For extra safety, use a locking
biner on key fixed anchors. Avoid clipping biners together
to form a makeshift quickdraw. A twist on the biners can
separate them.

Occasionally you'll encounter a bolt stud with no hanger.
Slide the nut down on a medium wired nut, place the wire
around the stud then cinch the nut tight against the stud. The
wire might stay on, especially if the stud is lipped. If you anticipate hangerless bolts, bring some keyhole hangers.

Some rules of thumb: Never trust fixed slings unless they
are obviously new, and you have inspected their entire length,
their knots, and the attached anchor(s). Slings left on the
middle of a pitch are normally retreat points ("poot" slings),
meaning the rope has been dragged through them, significantly weakening the nylon. Never trust fixed pitons outright.
Changes in temperature can transform a veritable Lancelot's
sword to stick in the mud. And everyone with a hammer has
tried to clean the pin as well. Cracked eyes are common on
fixed pins. I (C.L.) took a short fall onto a rusty antique pin
high on the Salathé Wall. The eye broke entirely and I pitched
30 feet, stopping just inches above a ledge system. Thank
God the next pin held, because all my nuts zipped out of the
crack. Always back up fixed pins.

A fixed nut is stuck, but not necessarily in a position that
will withstand the force of a fall. And like fixed pins, everyone
has tried to clean the unit, yanking on it every which way; the
normal result is a trashed cable, making the nut poor to useless. With all fixed gear, a close visual inspection is essential.

BAD GEAR

Be wary of protection placed in soft, rotten, hollow or frac-
tured rock. If you protect behind a big block or flake, you risk
pulling it down with you in a fall. Dubious protection that
inspires false confidence can be worse than none at all.
Sometimes, though, a bad piece is worth placing because it
might catch you, or at least slow you down. If the pro is

sketchy, place several pieces to achieve safety in numbers, and then do your damnedest not to blow off. One way to increase the strength of marginal anchors is to equalize them. Another trick is to clip them with a Yates Screamer. The Screamer is a fat quickdraw that self-destructs to absorb energy in a fall, limiting the load of a short fall to 550 pounds. For really horrible gear, equalize it and use a Screamer. And then make sure not to fall anyway.

The rope running around this lip has pulled the Friend into a horizontal orientation, and a fall after placing protection above will load the rope over the edge. A quickdraw would have cured both problems.

(Left) Even this much of a zigzag in your rope will cause big rope drag later in the pitch. The right piece needs a shoulder-length runner.

This mistake is going to cause huge rope drag, and it's possible the rope will jam altogether if it gets pinched between the rope and the carabiner.

THE RUN OF THE ROPE

Rope drag increases with each bend in the rope, so set gear in the straightest line possible. When sharp angles are encountered, use slings and quickdraws, or double rope technique, to straighten the run of the rope. Extend the piece no further than necessary, but make sure the sling extends beyond any edge or roof that may jam the rope. And always avoid loading carabiners over or across an edge. Work to keep the rope clear of sharp edges.

Belay anchors are properly a lifelong study. They are also the specific topic of the two anchoring books also in the *How To Rock Climb* series. Belaying and rappelling are also topics essential to master at the beginning to intermediate level. Still, these topics are worth a brief review relative to what the advanced climber must know.

Belay anchors can be subjected to loads of 3,000 pounds. Setting good belay anchors is one of, if not the most, important steps in climbing. Never take shortcuts. Strive to rig anchors that are clean, simple and absolutely bomber. Advanced climbing is largely a matter of efficiency with all aspects of the climbing game. Particularly on long adventure routes, where time is a factor, the efficiency with which you build solid anchors can sometimes mean the difference between a perfect ascent and a forced bivy.

Whatever the anchor configuration, three good downward pieces and one upward piece, opposing the downward anchors, is a minimum, no matter how inviolate the placements seem individually. Sometimes, three are enough. Sometimes that's all you'll get. In alpine situations I've (C.L.) settled for two, and on rare occasions, even one belay anchor, but only when no other option existed. In this extreme case, always hunker into the belay ledge to incorporate your physical perch as a component of the belay. The rule on rock climbs is to always use three or more anchors. Anything less is a crap shoot. Be sure the closest anchor(s)—the first to be loaded in a fall—are multi-directional. If you're on a bolt route you may have to trust a double bolt anchor, which is sufficient provided the rock is solid and the bolts are well-placed and at least ⅜" in diameter. Still, equalize the bolts, and back them up with a bomber chock if possible.

When rigging anchor systems, always consider the following details:

• Find a spot that provides convenient placements and a comfortable perch. Take a moment to plan the entire system. Analyze the situation and prepare the anchors for any possible direction of pull.

• Keep the system simple, so it is quick to set and easy to doublecheck and keep tabs on. Use the minimum amount of gear to safely but efficiently construct a bombproof, multi-directional system.

• Any anchor is only as strong as the surrounding rock, so make sure to set your anchors in the best available rock.

Whatever configuration we rig, we always strive after anchors that are Solid, Redundant, Equalized, and that allow No Extension, or SRENE. (This acronym is modified from one used by the American Mountain Guides Association.) The fundamental concepts behind SRENE are:

SOLID means the individual anchors and the system as a whole must be bombproof.

REDUNDANT means placing three or four solid anchors

SRENE

Solid

Redundant

Equalized

No Extension

(more if the anchors are less than ideal). Redundancy should exist through the entire anchor system: all anchors, slings and carabiners should be backed up. Redundancy also can include setting anchors in more than one crack system to avoid relying on a single rock feature.

EQUALIZATION means distribute the load equally between the various anchors in the system to increase the overall strength of the system and reduce the chance of a single anchor pulling out.

NO EXTENSION means that if one of the anchors or components in the system should fail, the system will not suddenly become slack and drop the climber a short distance, shock-loading the remaining anchors.

Though we will not always be able to construct anchors that conform perfectly to SRENE standards, that is our goal. You want an efficient anchor, not simply one that will bear the greatest impact. This means that whenever possible, the nuts should be straightforward to place and remove, and should be located as centrally as possible—a nice, tight grouping, rather than a baffling web of nuts crisscrossing the station. Once that first nut is set, try to rig the secondary anchors in close proximity, but not so close that they are cramped or virtually on top of each other. If the rock is less than perfect in quality, spread the anchors out to preserve redundancy; don't put your life in one basket.

Equalize, Equalize, Equalize

Even if the belay chocks are bomber, it's important to equalize the load on your pieces. Several possibilities exist—use the climbing rope, a cordelette, webbing slings, or a combination of these. With every belay system, make sure you're tied in tight to the anchors, in line between them and the climber, so you can't get launched. In some situations you may choose to sit below the anchors so your body can lift a bit

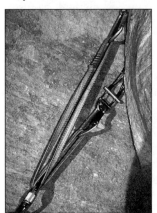

A slider knot on two thin pieces.

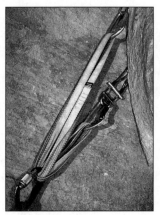

Double slings improve redundancy.

You can reduce the the possible extension of the slider knot if the upper piece pulls by tying it off.

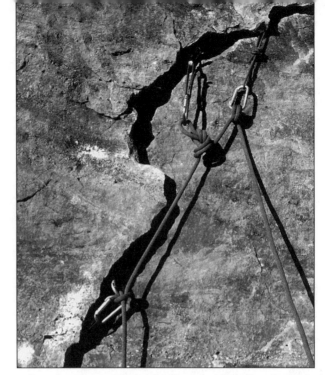

A slider knot tie-in, backed up by a high anchor. Two clove hitches provide easy adjustability. The locking carabiner at the slider knot tie-in greatly improves security.

to soften the impact of a lead fall—provided there's no roof or other projection to bean you. Avoid rigging that throws slack into the system if one anchor fails, which would shock-load the remaining anchors. The best method for equalizing is a slider knot, which maintains equalization even if the loading direction changes. You can reduce the potential extension by tying off the long leg of the sling. Rigging two slings identically in a sliding knot preserves redundancy.

Rope Tie-In

The popular rope tie-in, usually the quickest method, requires the least amount of gear and is preferred by both authors much of the time. In the best situation, the belayer will tie tightly to a bombproof multi-directional anchor set near his/her waist, then tie into two more bombproof downward anchors placed above the first, with the belayer's body in line between the anchors and the anticipated direction of pull. It's wise to tie into the most bombproof anchor with a figure-eight knot and a locking carabiner. Clove hitches should suffice for the remaining anchors. Some climbers prefer all clove hitches to keep the tie-in adjustable. Now feather the clove hitches so the whole rig is more or less under equal tension. Cinch the clove hitches tight and keep your eye on them—they have a tendency to unclip. Two biners, gates opposed, or a locking carabiner, add security to the clove. Incorporating a slider knot into the arrangement ensures equalization of two of the anchors.

You can also equalize the load by tying an equalizing figure-eight knot and clipping it into two or three of the anchors.

This knot requires a bit of rope, so make sure the next pitch isn't a full rope length. It's also best if the anchors are absolutely bomber and relatively close together. The primary disadvantage of rigging with the rope is that, if your partner has an accident and you need to escape the belay (more on this in the Self-rescue chapter) to initiate a rescue, you must completely re-rig the anchors to free the rope, which could be difficult, or even impossible.

Above, two belay bolts are tied off with an equalizing Figure Eight.
Right, step by step construction of an equalizing Figure-Eight.

1. Tie a figure eight on a bight with an extra large loop of rope.
2. Pass the bight back through the figure eight to create
3. Three clipping loops.
4. Clip all three loops to equalize three anchors, or collapse one clipping loop
5. And clip the other two to equalize two anchors.

Cordelette tie-in. Both the nuts and small Friend will hold a downward or upward pull, so no separate upward anchor is necessary. You would want to rearrange this anchor if you expected a possible sideways pull (the next pitch traverses). The cordelette, tied off as shown, will only equalize the load if the pull is straight up or straight down. If equalization is critical, this may not be the strongest system, but it's fast, clean, compact, and provides a single tie-in point.

Web-o-lette tie-in. The free loop is hanging loose, waiting for the second to arrive and clip in. The lowest anchors, two opposed nuts, make the anchor multi-directional.

Cordelette

Another useful system uses a cordelette—a 16- to 18-foot loop of 6mm to 7mm perlon (or 5.5mm Spectra or Gemini)—to equalize the load between two, three or four anchors. The cordelette creates a single tie-in point, greatly simplifying belay switch-overs when one climber is leading all of the pitches, or if the party consists of more than two climbers. The cordelette also requires less gear than webbing slings for connecting the anchors together, thereby justifying its size and weight. A cordelette can also be invaluable in self-rescue situations.

The cordelette is tied into a loop with a grapevine knot and clipped into each of the anchors. A loop of the perlon is then pulled down between each of the pieces. If you have three pieces in your anchor, you'll get three strands/loops that must then be ponytailed together and pulled tight toward the anticipated loading direction (put a finger or biner through the loop at the anchor point and pull slightly until the strands are equalized). Lastly, tie an Overhand knot, or if you have enough slack, a Figure-eight knot in the tripled strand to create the tie-in loop.

The biggest shortcoming of the cordelette system is that it

doesn't maintain perfect equalization if the loading direction changes. The first few times using a cordelette will seem like a pain in the ass. With practice it becomes quick and straight forward. While the cordelette is probably the best setup, and in time may well become standard, it is still a novelty amongst most climbers who, for the most part, opt for a simpler construct.

Web-o-lette

A Web-o-lette—a ten-foot piece of Spectra webbing with a sewn loop at each end—substitutes for a cordelette when rigging anchors. The Web-o-lette is slightly lighter, more compact and quicker to rig than a cordelette, and it is great for long anchor extensions on lead or at the belay. A cordelette serves better for rescues, so some climbers and guides carry a Web-o-lette for rigging anchors, and a cordelette for rescues.

Slings

The most gear-intensive, confusing and unfortunately popular method involves using an array of slings, quickdraws and carabiners to connect the anchors.

Nonetheless, slings are often invaluable in rigging an anchor, particularly when equalizing several components of a multi-component anchoring matrix. Aside from the fundamentals discussed in *How To Rock Climb: Climbing Anchors,* the business of "close" and "narrow

Sling tie-in. This system is nearly as bomber as they come, but it sure uses a lot of slings, carabiners, and time to arrange. A slider knot with double slings and carabiners provides equalization and redundancy at the clip-in point. The bottom anchors are held in opposition by a clove hitch in the slings, and the upper two anchors are equalized with a second slider knot. This rigging will place 50 percent of the load on the lowest downward anchor, and 25 percent on each of the higher anchors.

angles" should be understood. In simple terms, it works like this: whenever a sling or cordelette is used to connect two pieces of protection, you end up with a triangular configuration. The points of the triangle are comprised of the left-hand placement (A), the right-hand placement (B), and the point at which you secure the sling to the climbing rope—the anchor point (C). The triangle can be visualized as a piece of pie. All triangles and all pieces of pie form a "V". The branches of the sling coming from the left-hand placement (A) and the right-hand placement (B) converge like a "V" at the anchor point (C). The critical thing to grasp here is that the bigger the angle formed by this "V"—the bigger the wedge of pie, if you will—the greater the force placed on the A and B placements. Again, as the angle of the "V" increases, so do the forces placed on the placements. This phenomenon is known as "load multiplication," and it's sobering to see how quickly the forces increase as the angle of the "V" increases (as the piece of pie gets bigger).

Consider this: imagine a two-bolt belay. If a 1,000-pound force was applied to the anchor point (C), and the "V" formed by the sling was at 30 degrees, a load of 520 pounds would be placed on each bolt. At 60 degrees, the force increases to 580

Angle of Pull and Anchor Strength

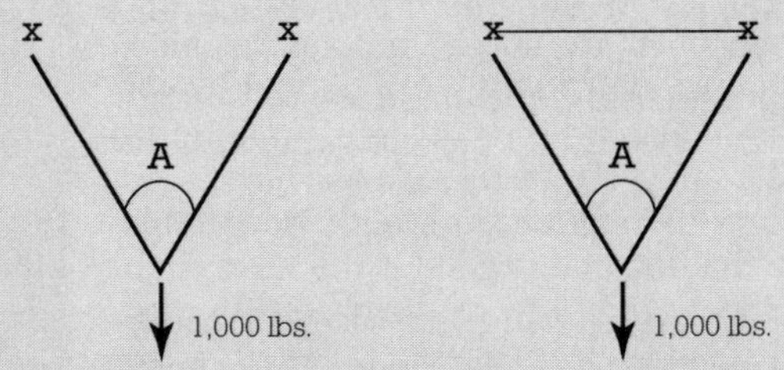

angle (A)	slider knot or independent slings (pounds)		American Triangle (pounds)
0°	500		707
30°	518	comfort	821
60°	577		1,000
90°	707	caution	1,306
120°	1000		1,932
150°	1932	danger	3,830
175°	11,463		22,920

If the anchor system is required to support 1,000 pounds, the figure shown in the table is the resulting force on each anchor.

Increasing or decreasing the load on the anchor system results in a proportional increase or decrease on each anchor.

pounds; at 90 degrees, 710 pounds; at 120 degrees, a load of 1,000 pounds is placed on each bolt. This tells us that the comfort zone is when the angle of the "V" is at 60 degrees or less. The caution zone is between 60 and 90 degrees, and the danger zone is anything over 90 degrees, where the forces are multiplied exponentially.

This gives us rule of thumb: whenever connecting two placements with a sling, strive to keep the angle of the V (at the anchor point) around 30 to 60 degrees. (Some guides tell students to try and keep the angle of the V less than 90 degrees, but this is pushing the system too far for my skin.) The reason we normally connect two placements with a sling is to equalize potential forces between both placements. If the radical angle of the triangular configuration formed by the sling actually increases the load on each placement, you've done yourself more harm than good and have defeated the concept of equalizing the load.

Of course, we can only take what the rock affords, and many times it's necessary to place nuts rather far apart (which creates the high angles) and connect them with a sling. The only immediate solution here is to use longer slings to decrease the angle of the V, to narrow that wedge of pie. Remember, the closer the anchor point (C) is to the individual placements (A and B), the larger the angle of the V, and the greater load multiplication. The thinner the slice of pie, the less force each placement will have to bear.

If the anchors are spread out horizontally, combine slings with the rope to anchor in. Or tie the climbing rope in a triangle, running to each of the anchors, then back to yourself so you are tight to anchors from both sides. This uses rope that may be needed if the next pitch is long, but the belayer can dismantle the last leg of the triangle when needed. If you have led the pitch with double ropes, connect one rope into the anchors on the right and the other rope into the anchors on the left. Or utilize your haul line for the same purpose.

MULTI-DIRECTIONAL ANCHORS

The belay anchor must be multi-directional. The most obvious multi-directional anchors are trees, chockstones and holes in the rock girth-hitched with a sling. Bolts and pitons also are multi-directional. Horizontal cracks sometimes work if they open in the back to accept a taper, but pinch at the edge to resist any direction of pull. A SLCD placed in a horizontal crack provides a somewhat multi-directional anchor. A well-placed Bigbro also serves as a multi-directional. In a pinch, a SLCD set in the lower half of its expansion range in a vertical crack can be aligned with its stem pointing out to swivel up or down toward the direction of pull, but use this only in perfectly parallel cracks, with the SLCD in the lower half of its expansion range (and understand that it's even-Steven that the unit will blow). Another option is to oppose two chocks against each other, connecting them tautly with clove hitches on a sling or the climbing rope to create a multi-directional anchor.

The rope triangle tie-in keeps you tight to two horizontally spaced anchor clusters. After clipping the second anchor, clip the rope back to your harness.

If you're using a cordelette, set the lowest two pieces in opposition and clove hitch them taut against each other. Now clip the remaining loop of cordelette through two higher, downward directional pieces, pull down three loops and tie them off as before.

Difficult Anchors

If you reach a ledge or obvious belay stance and suitable anchors are unobtainable, consider climbing higher, setting some anchors, then downclimbing (toproped) back to the belay ledge/stance. Tying into the rope descending from the high piece(s) provides a backup to the available anchors. It's essential to incorporate your body into the anchor if the construct is suspect and find the most secure seat or stance possible. As a last resort (emergencies only) it may be necessary

Two nuts held tight in opposition by clove hitches on a sling. Beware of increased force on the pieces because the sling is arranged in an American Triangle (see Chapter 5).

Eric Kohl and Pete Takeda returning to the bivy,
pitch 11, the Porcelain Wall, Yosemite, California.

Greg Epperson photo

for both climbers to climb simultaneously until the leader arrives at a suitable, or at least possible, belay. Obviously, if the second falls, he/she will likely pull the leader off. Simul-climb only if retreat is impossible. That's the law. If you get stuck on grim terrain and have to "simul" to the only anchor, or whatever situation might force you into simulclimbing, vaya con Dios.

Bunk Anchors

If the belay anchors are pathetic and no better possibilities exist—like a hanging belay from double ¼" bolts, a situation found on ancient slab routes—the leader should avoid clipping into the anchors before leaving the belay. If the leader clips the anchors and falls before setting another piece, the pulley effect increases the impact force on the belay anchors by almost two-thirds. No addition of force occurs if the leader is caught directly by the belayer, but the fall may be more severe for the leader, and is almost always a more grievous "catch" for the belayer.

Three-piece minimal anchor, clipped with a series of clove hitches. The first piece, a good Friend, is set horizontally so it can swivel and hold a downward or upward pull. The placement needs to be perfect for this to work.

Steph Davis belaying
Kennan Harvey on
"Hallucinogen Wall" (VI
5.11 A3+), Black Canyon
of the Gunnison, Colorado.

Belaying and Rappelling

CHAPTER 5

Communication

Good communication between partners is essential to safe, fluid climbing. Sometimes regular partners have their own abbreviated commands, but it's best to use the formal belay signals so your communication is standard and exact. To avoid confusion in crowded areas, follow each command with your partner's name. Twice I (C.L.) have been mistakenly taken off belay after my partner heard another leader cry "off belay." Cranking a crux and hearing your partner yell "belay off!" is about as comforting as a death sentence. Everyone does it differently, but it's safest to holler "off belay" before taking your partner off, to make certain you heard him or her correctly. Especially on remote adventure climbs, the wind can blow so loudly (river noise on short routes is also trying) that verbal communication may be impossible (except when both climbers are at the same belay).

Communication in these conditions can be frustrating and dangerous. The solution is to have a system worked out with your partner before doing a multi-pitch route. One universal signal is three or four hard, steady rope tugs from the leader meaning he or she is anchored, off belay, and ready for the second to climb. These tugs would normally be preceded by a few moments when the rope doesn't feed out— while the leader arranges belay anchors. Then the slack would be steadily pulled up until the line is taut. Another short pause while the leader rigs the belay device would be followed by three or four tugs. After this sequence, you're probably on belay— but never for certain unless the signals are arranged beforehand. If you start climbing up and the rope isn't going with you, you may not be on belay, so clip back into the anchors and wait until the rope goes tight. Again, the key here is to have something worked out with your partner and understood before you need to trust your life to it.

Good, attentive belaying. The belayer is tied in so there is no way the end of the rope can come through the belay device when lowering or at the end of a long pitch.

BELAYING THE LEADER

Some rules are made to be broken; belay rules are not. In review, the belay rules are: never take your brake hand off the rope; stay alert and focused on the climber; have bombproof belay anchors and tie yourself in tight, in line

Typical, bad belaying. The belayer has too much slack in the rope, is too far from the bottom of the climb, and is not paying attention to the leader.

with the anticipated direction of pull; double check anchors, harness buckles, knots, locking carabiners and belay devices before anyone leaves the ground; maintain a secure stance; keep excess slack out of the rope; keep the rope stacked so it feeds well; be tied into the rope or at least have a knot in the end of the rope; use proper communication signals that are concise and understood by both climbers; if the moves off the ground are bleak, spot the leader until he/she clips the first solid piece; and always, for you and your partner's protection, insist that the leader puts in solid protection straight off the belay.

Those are the basics that apply equally to a beginner and a World Cup champion. Once you're into the upper range of difficulty, other factors come into play.

Feed Me

Because pace is so important on hard routes, always feed the rope to match the climber's pace. The rope should never go tight against the leader, nor should too much slack be in the system. When the leader places pro or clips a quickdraw, anticipate feeding rope, especially when the clip is desperate. For a quick feed, extend your brake hand an arm's length away from the belay device on the brake rope, and bring your guide hand in right next to the device. As the leader reaches down to pull up rope, quickly fire an arm's length of rope through the device with your guide hand, while feeding with the brake hand, and return your hands to the starting position. If the leader reaches down to grab more rope, quickly repeat the process. When climbing or clipping, the leader should never feel resistance from the rope. If you don't anticipate the clip, or if the leader's arms are longer than yours, it may be hard to feed rope quick enough. If the clip is super-desperate, you may need to feed slack just before the leader needs it, so he/she can grab rope freely. Be careful doing this if the potential for a ground or ledge fall exists. If you're belaying on flat ground, you can also move in and out from the base of the climb to help feed out or take in rope.

Even worse. This person should not be belaying.

Stance

The belayer should always have a secure and comfortable stance. In extreme circumstances where good anchors cannot be found, brace your feet against a rock, sit your body in a depression, or wedge it in a crack to bolster the belay. When possible, especially if you're on soft or rotten rock, belay in a sheltered spot so you're not vulnerable to rockfall from the leader. I (C.L.) once caught a rock in the mouth while belaying below the leader on soft desert sandstone. A helmet can be useful for protecting your head, but on junk rock it's a poor idea to stay directly below the leader—or any climber in action.

Peanut Gallery

The belayer has a different visual perspective on the way the rope runs, and can often give useful advice to the leader. Some leaders will suffer no advice, though most will appreciate you mentioning things like: "Flip your rope off of that edge," when the rope is not running true; "Extend that piece with a sling or you're going to have nasty rope drag," if you can foresee the rope making sharp bends; "You're almost into groundfall range," if you realize that their highest piece of pro is soon-to-be too low to keep them off the deck; or "30 feet" when only 30 feet of rope remains, cuing the leader to start looking for a belay. Remember, belayers normally underestimate the length of rope left.

Lock Fast

In the days of hemp ropes, many arcane climbing textbooks espoused the idea of a "dynamic" belay, where the belayer intentionally lets some rope slide through the belay device when catching a lead fall. This softens the forces on the leader, belayer and anchors. Today, with highly engineered nylon ropes, ⅜" or ½" diameter bolts and chocks that will hold a battleship, the belayer gives a more "static" belay, and locks off the rope immediately if the leader falls.

If the lead protection is marginal, the climber isn't going to hit any ledges or other features by falling further, or if the leader is falling off a roof or bulge, some extra slack will soften the catch, increase the radius of the leader's swing and decrease the speed at which he hits the wall below, possibly sparing him shattered ankles.

Suck It Up

Sometimes you want to take in rope if the leader falls, especially if the last protection is far below and he's in danger of decking. More than one life has probably been saved by the Edwin Moses belay, where the belayer sprints along the ground to take up rope and hopefully keeps the falling leader off the ground. Bear in mind that this will significantly increase the impact force on the anchors and the climber, but it beats a sure-fire groundfall.

Two Lines

Double rope technique works well in some situations, but it requires extra effort to carry, stack and coil two ropes. Also, two ropes are four times more likely to get tangled and twisted than a single rope. When belaying with double or twin ropes, remember, each rope must pass through the belay device and your brake hand must always be on both ropes. If the leader clips only one rope above his or her waist, that rope must be taken in, while the other rope is fed out, until the leader's waist is above both pieces. Then you will feed both ropes out again. Usually you'll stack both ropes together in the same pile on the belay ledge, or in a lap coil.

Free Fall

Famous climbers are not exempt from forgetting—or neglecting—to always tie into the end of the rope when belaying.

If not properly tied in, the end of the rope can whistle through your belay device if the leader falls near the end of a long pitch, or if the lowering distance is a little longer than half the rope length. The frequency of this last scenario is alarming—especially at sport climbing areas—and has resulted in many grave injuries, sometimes to top climbers. Just last year, two of my (C.L.) friends were lowering off the top of sport climbs and, not having enough rope to quite reach the ground, were literally cut loose when the belayer unwittingly let the end whizz through the belay device. In both cases the belayers had over ten years of climbing experience and were 5.12 leaders. Again, always tie in to prevent the rope's end from getting away from you and possibly killing your partner. If sport climbing, at least tie a knot that cannot pass through your belay device in the end of the rope.

Belaying the second off the harness.

Belaying the second through a high directional anchor. The high anchor MUST be a good one, or you're at risk of dropping the second a ways if it fails.

BELAYING THE SECOND

Usually you'll belay directly off your harness. This always works best when belaying a leader or a slingshot toproped climber. When belaying a second, especially on hard routes where hanging is anticipated, run the rope from your belay device up to the bombproof anchors and down to the second (belay directional). If he falls or hangs on the rope, you'll get pulled up rather than down. The friction of the biner lessens his weight and makes belaying more comfortable if your partner "epics" on the pitch. Never use less than bomb-proof anchors as a directional.

Belaying directly off the anchors ("direct belay"), rather than your harness, also works well for a struggling second. Your anchors must be absolutely bombproof because your body is not in the system to cushion or resist the load. One quick way to rig this is to tie into the anchors with a figure-eight or an equalizing figure-eight knot. Just below the figure-eight, on the second's side of the rope, tie a figure-eight on a bight at chest level or so, and set up the belay device on this knot. Now if the second hangs, the anchors will directly hold his or her weight. If you use a GriGri for the direct belay, you can easily create a 3:1 pulley and hoist your partner up if they're in a jam (see Chapter 9, Self-Rescue). Anchors rigged with a cordelette also provide a convenient setup for a direct belay.

Belaying the second directly off the cordelette with a GriGri makes life easy for the belayer. Never let the cam get pinned against the wall, or it may not engage in a fall. The anchors must be absolutely bomber for this system.

Belaying the second directly off the rope, which is equalized to all three downward anchors with an Equalizing Figure-Eight. It's nice to have the belay device rigged slightly higher. Chest level works best.

Passing a knot on top rope.

(1.) Tie a backup Figure Eight into the rope that will jam in the belay device if anything goes wrong. (2.) Rig a second belay device on the other side of the knot and resume belaying. Keep the first device rigged if you plan to lower the climber. (3.) To pass the knot when lowering, ask the climber to get their weight off the rope, or have someone hold off the climber's weight. (4.) while you dismantle the second belay device. Now your friend on the ground can untie your backup Figure-Eight, (5.) and you can resume lowering the climber.

Slingshot

Consider the typical "slingshot" belay, where the rope runs from a belayer on the deck, up and through a toprope anchor and back down to a climber. We've all run this rig hundreds of times and yet many people are getting hurt with this set up. For that reason, the basics are worth reviewing:

When slingshot toproping a climb longer than half a rope length, you must tie two ropes together. A figure-eight backed

Lowering with both hands braking is safest.

up by Grapevines is the favored knot. This presents a problem when the knot gets to the belay device and won't pass through. A workable solution: have an extra device ready to rig on the other side of the knot while the climber is tied off on the first device. You might ask the climber to hold on for a minute while doing this—which may or may not be possible for them. If you're planning to lower the climber, keep the original device rigged for re-passing the knot. Sometimes you can simply walk down hill or away from the wall to take rope in without passing the knot. Or you can have the climber tie in mid-rope (with locking carabiners) while the knot connecting the ropes is at the top anchors. The excess rope can be clipped off to the back of your harness so you're not tripping over it on the way up. This eliminates the need to pass the knot, which will arrive at the belayer precisely when the climber arrives at the top anchor.

An effective method for tying directly into the middle of the rope when toproping so you can avoid passing a knot.

(1.) Tie an extra large Figure Eight loop and pass it through you harness tie-in point. (2.) Pull the loop around your head (3.) then step through it. (4.) Now the loop is girth-hitched to your harness. (5.) Work the Figure Eight knot closer to the harness and tie a loop to the back of your harness to keep the free-hanging rope away from your feet. One possible disadvantage is that you can't exit this knot quickly without a knife.

LOWERING

Every experienced climber knows never to lower with the rope running through a nylon sling or cord. But climbers still do it, and some are presently shoveling smelting coal or plucking the harp because of it. Lowering or toproping through aluminum rappel rings is likewise perilous, especially in the desert, where sand in the rope abrades the rings. Hopefully climbers will soon abandon these aluminum rings entirely in favor of steel links.

"Lower Me!"

Before you lean back to lower, always look down and make certain your belayer is with you. Say "Lower me" and/or give the "thumbs down" signal. Never say "Belay off" or "I'm off" at the end of a pitch if you intend to lower because you need to be on to get lowered. And don't yell, "I'm off," if you fall. Not few, but many top climbers have been busted up because their belayers prematurely took them off belay, or weren't holding the rope when they leaned back to lower. Best to always grip the belayer's side of the rope and ease into the tension, holding on until you can feel the belayer has you nice and tight.

Smooth as Single Malt Scotch

When lowering someone, nothing's more hateful than twists and knots tangling the rope and jamming in your belay device. Once the cord gets truly snarled, it's typically a nasty, two-hand job to get it straight, so you might have to call for help. The solution: avoid the tangles in the first place by stacking the cord for easy feeding. Skip this step through sloth or to save time, and live to curse the world.

As soon as the climber gives the command to lower, reel in any slack, lock off your belay device and lean back to give them tension. Don't leave slack in the line and make them "fall" onto the rope.

I (C.L.) use two hands on the brake side of the rope to give a smooth descent—a practice especially useful in preventing a rope kink from knocking a single brake hand off the rope. Lower your partner smooth as single malt Scotch, not too fast but not too slow. Never jerk him about like a puppet on a string. Slow him as he approaches the ground, and make certain he's solidly on his feet before feeding out a load of slack.

Plummet Protection

The gravest mistake in lowering someone is to drop them out of control, or to let the end of the rope pass through your belay device and lose them altogether. As mentioned, both of these mishaps occur far too often, even to the best climbers. The lowering anchors must be within a half rope length for your partner to reach the ground. Even if you're certain that the rope reaches the ground when doubled, tie into the rope and eliminate the chance of your buddy whizzing through your belay device if the rope is shorter than you thought. Also, don't stray too far from the lowering zone, in case extra line is needed. A middle mark on the rope can help determine if you have enough rope to lower the climber.

ROPE MANAGEMENT

No leader can crank through a bleak crux unless the rope is fed smoothly. It is the belayer's job to make sure it is. Before the leader starts, the belayer stacks the line in a loose pile, hopefully out of the dirt, with the leader's end (the "business end") on top. If you belay straight out of the coil, count on the rope to tangle just as the leader is trying an urgent clip. It's murderous to claw up a gruesome lead and have the rope repeatedly jam at the belay. If the rope is kinking, keep the snags several feet ahead of the belay device so the leader can move unimpeded.

If no decent ledge exists for stacking the rope, be careful not to let it hang down too far below your belay or it might snag, especially if the rock is featured. Getting the rope hung up below can put the leader in a straightjacket, unable to move up or lower down. Also, if the rope hangs too low, it's difficult to feed rope quickly. A lap coil helps here. On clean slabs you may only need to fold the rope once, near its midpoint. If the rock is more featured you might fold the rope back and forth several times to keep the loops short. The first loops should be the longest, with each successive loop made progressively shorter. The shorter loops get fed out first and shouldn't tangle on the longer loops. If you don't want the rope draped in front of you, or if you need to stack more than one rope, fold the rope back and forth through a sling.

Change Over

When swinging leads, once the second gains the belay, the rope will be set with his or her end on top of the stack. If the belay ledge is ample for both climbers to easily stand, quickly secure the climber with a figure-eight-on-a-bight tied into the rope just behind the belay device. When the new leader is set to cast off, simply untie the figure-eight and you're set to belay. If the same climber leads all of the pitches, restack the rope at each belay so the leader's end of the rope is on top of the stack. If not, the rope will surely tangle, most likely when the leader is cruxing. If the rope is already marvelously stacked on a ledge, you might be able to do the "pancake flop." Pick up the whole stack and flip it over flapjack style, so the bottom end comes out on top of the stack.

Hang

If no ledge exists at the belay station, you'll have to rig a hanging belay. As always, make sure the anchors are solid, multi-directional and well-equalized. Have a place ready for your partner to clip into when he or she gains the belay—usually a sling (with locking biner) pre-clipped into the anchor point. As things get more complex, systemization and organization become increasingly important.

Once you have climbed enough long adventure routes, you'll get a feel for how to set up an efficient system on the spot. Security is always first, followed by convenience and simplicity. By the time the second gains the belay, an experienced hand will already have scanned the next pitch and organized the leader's rack. Organization is crucial to keep the flow going. If you get to the belay and find the rack in disarray, with nuts and biners clipped everywhere and no order to

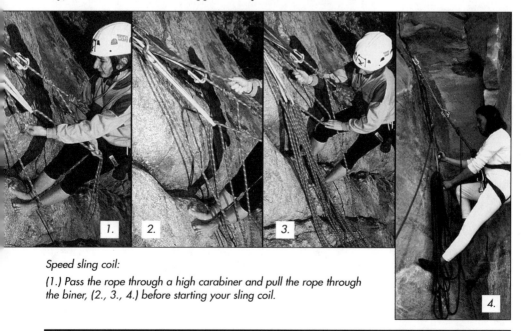

Speed sling coil:

(1.) Pass the rope through a high carabiner and pull the rope through the biner, (2., 3., 4.) before starting your sling coil.

1. 2. 3.

Hanging belay transfer.

1. The second arrives at the hanging belay and

2. clips into a pre-arranged sling.

3. The climbers quickly reorganize the rack, and the new leader casts off on the next pitch.

Rappel anchors: BAD

anything, you'll be in for a long and frustrating day. The ability to crank hard cruxes is only part of becoming an ace adventure climber (and adventure climbs are often where hanging belays are found). Staying on top of things, keeping well-organized and anticipating things before they become necessities are all crucial aspects of an efficient ascent.

GOING DOWN

We all understand that the tools and techniques for descending are fairly straightforward. Yet every year many experts forget that the cost of a mistake is extremely high. Good judgement, attention to details, awareness of hazards and religious double checking will keep you alive. Believe it: even a momentary lapse can put you in a pine box. If you're not confident that you can safely get back down to the ground, don't start up on a climb. Period.

Always have a plan for the descent. This was not so important when you were breaking in, when your usual route saw much traffic and the descent was generally common knowledge; but now that you're venturing onto test pieces, there will be less general info and less traffic on the descents, which are often devious and poorly marked, if marked at all (remember, experts are likely to leave the least amount of gear behind, such as rappel anchors et al). Descending long routes can be complicated, circuitous and dangerous. Innumerable epics have been suffered after a party neglected to do its homework per the descent. Consult guidebooks and fellow climbers for the scoop on descending a given climb. Usually there are several options, but often only one good—or at least established—route. If info is scant or unavailable, eyeball the cliff from the ground. Look for places to walk or climb down, or established rappel anchors. If you can't find an obvious descent, it's often best to rappel the climbing to avoid forging into unknown, and sometimes unforgiving, terrain.

WALKOFF

Walking down is always the first option, providing the walkoff is easy. On short routes, climbers frequently lower or rappel for convenience. The advice on walking down is basic: always be careful not to cut down too soon to avoid getting "cliffed," and always ferret out the path of least resistance.

RAPPELLING

We all know the score: rappelling forces us to rely completely on our equipment and the anchors, and can be a deadly proposition unless everything is exactly right. For the advanced climber—especially after cranking an exhausting adventure climb—rappelling often comes at the end of a long day, or in the face of miserable weather, two instances where our guard might be down. But we can never let our guard down when rappelling. We must maintain control until we're finished. As always, it's critical to double check every aspect of the "safety chain"—harness buckle (and your partner's), rappel device, locking carabiner, anchor, and all knots—before leaning back to rappel.

Rappel anchors: GOOD

Review

The following introduces nothing new, but since so many injuries occur from rappelling, the basics are worth reviewing, no matter how experienced we may be.

• At least two bombproof anchors should be established at rappel stations. If they're anything less than bomber, back them up if possible, and make sure everything is well-equalized.

• If you're relying on fixed slings, inspect them for UV degradation (the arch foe of nylon), varmint gnawing and fatal grooves left from previous ropes being pulled through. Check the entire length of the slings hidden from view, and any rappel rings or links. Add a sling if you question the existing ones (a dollar is a fair exchange for your life). Don't get into the catastrophic habit of trusting whatever fixed gear exists. Many climbers have been found at the base of cliffs, very dead from rapping off fixed gear.

• Avoid the American Triangle, where the sling(s) pass through both rappel anchors and the rappel point to form a triangle, especially if the anchors are suspect.

American Triangle on two good bolts with aluminum rappel ring—OK, but only because the anchors are bombproof. Otherwise you should not use the American Triangle. This setup is good for rappelling only; do not lower from the ring, and I'd back up the ring and sling.

Below: backed up rappel anchor.

• If you're forced to rappel on piss-my-pants anchors, back up all but the last climber down, setting additional gear in a crack; and if the anchors are truly bunk, leave that gear in the crack or get ready for Forest Lawn.

• Send all the heavy gear down with the first climbers. The first climbers down can then bounce test the anchors (with back-ups in place)

Never rappel below a rope snag. Clear the rope as you go.

before the last climber follows. Ideally, the lightest person should go last, though the smallest climber will likely feel otherwise. Make sure the backup anchor bears no weight because you want the first climbers down to test the fixed anchors. If there's any chance of the anchors failing, the whole business will shock load onto the backup system. Hence the backup anchors must be very bombproof themselves—not just a casual nut pitched into a seam.

• If the rappel is half a rope length or less, use only one rope so there's no knot to snag. Always set the middle of the rope at the anchors so one end won't be short. A middle mark on the rope is crucial here. (If your rope isn't pre-marked, mark it yourself with Carter's MARK'S-A-LOT, Sanford's SHARPIE, or Binney & Smith's MAJIC MARKER.) Otherwise, work your way from both ends to locate the middle. Careful not to burn the rappel slings as you feed the rope (read—"feed," not "drag" the rope through the slings).

• If the rappel is longer than half a rope length, tie two ropes together using a double fisherman's knot or a figure-eight

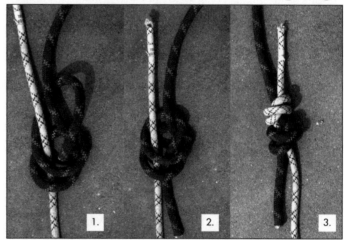

Double fisherman's.

knot backed up by two grapevines. Another choice is a square knot backed up on each side by a grapevine. The square knot is easier to untie after loading, while the grapevines secure the square knot. Many climbers tie their rappel ropes together with a simple overhand, which has a small profile. Make sure you tie a stopper knot in the end of each rope before tossing them, so you cannot rappel off the ends of the line. This is especially important during bad weather or when it's dark. The stopper knot does increase the possibility of getting the rope stuck, particularly if it's windy and the rope is blowing sideways. If you neglect the stopper knot, pay extreme attention to avoid rapping off the ends of the ropes many climbers have met God this way. If you're rapping with a figure-eight, beware: the stopper knot can whistle clean through the device. Fashion another backup in addition.

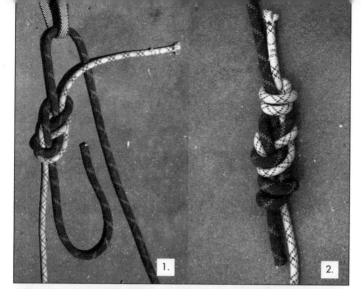

Figure-eight fisherman's.

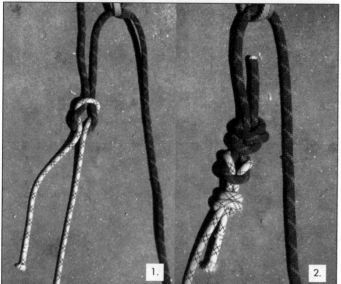

Square knot fisherman's.

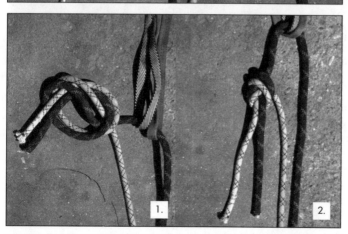

Overhand knot.

A carabiner clipped to one of the rappel ropes prevents twists from passing up the rappel line. It's not necessary with the tubular rappel device shown, but can be crucial if the last person down is rappelling with a Figure Eight rappel device, which does pass rope twists.

Stopper knots prevent rappelling off the end of your rope.

• When pitching the ropes off before a rappel, throw them one at a time. Coil and toss the upper half of each rope first, then coil and throw the free end and try to clear all obstacles. On low-angle rappels it will be impossible to get the ropes all the way down, so you'll have to untangle and toss the ropes as you go.

• Never rappel below a snag in your rope; you might not be able to untangle it from below, and you could pull a rock down on yourself trying. Instead, clear the snags as you go.

• Consider using a friction knot to back up your brake hand and increase your safety when rappelling.

Brake Hand Backup

Some climbers rig a Prusik on the rappel lines above their belay device to back up the rappel device. If you do this, be sure the sling connecting the Prusik to your harness is short enough that the Prusik can't jam out of your reach, leaving you stranded.

A much better and safer system is to rig the friction knot below your belay device and clip it to your leg loop, to back up the brake hand.

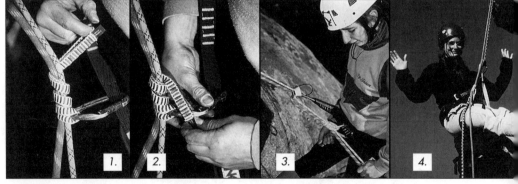

An Autoblock rappel backup is quick to rig on multiple rappels. It's nice to have a cord or sling that's just the right length for an Autoblock. (1.) Clip the sling to your leg loop and wrap around the rope. (2.) Clip the sling back into the carabiner. (3.) Rappel. (4.) the autoblock locks onto the rope to free your hands and prevents losing control of the rappel.

A Klemheist works well. Quicker is an Autoblock, where you simply wrap a few coils of a loop of cord around the rope, then clip it back to your leg loop. It's good to have a cord pre-tied to the proper length for this safety trick, though you can use a standard sling as well (⁹⁄₁₆" or ⅝" wide webbing works best). Make sure the Klemheist or Autoblock has enough wraps that it easily grabs the rope. To rappel, hold the Autoblock with your brake hand and slide it down the rope. Notice the greatly increased friction of the rappel setup. If you need to stop to untangle the ropes, the friction knot will hold you, freeing your hands. And if something like a falling rock causes you to let go of the rappel line, the friction knot will tighten so you don't go zipping down the rope.

An Autoblock clipped to the leg loop backs up the rappel device, adds friction to the rappels, and grabs the rope so you can let go of the rope to untangle the rappel line.

Nutshell

The rules of rappelling apply to both the green novice and the 5.14 leader: A) *Never let go with your brake hand.* B) Walk smoothly down the face—a bouncy or jerky rappel places withering stress on the anchors. C) Keep clothing and long hair tucked in while rappelling, as they tend to get jammed in rappel devices, which can be painful and dangerous.

Fine Devices

Some belay/rappel devices, particularly the flat plate variety, tend to bind and give a jerky rappel, remedied by clipping two carabiners into the rope (rather than one). The extra carabiner also adds friction. When rappelling with a figure eight device, be careful not to allow twists to pass through that could jam your line. To prevent this, clip a sling into your harness and then to one of the rappel lines above your figure eight, thus allowing the twists to get separated by the "keeper" sling.

Figure eights work better on icy ropes, but most rock climbers will never deal with iced ropes, so you're usually better off with a lighter, more compact device that will lock up a on stopper knot.

Standard carabiner rappel brake.

"Biner Brake"

The carabiner rappel is well known and functional, however many lightweight sport climbing biners are too small for rigging this system. If all you have are small biners (and no rappel device), a workable alternative is to set separate Munter hitches on each strand of the rappel rope. Use a locking biner or two opposing biners for the Munter hitches, and extend one of the Munter hitches out from your harness with another locking biner (or two opposed) so the hitches don't bind against one another. The Munter hitch twists the rope badly, but it serves as a backup rappel rig for lightweight biners. It's a symmetrical pain-in-the-ass to use, so carry a rappel device (or six large biners) if a rappel is needed.

Double Munter hitch carabiner rappel brake.

Speed on the Line

Rope weight decreases the farther you descend on the rappel; and the less rope weight on the belay/rappel device, the less friction it provides, translating to a faster rate of descent. Sometimes even modern rappel devices don't provide as much friction as you'd like, especially if you're rappelling a single or small diameter line, or carrying a heavy pack. Of course you can wrap the rope around your hip to gain friction, but that might scorch a hole through your favorite climbing breeches—or worse—your hide. Another option for adding friction is to clip a carabiner (preferably locking) on your leg loop and run the rope through this, then to your brake hand. For mega-friction, wrap the rope twice around a locking carabiner.

The GriGri works splendidly for rappelling a single line. It locks up when released, which is convenient and safe, but it heats up like a meteor and can glaze the sheath of ropes, especially if you rappel fast. To rap two lines (the normal case), rig said lines through the anchors as you normally would. Tie a figure-eight just below the knot joining the ropes, and clip it to the second rope with a carabiner (preferably locking). Now rappel on the second rope. After you reach the ground or the next rappel stance, pull on the knotted strand to retrieve the rope. Usually you can bring the biner down slowly. Inspect, and possibly retire, the biner if it smashes into the ground—a hard impact could cause damage.

Adding friction to the rappel with a carabiner on the leg loop.

GriGri rappel rigging. (1.) Set the GriGri on the rope that passes through the anchors. The rappel line is anchored by the grapevine knot which jams in the rappel ring. Back up the knot jam by clipping a figure-eight tied in the pull-down rope into the rappel line.(2.) Rappel with the GriGri.

Novice on the Line

When climbing with a novice rappeller, always belay them. On a multi-rappel descent, though, you shouldn't trust them to locate and connect into the next anchors. Better to pre-rig your partner's rappel device, go first, and give them a fireman's belay, where you hold the rope and pull it tight to stop the rappeller if he loses control. To pre-rig an inexperienced partner, girth hitch two good slings to his harness tie-in point to form a double "cow's tail." Connect his rappel device to the rope and both girth-hitched slings—before you rappel. Always double check both your partner's and your own setup before heading down. Now, as you rap down the rope and pull it tight, your inexperienced partner can stand comfortably without getting sucked into the rope, owing to the extension provided by the cow's tail. And once you've prepared the next anchors, he's pre-rigged and ready to go. Explain to him to avoid running the rope across the cow's tail slings as he rappels, and to keep hair and clothing away from the rappel device.

Stuck Line

If any doubt exists about the rope pulling through the rappel anchors, the first climber down should do a test pull for a few feet before the last person goes. If the rope won't pull, gradually tug harder to see if you can get it moving. If that fails, try extending the anchors with webbing, pulling or flipping the rope out of a crack or other snag, running the rope through a rappel ring or biner rather than the nylon sling, or setting the knot below the initial lip. To set the knot below the lip, the last climber must pull up some line and rig his rappel on the rope below the lip. Then he must downclimb or hand-over-hand down below the knot, then begin rappelling.

Pre-rig an inexperienced partner for a rappel with double slings girth-hitched to the harness to provide an extension for the rappel device.

Make sure you remove the stopper knots and tangles from the rope before pulling it down. Once you start pulling, keep the rope moving so it can't lodge in a constriction. An instant before the rope begins to fall under its own weight, whip the rope outward to help clear any obstacles. If you're on the ground, walking away from the cliff reduces the angle of the rope on the edges above, easing retrieval. Don't forget to yell "ROPE!" as it starts to fall, and take cover. Once at the Devil's Tower, my (C.L.) rappel line whipped down and cracked like a bullwhip on the ground, completely fraying four inches of the rope.

Efficient

One of the more exciting and terrifying predicaments in rappelling is the hanging rappel transfer, where no ledge exists and the climbing team must hang from anchors while they rig the next rappel. If you expect multiple rappels with hanging stations, both climbers should pre-rig a cow's tail by girth hitching one or two slings through the tie-in points on their harnesses.

1. The first climber, preferably the most experienced, goes down with the rack and ample slings to climb the rope if the rappel is a dead end. Clearing tangles and snags in the rope as she goes, the first climber locates the next anchors and evaluates them, adding slings or backup anchors as she sees fit. Then she clips the anchors with his cow's tail, hangs from them, pulls slack through his rappel device so the climber above can start rigging, and yells, "Off Rappel!'

2. Now the first partner double checks everything and disconnects his rappel device, but keeps the ropes in his hand to give the next rappeller a fireman's belay (whereby you pull tight on the ropes to stop an out-of-control rappeller.) As the next climber descends, he feeds the pulling end of the ropes through the new rappel point, and ties a stopper knot in that end of the rope.

3. When the second climber arrives, she clips into the anchors, double checks, and dismantles her rappel device. She removes the stopper knot from the free end of the rope and pulls the ropes down, while her partner feeds the rope through the new anchor.

4. After the free end is pulled down, closed with a stopper knot and tossed, the first climber rigs for the next rappel.

5. The first rappeller double checks her rigging and descends. The team repeats the above process until they arrive on the ground.

The last climber down must take great care to run the rope over smooth edges where it cannot cut or get stuck. The team should never lose possession of the rappel lines, lest they swing out of reach, stranding you. And always make sure to free the rope of twists and knots before attempting to pull it down.

DOWNCLIMBING

Imagine you're fifteen feet above the last sketchy piece and twenty-five above the next-to-last. You realize you're off route and you can't continue up or traverse. The great Tobin Sorenson used to jump off in these situations, but he died. The sane leader has one option—downclimb.

3.

4.

5.

Practice downclimbing on short boulders or on a toprope before you do much leading. It's also good to always keep something in reserve on serious (i.e. runout) leads, so you have the strength to downclimb if needed.

On low-angled downclimbing, face out or sideways so you can see where you're going. As the angle steepens, turn in and face the rock. To spot the holds below, especially the footholds, lean back and look down, then regain proper posture and place your feet where you remember the holds to be. It's helpful if you can remember the moves you did on the way up. Be especially careful selecting footholds, because it's difficult to see if things are loose from above.

Downclimbing is also often required when descending from a route, but don't be afraid to pull out the rope and rappel or belay if things get too hairy. Never downsolo anything you don't feel absolutely confident about. Likewise, never coerce your partner to downsolo anything he's not comfortable with. Instead, be the first to offer a rope for your partner. If you're the stronger partner, go down first to find the most logical route, and spot your less-experienced partner through the dicey stretches (provided you have a good stance!). Stay close together, so any dropped rocks can't gain too much momentum, and so both climbers have ready assistance if anything goes wrong. Never get separated. If you rope up for the downclimb, the weaker climber should go first, with a toprope, placing protection for the stronger partner to "down lead" on (hopefully the "weaker" partner knows how to place good pro). Rappelling is usually safer and quicker.

Herm Feissner dropping a
knee on "Third Millenium"
(13d/14a), The Monastery,
Colorado.

Sport Climbing CHAPTER 6

Sport climbing is covered extensively in both *Clip & Go,* and *Sport Climbing,* also in the *How to Rock Climb* series. However, a text on advanced climbing techniques that slights the most fashionable aspect of the game (sport climbing) is hardly complete, no matter what has been said in previous manuals. For those interested in a special study of sport climbing, refer to *Clip & Go,* and *Sport Climbing.* For our purposes, let's review sport climbing from the perspective of someone looking to move onto difficult, even world-class terrain, and focus on the key elements in getting there safely and quickly.

The Game

Some dozen years ago, sport climbing tore across the country like wildfire. Presently, new areas and indoor climbing gyms pop up almost weekly. Fun, relatively secure and accessible to the masses, the clip and go movement has done for climbing what the mountain bike did for cycling. No need for the thousand dollar rack for the sport climbing game. A rope, some rock slippers plus a handful of quickdraws and you're set to motate. Sport climbing means bolts, which usually—though not always—translates to straightforward protection and anchors. This allows sport climbers to cast off with less formal instruction than traditional climbing. With a bolt at the knees and another two moves higher, you can pull down without the heckling fear native to traditional, or "trad" climbing, where the leader, thirty feet out and quaking in her knickers, questions if the last nut will hold, and where the devil the next pro might be found. Let us not mislead you into thinking sport climbing is completely safe, or that gym climbing fully prepares you for sport climbing. There are plenty of ways to get hurt sport climbing.

Heavily bolted routes do mean less risk, which allows sport climbers to focus on gymnastic difficulty and fun. But what kind of fun? Today's foremost sport routes require days of work, then an Olympic effort, for a world-class climber to redpoint. Though sport climbs don't entail the commitment and jeopardy of being 2,000 feet up Mt. Asgard in a snow storm, hard sport climbing requires a commitment of lifestyle. Leading sport climbers follow a severe and barren diet, train like fiends and climb two hundred plus days a year, focusing on everything geared to mold their minds and bodies into climbing machines. They seek bolted faces, the steeper the better.

The new wave of climbers, weaned in rock gyms fashioned by the previous generation, are poised to push the standards to Mars, a certainty once they leave the gyms and bluffs and mount the high crags to make their own statements. Not until

Tommy Caldwell on his thin crack route "Country Boy" (13d), Lumpy Ridge, Colorado.

these young climbers take their awesome skills into the traditional climbing arena—following a sufficient apprenticeship—will the next page in climbing history be turned.

Perspective

Considering the entire arc of the climbing experience, sport climbing comprises a popular, if minor, part. To someone interested in the overall climbing game, solely emphasizing sport climbing is like a boxer developing a jab but never honing the hook, straight right or uppercut. Distinct and valid as it is, sport climbing doesn't overshadow adventure climbing, and never will—a perspective understood only by experiencing both games. Tastes differ according to temperament, goals and countless other factors. But whether you're an adventure maniac or strictly a sport climber, you must be versed enough to have tolerance for the complete game. Without this experience there's no true understanding, which has led some to try and impose specialized methods and techniques where they don't belong—sort of like trying to play hockey on a baseball diamond because you've never played baseball before. The results are not good. You simply can't go up on "Black Rose," Middle Cathedral—a long route with long runouts—and commence installing new bolts because your home crag has protection every body length. Nor can you justly start crowbarring the bolts out of a clip-and-go route because you feel it is over-protected. With millions of climbers presently in action, the days are gone where a self-appointed High Lama can declare how he feels things must be, and all the lackeys will fall in line. More likely is that the High Lama will be branded a crackpot and a has-been, out of step with reality. A climber is served well to regard every style of climbing with a perspective gained from doing. Like the song says, "If you ain't tried it, don't knock it; somebody else might want to rock it."

Roots

Sport climbing began in Europe, but caught on worldwide very quickly. Briefly, prominent European climbers visited Yosemite in the '70s, when Yosemite climbers walked the cutting edge. The Europeans returned home inspired by what they saw. Countless small limestone cliffs are peppered throughout Europe; however, transferring the concept of hard free climbing to these bluffs was impossible—at least on traditional terms—since there were not cracks enough to arrange adequate pro, and no way to stop on the lead, hanging from a mono-doigt, to drill a hole. The Continental Euros would have to forego the American and British ethic of the on-sight, ground-up approach, if they were going to exploit their resources. The result was that they began pre-placing bolt protection via a toprope. The clip-and-go route was born and the sport climbing revolution began.

Hit the Road

For a sport climber to grow, he or she must travel far and wide, visiting the famous areas and dusting the celebrated routes. Keep clipping up the same line of bolts and the tedium will burn you out. Indoor gyms have alleviated this problem somewhat by changing routes regularly; but still, new areas, new routes and new people are what keep climbing fresh and exciting.

North America hosts a rich collection of sport climbing areas in every region of the country. Tim Toula's *Rock 'N Road* rock climbing atlas lists over two thousand throughout the continental United States. The renowned sport climbing areas are well-traveled, and many feature traditional routes as well as clip-and-go projects: Smith Rock, Red Rocks, Rifle, Shelf Road, American Fork, Austin, Owens River Gorge, Virgin River Gorge, Red River Gorge, New River Gorge, to list a few.

Gary Ryan rides the "Soul Train" (12b), Mickey Mouse Wall, Colorado.

Patrick Edlinger on "Father Figure" (12c) in Joshua Tree.

Beth Wald photo

Danger

The premise of sport climbing is security through bolts. But not all sport climbs are safe. ("Safe" is an inappropriate word to apply to any mode of climbing.) Poorly bolted routes are too common. Runouts, bad bolts and hard clips, especially for shorter climbers, can turn a casual route into a mother's lament. And there are gray-area routes, part sport, part adventure climb. Here, existing bolts require intermediate protection, meaning you must place wired nuts and camming devices in addition to the bolts, to achieve adequate protection. Don't mistake a mixed-pro route for a benign sport route. And don't venture onto a mixed-pro route until you have the science of setting protection and anchors down cold.

Cheops

If your goal is to climb higher grades, consider the notion of a progression pyramid. Say you want to break into 5.12 sport routes. First, get a bunch of 11b, 11c, and some 11d routes under your harness. Now you're ready to try a 12a. After that first 12a, climb a load more 12a routes, until you feel comfortable at that grade. Then boot it up to 12b. The key is to develop patience for your own development. Everyone's learning curve is different. The fact that Jack Rabbit got to 5.12c in sixteen months doesn't mean that he won't plateau there for years. I've seen climbers who improved in the smallest increments, so slowly that their improvement seemed imperceptible. And yet they never reached a plateau. Ever so slowly, they kept getting better and better. With a steady progression scheme, you gradually build a base from which to launch onto harder routes. Push your limits only on well-protected routes on which you can't get injured (avoid, say, climbs requiring continuous one-finger pulls). At some point we all plateau, and progress slows down. This is where cyclical training might help (see the Training chapter). The point is to be patient, stay focused on your goals, and understand your limitations.

OVER YOUR HEAD

Avoid spending all your energy on routes that are too hard. If you rarely send routes or boulder problems, you'll lose the flow, the knack to move smoothly. You'll actually adapt to failure by programming yourself to make mistakes and hang, rather than climb smooth and confident on a route you can handle. A good mix of projects and onsights is the proven way to improve most rapidly.

Choosing a Route

What are your goals? What is your current ability? How familiar are you with the area? Are you trying to onsight or redpoint? Most climbers redpoint at least two letter grades harder than they onsight. These variables determine which routes you can and should climb, and allow you to target routes approximate to your skill level. When new to an area, start off easy to get a feel for the rock, the routes and the ratings. Most climbers compose a "hit list," an inventory of routes they'd like to try. Concrete goals breed motivation.

Warmup

Warmup with a couple cruiser routes to get your muscles, joints and brain primed for cranking. If you have a project that day, warm up well, get the blood flowing to avoid the dreaded flash pump, then head to your project. If you're route bagging, trying to tic off perhaps a dozen different lines, figure out the best order to bag the climbs. Start easy to get your psyche and your body up to speed, then hit it hard, cranking the grimmer routes on your list, then winding back down to casual turf. The easier, final routes warm the muscles down, and allow you to regain any "flow" you might have lost while sketching on the ghastly lines. A thirty-minute rest between burns gives good recovery, without allowing your muscles and joints to grow cold. For a serious, withering pump, you may require more recovery time, followed by another brief warmup. The rope also benefits from resting between gut-wrenching falls.

left hand, gate facing right.

right hand, gate facing right.

right hand, gate facing left.

CLIPPING

Is the route prearranged with draws? If not, and you question whether you can place them as you go, take a low energy run up the route, hanging the draws and resting on the cord as you learn and rehearse the moves. You can also aid climb between bolts. Another option is to swindle someone else into hanging the draws for you, so all you have to do is clip them.

Face the gates of the biners opposite your intended direction of travel to minimize the chance of the rope unclipping during a fall—when moving up and right, face the gates to the left; when moving up and left, face them right. When heading straight up, face the carabiners either way. It is best if the lower biner—which is often dog-legged for easy clipping—is held tightly in the draw, so it stays properly oriented. Make sure the dog-legged biner is on the bottom, or rope side, with a straight gate carabiner attaching the quickdraw to the bolt, and never backclip.

Sometimes it's wise to clip critical bolts with a locking biner, to eliminate the risk and fear of accidentally unclipping. Another way is to clip a second, slightly longer quickdraw to the bolt, just above the initial quickdraw, with the biner gates opposed. The longer draw is never loaded lest the lower draw fails, which is the intention because the upper biner would be loaded at a strange angle, as it's sitting on top of another biner in the hanger.

On bleak terrain, clipping proficiently can make the difference between sending the route and pitching off. It's hard to say what spanks climbers more frequently—blowing a clip, or bungling a move. Many are the tricks to clip fast and clean.

For a high, reachy clip, the standard method is to pull up a bight of slack, hold the rope with your teeth while you grab more, then pull it up and clip. Faster is to pull the rope up in one smooth motion, letting it slide through your hand, until you clip. A slick rope and on-the-ball belayer help here.

If the biner gate opens right, and you're clipping right-handed, or left and left, drop the rope into the carabiner with your fingers. Whenever clipping with the opposite hand from the direction the gate opens, push the rope through with your thumb. Again, a snappy clip is crucial on steep sport climbs. When attempting a route near or at your limit, a blown clip will usually cost you the very strength needed to send the route. Developing the dexterity to clip quickly, and from the least strenuous body position, are vital factors in mastering the art of sport climbing.

Avoid making high clips from tenuous stances. If you blow the clip, you'll fall further than necessary. It often burns energy to make high, reachy clips. And a whistler will always sap your psyche. Better to climb higher to a good clipping hold. Ninety times out of a hundred, the closer your waist is to the bolt, the easier the clip. Of course, when you're standing on good holds and launching into a grisly sequence, clip high whenever possible. Shorter climbers often get hosed on

left hand, gate facing left.

clips—the bolt has been placed too high for clipping from the good stance, so the clip is desperate and sometimes dangerous. Some climbers carry a couple of tape stiffened quickdraws so they can clip bolts several inches above their reach.

Occasionally, (or often, depending on where you climb and how bold you are) the first bolt is higher than you care to climb without protection. Here, stick clipping is the trick: pre-clip the first bolt before leaving the ground, thus scoring a top rope for the opening moves. Some modern routes were designed to be stick clipped, a tactic that spared the first ascentionists the time, cost and energy of placing another bolt. You can even buy a fifteen-foot tentacle to clip the bolt. Or simply fashion one from a stick or a marlin rod. To do this, put the rope through the lower biner on a quickdraw, and lightly tape the upper biner onto the stick, with its gate held open by the tape. Reach up with the stick, clip the bolt and pull the stick away. The tape will come free so the carabiner closes on the bolt hanger. Make sure the gate closes fully or the biner will lose more than half its strength.

Stick clip rig.

ONSIGHTING

An on-sight lead—where you flash the route first try with no falls, hangs, or Beta from other climbers—is the premier style to climb a route. Note that climbing competitions are structured to reward the onsight, with competitors held in isolation so everyone climbs without having seen anyone else on the route, which can reveal secrets per the sequence, et al. If you have any prayer of onsighting a route, try and do so. You only get one shot at an on-sight lead, so make sure it's your best one.

The "importance" of an on-sight ascent hinges entirely on how meaningful the route is to you. If the onsight is "The World," be patient. Wait until you're fit for the task—strong and well-versed in the given style of climbing.

When preparing for an on-sight ascent, study the route from the ground, learning whatever you can before the clock starts ticking. Ask yourself every question that's germane to you flashing the route: How many quickdraws do I need? Are there any rests? Where is the crux? What can I decipher about the moves and sequences? Are there any key holds that will be difficult to see while I'm cranking my liver out? Process this information and form a strategy for the on-sight attempt. Wait for cool, crisp conditions to maximize your odds for the flash ascent. And even if the conditions are ideal, if the route is at your max, both your mind and body need to be in the right mode. You need to feel like you are in top form. So the timing has to be right, which means you must know how to read your body. Often, climbers are so anxious to get cranking on a test piece they will cast off prematurely, without properly inspecting the route, or warming up, or waiting for better conditions, or when they physically and mentally feel primed to give their best effort. Such bids are bound to fail. When pushing your limits, stack the deck in your favor. Be patient until everything feels on.

RELAX YOUR MIND

When scoping a route from the deck, relax your mind and visualize yourself sending the route move by move. Once you commit to an earnest effort, make sure you've warmed up adequately, and that you feel calm and confident before stepping off the ground. Once you begin, focus on the moves in front of you, climbing bolt-to-bolt, or rest-to-rest. Strive for maximum efficiency, good footwork, body position and confident movement. Try to keep up your momentum. If you bungle a move you might go back to a rest and shakeout. Remember, however, that too much hesitation has caused legions of climbers to pitch off, where momentum and tenacity might have carried them through. Fight hard and give it your best, but if you fall, remember it is you, and not the sky, who has fallen. Don't regard an unsuccessful flash attempt as a failure. Consider the route as a project and your "failure" turns into your first burn to redpoint the route. Unless you think you can fire it off next try, switching to redpoint tactics will minimize your effort to send the route. There are many different methods of climbing a sport route, but redpoint tactics are key.

REDPOINT TACTICS

It is now accepted to declare a redpoint with the draws pre-placed on a sport route. Initially, redpoint meant leading from the ground, placing all the gear, including quickdraws, on lead, and never weighting the rope. This still holds for traditional climbing, where the difference between wiggling wired nuts into a slanting, overhanging finger crack, and clipping pre-placed gear, can be two or three letter grades, if not more.

The precept of redpointing is to climb harder routes than you can onsight, while minimizing the struggle to do so. If a route is an obvious redpoint—meaning you don't have a Gypsy's chance of sending it straightaway—don't waste energy trying to flash it. Work it from the start. Gain as much Beta as you can, but don't take someone else's Beta as truth etched in stone. Be flexible, willing to explore your own solution if someone else's Beta isn't working. Break the route into sections, and work the sections, spending extra time on cruxes, especially those toward the end of the route, when your arms will be full of lead. Work out the moves, exploring to find the most efficient sequences, then link the moves into sections, and link the transitions between sections. Don't skip moves, or you'll likely get spanked on the redpoint attempt. When resting on a bolt, clip a draw directly from your harness to the bolt or draw, thus relieving the belayer of your weight.

When hanging on the cord, sort out the moves you've just made, memorizing them, rather than just looking ahead. Try

Sylvia Mireles making the clip on "Rip-off" (12), Owens River Gorge, California.

Greg Epperson photo

to eliminate errors. Look for and practice rests—both good rests and quick shakeouts. Finally, when you think you've got it dialed, rest—two to three days if you need full recovery, or one-half to three hours if you're trying to finish that day. While resting, visualize the moves, exactly as they are on the rock. Try visualizing the whole route (like a movie), beginning to end, with no interruptions. Practice in your mind while the body recovers. A Beta map may help you learn and visualize the sequence. Draw the route as a very detailed topo. Number the moves, and describe the route move by move.

As mentioned, before going for the redpoint, wait for cool weather whenever possible. Warmup well, getting a mild pump to avoid a flash pump on your redpoint. Visualize the route one or two final times before leaving the deck. Relax and breathe consciously as you start up. Focus on the route section by section. And don't get ahead of yourself. Think about breathing, and moving efficiently, the way you learned the moves. Give it your best shot. If you're blowing the sequence and splurging strength, consider dropping off (if the fall is safe) and starting over. No sense in losing potency on a false start. Sometimes, you can battle through a blown sequence, to finish the redpoint by the skin of your tips. More often, however, you'll blaze out before the anchor.

Avoid climbing with the rope under your leg.

FALLING

In high end sport climbing, falling is far more routine than sending a route. A single hard route can require dozens, or hundreds, of falls. So it's important that a sport climber knows how to fall. Learn when it's safe to fall, and when it's not. A twenty-footer into a ledge will stop your progress faster than a costly wedding. If the fall is vertical, and you're directly above a ledge, you may be nimble enough to jump out and avoid a bone-crusher. But don't count on it. Better to pick safer routes, or not fall. On steep routes, there's nothing to hit but air, so many imagine they're home free no matter what happens. Not so. Overzealous belayers often pull rope in when the leader falls. On overhanging rock this tightens the leader's falling radius, and can send her slamming into the wall below. Many ankles have snapped this way. Instead, the belayer should release some rope as the leader pings off to soften the fall and keep the leader from penduluming into the wall. Obviously, don't pay out rope if it's going to cause a groundfall or ledgeout.

Whenever falling, try to maintain control, keep your head upright and legs poised catlike to absorb any impact against the wall. With practice, this all becomes instinctive, and you learn to relax when falling while still maintaining the catlike posture. Avoid climbing with the rope under your leg which sends you upside down in a lead fall.

RIGGING TO LOWER

Once you gain the top of the pitch, you must get down, and this is where countless climbers have blown it. Usually you'll lower off double or triple bolts. Clip into the anchors with a sling, and hang from the sling. If the hangers, chain links or other connecting hardware have a large opening:

1. Pass a bight (loop) of rope through the anchors and extend the bight down to your harness.

2. Tie a figure eight in the bight and clip this knot into a locking biner on your harness tie-in point or belay loop.

3. Double check everything, then dismantle your original tie-in knot.

You're now connected to the rope through the locking carabiner and figure-eight knot. Pull your end of the rope through the anchors and yell "Take!" Make eye contact with your belayer to be certain they're with you, then disconnect the tie-in slings, yell "Down!" and lean back. If it's impossible to make eye contact with your belayer, hold their side of the

1.   2.   2.   3.

rope as you lean back until you feel that they have you (many climbers do this regardless of having made eye contact with their belayer). This rigging system is quick and safe because you are never untied from the rope or off belay. If lowering requires the entire length of the rope, this method may leave you a little short of the ground, however.

    Another alternative—especially good if a bight of rope won't fit through the anchors, or if you need the entire length of the rope to lower—is to clip into the anchors with a sling or two, then:

1. Tie a figure eight in the lead line, four or so feet from the tie-in point, and clip it to your harness with a locking biner. This clip-off keeps you backed up by the higher pieces in the pitch, and will safeguard against dropping the rope, which would be mortifying and potentially dangerous.

2. Double check everything.

3. Untie from the end of the rope, pass it through the anchors, and tie back in.

4. Untie the backup knot,

Passing a bight to lower.

Passing an end to lower.

1.   2.   3.   4

Passing an end to lower (cont'd).

5. disconnect the slings, and

6. lower off.

A third option, which is quick but not as safe, is to clip into the anchors with slings, untie the rope from your harness, pass it through the anchors, and tie back into it. The main problem here is the potential for dropping the rope and becoming stranded. Believe it—this has happened often.

COLD SHUTS

For convenience, some sport climbing areas feature open cold shuts at the top of many routes. It is quick and easy to flip your rope through a couple shuts and lower off. While the folk who set cold shuts seem to have total confidence in them, it's a perilous practice to toprope through cold shuts because they aren't particularly strong, and toprope falls can reportedly put up to about 1,000 pounds of force on the top anchors. Also, cold shuts do not form a complete enclosure around the rope. And given that countless cords have most likely been pulled through the shuts, the once burly shuts could presently be worn into veritable paper clips. Watch it carefully whenever cold shuts are involved. None were made to climbing specs.

CLEANING A SPORT ROUTE

If the angle of the route is 90 degrees or less, it's typically easy to clean. The leader simply pulls the draws off as she lowers, or the second cleans them as he climbs. Often at sport areas, both climbers will lead the pitch. The first climber ascends the route, then lowers off two quickdraws at the top. The team then pulls the rope so the second climber can lead the pitch, which is cleaned as she lowers off.

Aerial Tram

If the route is steep and/or traverses, "tramming" is the trick for cleaning the draws. Clip a quickdraw from your waist to the rope, which runs through the quickdraws on the route. This allows you to pull into each bolt and clean the quickdraw. If the route overhangs, be careful unclipping the lowest draw—an excess of slack will come into the rope, possibly sending you into a big, swinging fall, into the ground, or nearby boulders and trees. It's often safer to clean the lowest draw (or two) with the rope still clipped through a higher bolt. Clean this high quickdraw last, so you're well above the ground when you cut loose and swing into the air.

RETREATING

Retreating from a pitch is simple if you have good anchors and are less than half a rope length off the deck; simply leave a carabiner on the high anchor and lower back to the ground or the belay. This method is expensive if you retreat often, but it's quick and failsafe, provided the top anchors are good. If the top anchor is a bolt with a welded cold shut hanger, or other ring-type hanger (fairly rare), you can pass the rope through the hanger and lower. First, make sure the anchor is bomber, otherwise back it up. Don't be cheap when your very life hangs in the balance. If the anchor or bailoff point is a bolt, a backup might not be available, so the best you can do is to leave a biner on the next lower bolt, hoping this anchor will stop you if the highest pro fails while you're still a ways above the ground. You can then clean all the lower pieces as you return to the belay or the ground.

Tramming to clean.

If you don't want to leave a biner, hang from the top anchor and thread it with a sling, then feed the rope through this sling and rappel on the rope. This method clogs bolt hangers with trashy slings; but owing to the cost of biners, leaving retreat slings is common. Again, never lower with the rope running through a sling, or you'll likely get down quicker than a candle blowing out in the wind.

No Trash

A technique exists for retreating from a bolt, or other good anchor, and then retrieving your sling from the hanger. However, the method is complicated and must be rigged perfectly. This technique is handy if you want to avoid leaving a trashy sling or a biner, but it forces you to totally rely on the top retreat anchor, a situation that often can't be avoided when retreating. If you have only one rope, you must not be more than one-third of a rope length above the ground; with two ropes, you can be half a rope length up.

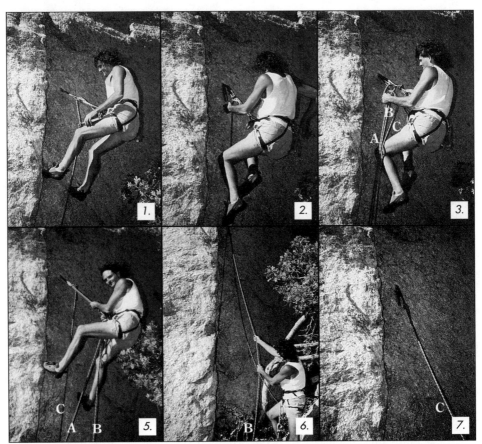

Sling retrieval trick, step by step.

At the point of retreat you'll probably be hanging on a bolt. To do the "sling retrieval retreat trick" with a single rope:

1. Clip the bolt to your harness with a sling and hang.

2. Pass a loop of sling through the bolt hanger and fold it in half. Untie from your climbing rope. Don't drop the rope! Tie it off somewhere before untying it from your harness.

3. Take one end of the rope and pass one-third of the rope length through both loops of webbing. This is strand A. Tie the other end of the rope, strand C, to the sling, on the same side as the knot or stitching in the webbing. Otherwise, the rope won't pull in step 7.

4. Have your partner check to be sure that both strand A, and the loop formed by strands B and C, reach the ground.

5. Double check everything thoroughly—your life depends on this setup being exactly right. Rappel to the ground on strands A and B, not C.

6. Pull on Strand B to retrieve strand A through the sling.

7. Now pull on strand C to retrieve the sling.

With two ropes you can set one rope at its middle for rappelling, and use the other rope for retrieving the sling. This requires pulling the rope through your sling, which will cause abrasion. Be sure to inspect the sling before you use it again. It may be dumpster material after the rope has been yarded through it.

A potentially more frightening and dangerous retreat would involve downclimbing a pitch, or making two rappels to retreat if you have only one rope and are more than half a rope length from the belay. As mentioned, if you can't find good anchors, the best option may be downclimbing.

THE MENTAL GAME

It's been said a thousand times: sport climbing is as much mental gymnastics as it is a physical endeavor. Visualization, relaxation, tenacity, control and attitude happen in the mind. You may have more endurance than Father Time, but if your mind's not centered you're going to flounder. First, climbing should have a strong aspect of fun. Too much pressure turns pleasure into work, and makes success more difficult. Visit the Training chapter for more on sports psychology. An adage worth remembering comes from Todd Skinner, who said, "If you think you're strong, you are strong." Herein lies one of the benefits of training. It makes the body feel strong, giving you the confidence to crank moves and cruise on through, saving bundles of energy.

When looking back on my (J.L.) own climbing career, I realize that persistence and patience were the two most valuable factors. I started as a hyperactive teenager hell-bent on ripping the walls down. It took five or six seasons before I started climbing on anything but energy and fitness. Once I slowed down, and in a sense let the game come to me, my climbing improved. Years later, the concepts of persistence and patience took on new meaning. Chronic tendinitis and trashed finger joints pretty much shut down my climbing in 1984. For a dozen years I could only do a day's worth of cranking and the old injuries would flare up. When an indoor climbing gym was installed only three miles from my house, I started back. My injuries still hurt, but no longer crippled me. Though I still remembered how to move and crack sequences, my finger strength was pathetic, despite having been a gym rat, kayaking buff and devoted cyclist over the previous decade. That first month in the gym I could barely climb at a grade I used to free solo. I thought about bagging it out of wounded pride, but I was having too much fun. I was also getting incredible encouragement from everyone I met. "The strength comes back," they all told me. And it did. But I had to be patient and stick with it, taking rest days and working back up the ladder. In a real sense, I had to start all over. No matter how hard I tried or fretted or cursed, my strength returned at about two foot-pounds a week. Time seems to have its own agenda. Patience...

Generally, sport climbs are engineered to help eliminate danger, but this is impossible in a sport where climbers continuously fall, and not just onto the last bolt. An alarming number of sport climbers have thumped straight onto the deck. The ways to get hurt while sport climbing are many. Knowledge of these hazards is decisive in avoiding dangerous situations. The current sport and gym climbing scene has bred an irreverent sense of complacency in some climbers. Every climber should know that if you commit a major safety error, the ground comes up fast and hard—even on so-called "safe"

Common Mistakes

Some of the most common ways sport climbers may be injured or killed include:

1. Bad communication which causes the belayer to take the leader off belay. The leader leans back to lower and plummets straight into the ground. Never say "Off belay," if you're expecting to be lowered.

2. Belayer not paying attention drops the leader. A GriGri helps solve this problem.

3. The belayer stands too far from the base of the cliff, and gets yanked into the wall, adding slack in the lead rope, maybe injuring the belayer and possibly causing the leader to be dropped. Stay close to the wall when belaying, or anchor to the ground.

4. The belayer sets up belay device incorrectly and can't stop a fall. Always double check.

5. Leader gets desperate, throws slapdash moves and falls out of control. Try to never abandon your form and keep the rope out from under your leg.

6. Leader forgets to complete her tie-in knot. Always double check. Once you start tying a knot, don't allow any distractions until you have finished. Then look it over to make sure it's properly tied.

7. Leader or belayer fails to double pass their harness buckle (very common). Double check.

8. Leader backclips a Quickdraw and the rope comes unclipped. Pay attention to the run of the rope through the draws. Use locking biners on crucial placements.

9. A carabiner gate gets forced open and the biner breaks. Be careful how your biners lay, replace abused carabiners, and buy carabiners with a high open gate strength (9 KN at least).

10. Climbers toprope off unsafe anchors. Get a clue.

11. Leader lowers with the rope running through slings. Natural selection.

12. The end of the rope passes through the belay device while the leader is being lowered, dropping him to the ground (more common than you think). A knot tied in the end of the rope will avoid this inexcusable mistake, as long as the belay device is not a figure eight. If it is, the belayer should tie into the rope.

sport routes. Good communication between belayer and climber is absolutely essential, as is double checking harness buckles, tie-in knots, belay devices, and locking carabiners before leaving the ground.

STYLE

In sport climbing, anything goes. The end goal is to redpoint the route, using whatever tactics you want. The only truly "bad style" in sport climbing is to alter the rock or misrepresent your accomplishments. If you say you did a route, that means you redpointed it. If you haven't redpointed the route, saying you did will be found out, and others will question your integrity. Nothing wrong with saying a certain route kicked your butt, or that you had a couple of hangs. It's far more noble to be honest with yourself and others, than to create a mythical reality that you have to try to live up to. This tactic not only isolates you from the climbing community, but moves you away from the Prime Directive—we climb to have fun.

Many sport climbers put immense pressure on themselves to perform well. If things aren't going swimmingly they become such brooding sourpusses you want to take them behind the shed and spank them. We've all seen it—tantrums on the rock, sulking, and the asinine whining that follows. Avoid taking the sport, and yourself, too seriously. If it's not fun, why bother?

One of the psychological pitfalls that most every climber falls into is comparing yourself to others. This is useless, self-defeating and it stifles your growth and enjoyment. It is one thing to be inspired by Sonja Hardbody floating up a 5.12 as though it were a step ladder; it's quite another thing to kick the shit out of yourself because you cannot make it five feet up the same route. The thing to keep in mind is—"Not yet." We can't climb that 5.12—yet. Give yourself time and enjoy the process. Celebrate every accomplishment and the process becomes exciting. Grieve the fact that you're not the best and climbing becomes no more than a rat race after meaningless numbers. Ultimately, everyone must answer the question as to why they are roping up in the first instance. If the answer is anything but to relish the experience in our own unique way, we're in for more anguish than fun, and it's worth reevaluating our motivation. In twenty-five years of climbing my (J.L.) most cherished memories are of the experiences—both victories and defeats—shared with friends.

Topher Donahue and
Kennan Harvey on the
first free ascent of
"Lovelace" (IV 12d),
Zion Canyon, Utah.

Adventure Climbing

Prior to about 1980, the term "adventure" climbing had not been coined, since virtually all climbing was an adventure. Certainly, a climber could stitch a crack with nuts, or stick with benign slabs, but generally, doubt, commitment, jeopardy and a solid ration of fear and exhilaration were the things that vitalized the game. Hard climbing was equal parts confronting your own fears and linking a series of moves. In decades past, "working" a route meant returning a second time for a "no-falls" ascent. Throughout the '70s and early '80s, prestige was garnered not so much by a climber's ability to eventually tic an impossibly hard route, as it was in cranking a confirmed test piece perfectly via an onsight flash ascent. With the advent of the clip-and-go route, focus quickly shifted away from traditional adventure climbing and the onsight flash mentality, except in the exacting competition arena. Presently the most difficult free climbs are so technical and complex that success is often measured in terms of days, rather than attempts.

Another major shift concerns the scope of many present-day climbers' dreams—what they have their hearts set on. The once-sacred credo—that an active climber must tackle long routes to be "real"—is a quaint notion, and has been for over fifteen years. A grace note of the sport climbing movement is that macho posturing has been replaced by the saner orientation of having fun. And yet there was something to the old credo, namely that climbing a long route often requires, and in fact summons, life-affirming rendezvous not found on short cliffs, no matter the grade or gravity. And such ordeals—from the terror of running the rope out over loose rock, to the elation of pulling over the summit of a monolith that exhausted you of every reserve and resource—must be experienced first-hand to be known. Reading about or dabbling in adventure climbing will never betray its magic. You simply must tie in, cast off, and come what may. And what inevitably comes is the Holy Grail of all climbing, that trial by fire that requires and ultimately allows a person to become more than he/she ever thought he/she could be. This can never be found through physical effort alone, but is sooner or later encountered when a climber's most basic stuff is challenged in a threatening arena in which rigid personal control is lost entirely, and the climber proceeds on faith alone. Here, the summit is not simply the apex of a titanic rock, but the Promised Land of Self. This is the boon of adventure climbing.

Craig Luebben and Jeff Achey off route on "Astrodog" (11d), Black Canyon of the Gunnison, Colorado.

HIGH AND WILD

Getting stale from frigging up another forty-foot tendon buster? Jump onto something long and wild, where you deal with things on sight, without the option to yell "Take!" and lower to the deck. This is an almost certain method to pump volts into deadened ambition. When you see big name sport climbers free soloing, speed climbing big walls, or alpine climbing, they're doing nothing more than what we're suggesting here. When you get a chance, jam out to Zion, Yosemite Valley, Moab, Devil's Tower, or the Alps. Drive a junker down to Mexico and climb at Trono Blanco. Head up to the Diamond, the Wind Rivers, Tetons, Bugaboos, Baffin Island, or Cirque of the Unclimbables. Save your cash and travel to Patagonia, Dresden, Arapiles, the Caribbean. You'll never regret it, and you'll appreciate sport climbing all the more.

What is adventure climbing? It is a slippery term, but most agree that if you place clip-and-go, gym climbing and bouldering (excepting high bouldering) into one category, every-thing left is adventure climbing—cragging with clean or mixed protection, crack climbing, desert climbing, seacliff climbing, alpine climbing, long free routes, speed climbing, aid climbing, wall climbing, soloing, free soloing, expedition climbing, altitude climbing and ice climbing. The platter of opportunity for an adventure climber is a full one. Given the many entreés, it is obvious that we could never cover the full menu in this book. Herein we've limited our focus to tradi-tional free climbing.

DEEP QUIVER

While success in sport climbing hinges on fitness, face tech-nique and tenacity, adventure climbing requires a deeper quiver of skills and knowledge. As a generalized art, genuine adventure climbing is not and cannot be performed at the stratospheric levels of sport climbing. Compare a sprinter to a decathlete. The sprinter, completely focused and trained specifically for his chosen event, will run the socks off the decathlete every time—in a sprint. But the sprinter can't throw the javelin to save his life, nor can he put the shot, while the decathlete can do these events fairly well. And chances are, the sprinter will foul his trunks at the thought of trying the pole vault.

In addition to requiring wide-ranging skills, adventure climbing is more dangerous than sport climbing. Though def-initions vary, fear, and an unpredictable outcome, remain the hallmarks of all adventures. As the ranks of sport climbers swell beyond the capacity of available areas, and as some sport climbers become bored with clip-clip-clip climbing, the overflow is spilling out into the various facets of adventure climbing. Growth is also coming from new climbers drawn initially to the adventure side of things. More climbers than ever are buying big racks of hardware and heading out onto the high and wild.

GROUNDWORK

Good judgment will keep you alive adventure climbing; poor judgment can kill you fast. The challenge is to safely acquire the experience to tune your judgment. A climber schooled in the gym or on the sport crag should approach adventure climbing conservatively. In plain language, no matter what level you've achieved in sport climbing, do not, under any cir-cumstances, jump onto a long trad (trad = traditional, or adventure climb) route until you've worked up to it. Do so and invite disaster. Sound knowledge in placing bomber protec-tion—tapers, SLCDs, and other pieces—is crucial for all adventure climbing, as is knowing how to rig complicated belays. Bolts are the exception in the big wild. Other crucial factors include route-finding skills, knowledge of weather, efficient ropework, crack climbing ability, and a solid partner.

Controlled Progression

As a rule, the longer the climb, the more serious the endeavor. A strong background of cragging on small cliffs is prerequisite to tackling longer routes. No one goes from arithmetic straight to calculus. First you must learn algebra, geometry and trigonometry. The same applies to climbing. A handful of grade II rock climbs does not prepare you for El Capitan. An attempt to make such a quantum leap will likely land you in quicksand. Slowly but surely, tackle longer and more serious climbs. A controlled progression keeps the process fun and greatly reduces the chance of epics.

Once you feel sound with the basics—protection, anchors, route finding and general rope management—it's fine to select routes that will challenge you. But always remember this: judge your competence not in terms of a letter grade (5.11a, say), but by your experience in handling that grade of difficulty in the adventure arena. And before heading up a route, seek information from guidebooks and other climbers. What's the climbing like? How about the approach and descent? How's the pro? And what about objective hazards? Is the route finding tricky, and if so, where? What gear is needed? Always learn as much as you can before heading onto a challenging adventure route.

Cragging

Cragging conjures up images of fun-in-the-sun climbing on shorter cliffs. Because the commitment is usually low, crags are the place to hone your skills. On crags, you can pick and choose—cracks, slabs, steep faces, runouts, etc. Whatever skill you lack, hone it on the crags. No clear-cut definition exists to delineate a short crag route from a long one. Much depends on the climbing and the climbers. The four pitches on "Standing Rock" have taken some parties four days; Rolando Garibotti led all thirty-four pitches on the Nose in less than five hours.

Varied Rock

Each rock type has unique characteristics, and fluency on a given type requires practice on that medium. The three most commonly climbed rock types are granite and "granite-like" rock, sandstone, and limestone/dolomite. Viable but less traveled rock includes basalt, welded tuff, quartz monzonite, quartzite, gneiss, and a host of conglomerates. Even among rock types, each climbing area has its own character. The granite in Yosemite is different than the granite at Suicide Rock. Even world-class climbers find it often takes a few days to settle into an area, where standard moves become instinctive according to the rock's friction properties, features and so forth.

Many of the world's great monoliths are granite—El Capitan, Cerro Torre, Trango Tower, Mount Asgard, the Dru... The list goes on. For most adventure climbers, bulletproof granite is the preferred medium. Quality granite often forms into perfect faces and laser-cut cracks that swallow bomber pro. Conversely, decomposed granite is fraught with monstrous teetering blocks and rotten, bottoming cracks. Seek out the good stuff.

Cracks

Crack climbing and granite are almost synonymous terms. Granite cracks usually vary in size, so a set or two of cams and wires does the trick on most pitches; a couple of medium hexes can also come in handy. Still, do some research to insure you have the appropriate rack. Beware the wide crack, and remember that cracks are often wider than they appear from the ground. On granite slabs, watch out for "coffin nail" ¼" diameter bolts still in place on many older routes. Experienced bolters should feel free to replace them with ⅜" or bigger bolts whenever possible.

If cracks are your passion, head to southern Utah. Wingate sandstone is the name, and climbing beautiful desert cracks is the game. The highest concentration of good desert cracks is in Indian Creek, where you can't walk twenty feet without passing beneath another beautiful splitter or corner. Wingate cracks are so pure, so uniform, they demand exacting technique. Here, crack climbing has been refined to a science, spawning new skills, gear, and even new taping tricks. Most of the cracks are on buttresses, but some lead to the top of spectacular towers.

Like any rock, Wingate varies in quality from horrible to good. Even the densest Wingate is far softer than granite, however, and camming units have been known to skate out of the crack in a leader fall, leaving cam tracks down the sides of the crack. On all sandstone (and soft rock), place ample gear, climb in control, and avoid casual whippers. One problem with climbing Wingate cracks is rounding up enough pieces the same size to protect the pitch you want to lead. Mia Axon needed 30 small cams for her ascent of "Tricks are for Kids," and I (C.L.) used 12 Bigbros on the first ascent of "Sidewinder" in Long Canyon.

Other crack meccas include Devil's Tower, Fremont Canyon, and Vedauwoo, Wyoming; Lumpy Ridge, Turkey Rock, and Unaweep Canyon, Colorado; Tahquitz/Suicide, The Needles, and Yosemite, California; plus a host of other western United States climbing areas.

Steph Davis making "Coyne Crack (11d) look like a day hike.

Tradition

Older, traditional climbing areas are a rich mine for adventure, classic routes and climbing history. Areas such as Eldorado Canyon, Tahquitz Rock, Granite Mountain, Stone Mountain and the Shawangunks have been preserved for traditional climbing, and they offer an aesthetic alternative to the clip-and-go. There's always something special about bagging a route that Layton Kor, Royal Robbins, or Fritz Weissner put up decades ago.

LONG DAY ROUTES

On long routes, efficiency is key. Start as early as safety allows. One hour lost in the morning can trap you in the afternoon storm, causing a hateful epic costing you several hours, if not more. Getting up and off a long day route isn't so much a matter of running up pitches, as it is starting early, making sound route-finding decisions, setting and removing anchors efficiently, handling the rope well, climbing confidently, and utilizing every moment toward the goal of getting up the climb.

Light is right, but one can trim things back to the point of having no resources at all. If everything goes perfectly, you'll merely suffer. If the unexpected happens—as it often does on adventures—you have no insurance because you're unprepared. When I (C.L.) climbed the Nose in a day with the late, great Derek Hersey, he brought only a 12-ounce Pepsi to drink. Though he climbed brilliantly all day, guess whose legs were cramping on the descent. Grub is a matter of taste and opinion, but fluids are not. Most climbers haul at least a quart to a half-gallon of water (each) for a full day's climbing, and all climbers could drink twice that amount. When the temperature soars, take all the water you can bear to haul—or suffer mightily. Some climbers report good results with the new backpack hydrating systems on long routes.

Lug It

Depending on the amount of gear you bring, you have three options for carrying it: a daypack, a fanny pack, or you can clip accessories on the back of your harness. In an alpine situation you'll need extra clothes, so a pack is mandatory. While it keeps everything tidy, a pack puts the weight where it adversely affects your equilibrium. A fanny pack is kinder to your center-of-gravity, but is less comfortable than a small backpack. When I'm (C.L) trying to go light and fast, I leave the pack on the ground. I clip a small rainsuit, stuffed with one or two energy bars, a half roll of tape, and a very small knife, onto the back of my harness, along with 1 to 1½ liters of energy drink in a duct-taped bottle with a carrying sling, and sixteen feet of 5mm cord for emergencies. I usually wear comfortable rock shoes that I can do the approach and descent in, and don't have to fidget with all day. I also wear long, light-colored pants if I'll be in the hot sun. I go with whatever shirt is appropriate for the weather, and tie a polypro shirt or jacket around my waist. I might also tuck a small balaclava hat, pair of gloves, and a lighter away some-where. This is my compromise between the balls-out, early Black Canyon of the Gunnison-style "a rope, a rack, and the shirts on our backs," espoused by Jimmy Dunn and Earl Wiggins, and the "Be prepared" motto I learned as a Boy Scout. Since everyone's skill and orientation is different, only experience dictates what to carry and how to carry it. Going light increases your commitment, but helps you move fast and free.

Whenever you carry a day or fanny pack, you'll inevitably come upon a squeeze chimney where the pack hangs up. Solution: Tether a line from your pack to your harness. This lets you drop the pack and trail it a few feet below, allowing you to slip through the crack, rather than fight desperately to drag yourself through while wearing the pack. Make sure the tether is well secured—with either locking biners or girth hitches at *both* ends—before dropping the pack.

What Rope?

Rope options are almost endless. A single standard 50-meter (165-foot) rope will take you most places, but may occasionally leave you short on some rappels. Sixty-meter (200-foot) ropes are gaining favor because they allow longer pitches and rap-pels. Whatever the length, most teams carry two ropes on multi-pitch routes for ease of descent or retreat.

Three basic rope systems exist: a lead line and haul line, which is necessary if you might need a gear re-supply mid-pitch, or have a pack to haul; double ropes, which can be routed separately to manage rope drag; and ultra-light twin ropes that save weight and must both be clipped into each piece of pro. Both the type of climbing and your personal style deter-mine which system works best. Experiment and see what option best suits your needs. If you only own two ropes, con-sider a 10 to 10.5mm lead rope, and an 8.5 to 9mm haul line that can also serve as a double rope to give you more options while reducing weight. This is the standard tackle. For occa-sional hauling and rappelling, a 7mm rope is light, and can be butterfly-coiled onto the second's pack to avoid futzing with two ropes while climbing. Remember, a 7mm rope must be used with great caution. It will part like dental floss when weighted over a sharp edge.

Prep

Tank up on carbos and liquids (not booze), and pack your gear the day before your big climb. Sort out the Beta and topo, then plan a realistic time schedule to insure you're on track for the summit as the pitches whizz by. Get the best night's sleep you can, and start as early as possible—at first light or earlier if a long approach is required. While gaining the wall (if the light allows), study your line and try to decipher any tricky route-finding areas. A few minutes scouting below can save hours, not to mention terror, above.

At the base of the climb, toss out the ropes, eat and drink a little, then cast off. Remember, the tortoise beats the hare. Steady and deliberate prevail over hasty and inefficient every time. On the route, each climber should continually ask, "What can I do right now to speed the team up?"

Belay Changeover

Picture yourself just finishing a lead. The first thing to do is fire in a couple bomber pieces and tie into them. Once you get the hang of it, you can take yourself off belay long before you're finished tricking out the anchor (again—providing you've clipped off to two bomber pieces). Remember, bolt anchors are not the norm on adventure climbs. Some adventure climbs have no bolts at all, and belays are often complex. Once you're tied off, you can fiddle with equalization and what not as the second cleans the lower anchor down to one bomber piece (more in a hanging belay). Once the higher belay anchor is completed and "Climb!" rings out, the second cleans the final piece of the lower anchor, and moves out. As the second follows, he's careful to rack cleaned gear in some semblance of order. Cleaning pro in a rush and clipping it on any old place can require extra minutes when you gain the belay and have to rerack.

At the belay, the leader has arranged a place for the second to clip in, and she backs him up by tying a figure eight in the rope where the brake hand grasps, essentially keeping him on belay. One climber feeds the cleaned gear, one piece at a time, to the other for reorganization. All gear is racked according to size and all biners face the same way on the rack. After a glance at the topo to prevent route-finding errors, the second is off, leading the next pitch; and so it goes, the team swinging leads to the summit.

Block Those Pitches

If one climber is stronger or more experienced, she may lead all or most of the pitches, or perhaps just the harder ones. A common practice is to lead in "blocks," where one climber leads several pitches in a row, then follows a block. Many consider this the fastest method to climb long routes. For a superstar team trying to maintain breakneck speed, blocking out the route is best. However, for a normal climbing team on a typical multi-pitch route, it's often just as fast or faster to swing leads.

Carabiner tie-in for block leading.

While "blocking," consider switching rope ends at each belay. Each climber clips a figure eight in the end of the rope, securing it to his/her harness with two locking carabiners. (Clip directly into the harness belt and leg loops, *not* into the belay loop.) This tie-in breaks all the rules of attaching yourself to the rope, because it adds otherwise needless links into the tie-in chain; but it's reasonably safe with beefy, doubled locking biners. The leader ties into the belay with the rope, then while the second climbs, he additionally anchors in with a daisy chain girth-hitched to his harness. When the second arrives at the belay, the leader unclips from his end of the rope, and hands it to the second, who immediately clips into the loop, one biner at a time, and is thus anchored. The second gives her end of the rope to the leader, who clips it into both biners. This end of the rope is already stacked on top, so the leader can set off leading the next pitch after four quick hands rerack the gear. Doublecheck religiously when switching rope ends. Though this procedure sounds involved, the progression is clear and logical if you visualize the process and work through it step by step.

Block leading belay transfer.

Off on the lead after a block transfer.

Efficiency

A skilled leader places enough gear to keep the pitch safe, but whenever possible, avoids burning time fiddling with pro. If the gear doesn't go in fast, do you really need it? Maybe there's a better placement a little higher. Avoid tough-to-clean placements, and don't overprotect. Every nut that goes in has to come out, so when you're on comfortable terrain, go for good, but not excessive, pro. Forget about running out the rope needlessly. Few adventure climbs are continuously grim, bottom to top. Protect difficult leads just as you would on a crag. It is on moderate pitches where a team can make time, and where overprotecting becomes a detriment.

Constant awareness of the route is critical. When following a single crack, route finding is easy. But most long climbs involve some nebulous sections. Getting outright lost is improbable if the topo is at all accurate and you continually refer to it. The tricky sections are often found on face climbing sections not featuring bolt protection. You might see the very ledge or crack you're going for, but in the absence of bolts to mark the way, one line of holds can look as promising, or bleak, as another. Another vexer is that several different ways might be chalked, and there's simply no knowing the easiest path until you start climbing. Here you are faced with the same challenge of the first ascent. The trick is to proceed with caution. So long as you arrange adequate protection, there is no harm in investigating. People get in trouble when they rashly commit to an improbable section that is poorly protected. This can lead to panic and desperation that the leader has created for himself. Topos can only be so detailed, but a good and trusted topo never fails to mention poorly protected sections of a climb because there is nothing more important for climbers to know. If the topo doesn't mention a thirty-foot runout on slippery 5.10, and that's what you are gawking at, it's pretty certain that you are off route. Downclimb a little and look around for options. Moving as little as ten feet to either side can make a huge difference. Getting lost can cost you hours, and taking long falls will always sap your psyche.

Sometimes the leader may choose to combine pitches to shorten time at belays. This works occasionally—principally on straight lines—although when you're 180 feet above the belay, the line feels like a tugboat tether. Little is usually gained by passing fixed belays. When only thirty feet of rope remains for leading, the belayer should yell "thirty feet!" so the leader can start looking for a belay site.

Simul With A Prayer

Occasionally on a long pitch, two ace and experienced climbers may simul-climb—both climbers moving simultaneously, a rope length apart. This is ill-advised for all but world-class climbers, who can decide for themselves what technique is best. Believe it—simul-climbing is sketchy work, to be used only on very easy terrain by full-blown experts accustomed to climbing together. Every time I've (C.L.) simul-climbed lately, my second has freaked. That's because if the second falls, she'll probably pull off the leader. Then both climbers fall until the leader gets stopped by his last piece—providing it holds. It's double jeopardy for the second, as the penalty for a mistake is two lives.

That much said, people do simul-climb, though most must be driven to it by, say, an impending storm or fading light. If you're ever pressed into simul-climbing, the leader should place gear frequently, and the second should never climb faster than the rope moves, making certain no slack accumulates between climbers. Continual communication and excellent terrain reading skills are essential. The leader can throw in a bomber piece or two to belay the second through the hard sections. On easy terrain (and "easy" is entirely relative to the given climbers), most teams dispense with the rope and third class, rather than simul-climb. Even masters are conservative with this call, however. Soloing beyond the comfort or skill level of any climber on the team is no place to make time.

Station to Station

On the way up, take a mental note on the fixed anchors and landmarks, so you'll know the best line of retreat if you get slammed by a storm. Always watch the weather, so you can bail or speed up as need be. And try to set belays out of the direct line of fire if the leader should pull off a rock.

Surpass

Any team that climbs quickly and efficiently on classic routes is bound to face this dilemma: "Should we pass?" In Europe, the answer is well-known and accepted, if grudgingly. Long alpine routes in the Alps are dead serious, and hordes of climbers endlessly swarm over them. Ascents of these routes can take on the aspect of love and war, where it's each team for themselves and anything goes. Bugger the other guys. Your priority is that you don't die—a method that evolved directly from the brotherhood of corpses who were more polite, but slower. The result is that the fastest team passes at will, often using your anchors for pro and your head as a

Melissa Quigley and Scott Carson climbing "Ankles Away" (11), The Needles, California.

Greg Epperson photo

foothold. In the States this tactic would result in immediate fisticuffs—as it should—so another ethic is generally followed: whatever team first drops their rope at the base of a route, starts first. But with the growth of climbing, especially in alpine areas, the ethic is edging toward the Euro method. If the faster team can pass the slower team without a major jam up (depending on the route and situation), the slower team often consents to being passed. The worry here is that the slower party is now exposed to rockfall from the passing party, suffering a risk they didn't originally bargain for. Who cares if a passing team takes responsibility for kicking rocks off? Their sense of blame means little if your skull's bashed in. For this reason, most American climbers reserve the right to deny passage to a faster party—and most teams accept this, especially on loose routes. The rule does not wash for one-day ascents of big walls, however, when a climbing team has no choice but to pass teams doing a multi-day ascent. A team is wise not to start a speed ascent on a route where six parties are strung out its length. However on classic walls, especially in Yosemite Valley, big climbs always see heavy traffic. Most classics are relatively free of rockfall, so the main hazards are tangled lines.

Pick It Up

To move faster on rock, practice bouldering fast and pulling speed laps on favorite routes. Since adventure climbing is typically on-sight, pick a few routes you've never done before (at least two full grades beneath your maximum) and dust them at speed. Polish easier pitches at pace, and practice rapid fire climbing on a toprope. Climb lots of pitches and get into the flow, concentrating on moving steadily and efficiently, rather than hurried. Slot gear where it's quick, convenient and solid. Always be thinking of creative (but safe) means to speed up the pitches. Try not to stall out or hesitate, but never rush things to the point of danger. It's amazing what a hundred-foot fall will do to someone chasing a speed record.

Amigo

For over a dozen years, checking off long free climbs was a top priority in my (J.L.) life. And while tackle, technique and experience supported a successful ascent, the crucial factor was always the person on the other end of my rope. On cragging routes, shagging a belay from any Joe with a Gri-Gri is tolerable—though more than a few climbers have been dropped by strangers who talked, but could not hold, a good line. Choosing a partner for an adventure climb is truly a matter of life and death. And since you're climbing to have fun and feel quickened—or should be—a partner's temperament and compatibility become as key as their flair on the sharp end. What happens in a pinch? Adventure climb enough and at sometime you'll find yourself fjording through Shit Creek—no way around it. How will your partner fare when the water starts rising? If you get hurt? If he gets hurt? Will he want to bail when cloud one shows in the sky, or will he drag your weary ass through a lightning storm to gain the top? You want to be on the same page—or climb, if you will—with your partner. This is discovered by doing a series of routes in various conditions, where the hero and the coward in you both will emerge. Beyond that, there is no telling what combination will create the right chemistry. Your ideal partner might be your total opposite or your twin sister. Though serious partnerships are developed over many years, you'll usually know after a few pitches if the magic is there.

HANGING BELAYS

Hanging off a few bits of aluminum and nylon, hundreds of feet in the sky, with only a tiny perch for the feet, is one of the most exhilarating experiences of climbing. Ledges are more convenient and comfortable to belay from, so try to reach a ledge whenever possible. Sometimes, though, you must hang it out. It is crucial to know that climbing ability (or lack of it) is rarely the factor that skunks teams breaking into adventure climbing. Even great climbers can fail miserably at adventure climbing if they manage belays poorly. If too much time is wasted arranging and sorting through byzantine belays, there simply isn't daylight enough to crank a long adventure climb, no matter how fast you lead individual pitches. And without exception, the one thing an adventure team must have down cold is how to transition smoothly and quickly through hanging and semi-hanging belays.

Organization is the key to all hanging belays. Without organization, belay transitions are difficult and aggravating—ropes going every which way and things clipped in over each other, entangling the whole shebang till you've got a befuddling snarl of crisscrossed gear. To avoid this madness you need to understand several generic principals that can be systematically applied to all hanging belays, no matter how that belay is rigged.

Swinging leads gives the easiest transition at hanging belays. It is worth mentioning again: the second arrives at the belay and clips into a sling already prepared by the leader. The leader

Tommy and Mike Caldwell on "Country Boy" (13d), Lumpy Ridge, Colorado.

backs up the second by tying a figure eight in the rope behind the belay device. The climbers exchange and organize the rack, then the second leads up the next pitch. As with all systems, efficiency comes through doing things the same way every time until the steps are instinctive. Every sling belay has special demands, but the basic steps remain the same.

Cord Vigilance

On big, open slabs, where the features are smooth and rope snags improbable, let the rope hang down the face in one or two big loops. If the face is featured, sling or lap coil the rope so it can't jam below while the leader is midway up the next pitch. If you have two double ropes to stack, fold them together into the lap coil. If you have a haul line and a lead line, separate them, lap coil one and sling coil the other. Whenever long lengths of rope are required, it takes practice to efficiently manage lap coiling and creative stacking techniques. Because these skills are basically easy, they become automatic after a few long routes. Allow yourself permission to make initial mistakes, knowing that you won't have to repeat them later on.

ONE LEADER

If one climber does all the leading, the belay transitions are more complicated. Options: either switch rope ends as described above, or perform the following ritual. After clipping into the anchors with a sling, the second ties his rope into the anchors. Now the team restacks the lead rope so the leader's end is again on top. The haul line is either restacked, or the leader switches ends of the haul line so it feeds off the top. After organizing the gear and being put on belay, the leader unties from the belay anchors and leads off.

NEW ROUTES

Climbing a new route from the ground up, with little or no knowledge of what to expect, is the last statement in adventure climbing. Whether you're cragging, or 20 pitches up a wall, clawing onto unknown terrain invigorates the soul like little else. At popular areas, obvious crack lines were climbed long ago, so establishing new routes today typically involves long runouts, creative protection, bolting, or all of the above.

When tackling a new adventure climb from the ground up, scope the route as thoroughly as possible. Whenever I (J.L.) used to prepare for a new climb in Yosemite, I'd borrow the Questar telescope from the Park Service rescue cache and spend an entire afternoon eyeballing every inch of the proposed line, often taking detailed notes and drawing tentative topos.

You never truly know what you're up against until boot meets rock, but locating big features, such as flake systems, cracks and ledges will almost always allow you to plot the most probable line. Things will inevitably change once you rope up, but the location of those features will not. Once you have identified the landmarks, you need only find the most practical or possible way to link the features together, something you can never fully determine beforehand.

During your recon of the new line, note what kind of climbing you'll encounter, and what manner of protection seems

The legendary Jimmy Dunn launching up yet another new route, "Kiss of the Spider Woman" (12b), Day Canyon, Utah

likely. If adequate protection and holds seem to exist, put together an ample rack to cover unexpected protection opportunities, and go for it. (Depending on the line, you might want an extra rack at the belay; it's common to underestimate the gear required to lead a new pitch. If you run low on some sizes of gear, resupply using the haul line.)

If the "line" lacks cracks, and therefore opportunities for natural protection, you'll have to install a load of bolts, and you face a judgment call hinging on personal ethics and the area's tradition. There's also the question of personal time, effort and money. Increasingly, wilderness areas are outlawing power-driven bolt guns. That means you're left to hand drill, and hand drilling bolts is a load of work. And expensive. However, some new lines are clearly worth the toil and the dollars. One advantage is that today's high-tech chocks offer protection solutions that often make bolts unnecessary. But not always. If you do place bolts, make sure to place them correctly. You're creating a permanent fixture on the rock, and other climbers will trust their lives to your handiwork. Install enough bolts to make the route reasonably safe for others. Bolted death routes, especially when the first ascent pre-rehearsed the leads, show fatal disregard for others.

Again, most federal lands have bolting policies that zealous officials are eager to enforce. It's your responsibility to learn these regulations before shotgunning a line of bolts up a blank face. In National Forest Wilderness areas and National Park lands, motorized drills are banned, and there's talk of outlawing bolts altogether. Although power drills are quieter and drill better holes than hand drills, hand drilling limits the number of bolts that go in because it's a major effort, and it compromises the quality of the bolts. Nonetheless, hand drilling is an essential skill for any serious first ascensionist.

Lead drilling setup.

Machine on the Sharp End

Leading with a power drill is an exciting duty. There you are, perched on tiny dimples, or possibly hanging from a wobbly skyhook, struggling to pull a $500, eight-pound drill over your head, get a hole started, then drilled. Now you must back the drill out and sling it back over your head, which could pitch you over backwards when the bit pops out. This was the stage I (C.L.) was at on the first ascent of "Blood for Oil" at Combat Rock, when the skyhook popped, sending me into a fifteen-foot, head-first fall. As I stopped five feet short of the ground, the burning hot drill bit augered into my thigh, leaving a permanent bullet-hole scar. After limping around for 45 minutes, I went up and finished the pitch. To this day I hate skyhooks.

After drilling is complete, you then have to blow the dust from the hole, slam the bolt home, and finally, clip into it. Depending on the exertion, you may find yourself hanging on many of the bolts you place to recover your arms and wits.

Climbing with the extra weight of the drill can be avoided by leaving the drill hanging from a fifi hook at the last protection. The haul line runs up to a quickdraw or pulley on the back of the leader's harness, then down to the belayer. Beware: if you're not careful, the haul line can pull the fifi hook off and send the bolt gun plummeting. When the gun hits the end of the trail line, you're as good as off. Another method is to have the second "belay" the drill gun, halting the haul line if the gun lifts off. When it's time to drill, the leader pulls the drill up and goes to work, then leaves the drill (via the fifi hook) at that bolt and climbs higher. The belayer can also pull the drill up to the leader by yarding on the haul line running through a pulley on the back of the leader's harness. Though this is occasionally done when the leader is on solid ground—or hanging for his life on bleak holds—it loads the leader ferociously. Electrical engineer types can rig an exterior battery that fits in a fanny pack or hangs at the previous anchor, providing juice to the drill through a short extension cord. This allows lead drilling with a much lighter, battery-less drill. You're on your own for working out the wiring, and proceed at your own risk.

ROPE SOLOING

Can't find a partner? Don't want to find a partner? Roped soloing is an option. It is also dangerous and lonely. It does, however, serve a purpose for some climbers searching for an extra challenge. Soloing comes in two versions: rope soloing and free soloing. Rope soloing allows you to climb alone and still maintain some security by belaying yourself. Any way you slice it, rope soloing is a lot of work. You must lead a pitch, while managing your own belay, then rappel, clean, and reascend the pitch.

When free climbing, the self-belay system must feed easily, keeping rope drag manageable. No self-belay rig performs these duties as well as a competent belayer, and no belay rig can help you if you get hurt. But for those who must go it alone, several options exist for self belaying. And one inviolate rule for all rope soloing: Always wear a helmet.

Because of the complexity and hazards involved, rope soloing on lead is for experts only. Rope soloing techniques could cover a full chapter, or a whole book, which has yet to be written. Here we only briefly cover the nuances of rope soloing, so the expert climber must still dabble with various systems, and develop his or her own approach by way of trial and error. The best bet is to approach rope soloing far more conservatively than normal climbing, at least until you have it dialed in.

It's generally easier to rope solo an aid pitch than a free pitch, because aid climbing leaves your hands free to feed rope through your self-belay rig, tie backup knots, and manage the rope. When free climbing, you'll inevitably run out of rope in the middle of the crux, and get hugely pumped trying to get slack. This will happen the first few times you rope solo, until you work the systems out, so keep the routes easy.

Systems

The safest and simplest way to climb solo is with a top rope. Things get dicey on lead, and everything feels harder. When lead soloing, all self belay systems start with a bombproof, multi-directional bottom anchor to secure one end of the belay rope, as well as to hang extra gear from. The anchor must be beefy in both the upward and downward directions. If the pitch starts off traversing, the anchor must be beefy in all directions. You'll tie off one end of the belay rope to the anchors with two locking carabiners, and secure yourself to the line with knots or a self-belay rig that moves along the rope with you, and automatically locks onto the rope if you fall. No matter what system you use, religious use of backup knots clipped to your harness is essential when rope soloing.

Before beginning, stack the rope very carefully at the belay. Flaking the rope into a rope bag works best for rope soloing once you're above the first pitch—a rope snag at the

Soloist and Silent Partner.

belay can cause you a lot of trouble on the sharp end. As you climb, place protection, and clip in the rope. When self-belaying, with the rope fixed below, it never moves through the protection, so you can use short slings on protection because rope drag is not a problem. However, still use slings to keep the rope away from sharp edges.

If you've climbed past sharp edges that threaten the rope, set a stout multi-directional anchor and tie the rope off mid-pitch, to isolate the rope from the sharp edges. This essentially creates a new belay, and if you fall, the fall factor is increased because there's less rope to cushion the fall. This can dramatically increase the force on your anchors, and decrease the distance you drop due to rope stretch (unless the extra force rips your protection out). Nonetheless, it's worth it to protect the rope from a sharp edge.

A GriGri on your harness can work for a self-belay, although it was not designed for this purpose. Once you have a lot of rope weight hanging on the GriGri, it's difficult to feed slack through. Three devices designed specifically for rope soloing–the Soloist, Soloaid, and Silent Partner–work better.

The Soloist works well for top roping and free leading, because the rope feeds automatically as you climb. It has one major downfall–it's locking cam won't engage if you're falling upside down. Also, you need a chest harness to rig the Soloist.

The Silent Partner—a rather new entrant of high tech gadgetry–reportedly feeds rope easily, requires no chest harness, locks under any body position, and releases easily after a fall, which make it a dream for free climbing. It's also pricey.

The Soloaid requires one hand to feed the rope, so it's not great for hard free climbing, but it locks up under any body position, and can be used with or without a chest harness. It's also fairly compact, so it's good for aid soloing and easy free climbing.

Each of these commercially available self-belay devices comes with extensive directions to it's use, along with tricks and techniques for rope soloing. Only a fool would use these devices without fully understanding the instructions.

With all of these self-belay devices, rope drag can become severe halfway up a pitch, unless you occasionally tie the rope into intermediate, multi-directional protection. Remember, though, this increases the fall factor. One way to relieve the weight of the rope without increasing the fall factor is to wrap a friction hitch onto the rope and clip it into a piece of protection. Use a shoestring-size cord that will break if you fall. A stout cord will increase the fall factor, and possibly damage the rope in a fall. This system does not protect the rope from sharp edges below.

Plate and Tube

An improvised self-belay method involves rigging a belay plate or tube on the lead line, with an ascender behind it to serve as a brake hand, and a figure-eight knot every fifteen or twenty feet to back it up. This system allows you to feed rope one-handed, by first sliding the jumar down the rope, then pulling slack through the belay device. As you can imagine, it's a poor system for fast clipping, and no manufacturer would recommend using their ascenders in this manner. I (C.L.) have used it, and it works, though halfway up a long climb I always question why I didn't try harder to round up a partner.

Clove Hitch

Another improvised system uses a clove hitch connecting the lead rope to the soloist's harness, with figure-eight backups every fifteen to twenty feet. To feed rope, the soloist passes line through the clove hitch. This is dicey work with one hand, so the soloist is typically left to feed extra rope through at stances and ledges, allowing a few feet of climbing with no rope hassle. The liability in this method is the likelihood of taking a big fall, owing to the extra slack in the rope. This system works better for aid climbing, when you can momentarily get two hands free to slide the clove hitch down the rope.

No matter how much you practice roped soloing, free climbing with a self-feeding system remains the principal challenge. Pull out too much slack and you risk taking a longer fall than necessary; pull out too little slack and the rope comes to a halt in the middle of the crux. It takes time to develop the knack for estimating just how much rope to feed out. Even more reason to learn the art on routes well below your limit. This is serious work and should be approached slowly. Practice on crag routes that are simple for you until the procedures become fluid and automatic, and your ability to judge distances—and the amount of rope to feed out—becomes increasingly precise.

Top: plate and jumar self-belay.
Bottom: clove hitch self belay.

Rappel

Whatever rope soloing method you adopt, at the top of each pitch you must establish another multi-directional belay, then rappel back down on the lead rope. If the pitch is straight up and down, often it is easiest to clean the gear on rappel. If the pitch traverses or overhangs, use the belay rope to pull into the anchors at the bottom. As you rappel past each piece, you must unclip it. If the route wanders and/or overhangs, you may have to reclip each piece into the rappel line (once you have rappelled past it). Otherwise, once you start jugging

The late Derek Hersey free soloing "Fat City Crack" (10c), Lumpy Ridge, Colorado.

back up the pitch the protection might be out of reach. You may be swinging out in space or off to the side and if you're not clipped into the pro, there's simply no way to swing in to clean it. The situation dictates which tactic works best. After ascending the rope, re-rack, and head off on the next pitch. Make sure you plan the whole operation out in your head, from beginning to end, before embarking. And always doublecheck every step. One oversight and you're dust.

FREE SOLOING

Free soloing is the act of climbing without a rope. And every free soloer is entirely on his own. Free soloing can be a thrilling experience for a competent weekend climber who casts off on something far below his limit. He might experience beautiful, flowing motion, with no pausing to hassle with gear. He might also see the ground so very far below, freeze up, pitch off and die. At the far end of the scale, where most of the free soloing takes place, the absolute expert fancies he has chosen to free solo for the "right" reasons (whatever those are). Whatever the motivation, free soloing is entirely unforgiving, and climbers at all points of the skill scale have fallen and died while free soloing. Two days after I (C.L.) climbed the Nose with master soloist Derek Hersey, he died soloing the Steck-Salathé. I drove home alone. Such are the risks of the game.

No one argues that free soloing is not climbing in its purest form. That so few soloists fall suggests that sober judgment prevails over the naive notion of the foolish daredevil going off half-cocked. Herman Buhl, Reinhold Messner, Royal Robbins, and more recently, John Bachar and Peter Croft—some of the true legends of our sport—all have reputations fashioned, in part, from soloing. Still, while we laud these climbers, a definite taboo shrouds their exploits. Certainly, difficult soloing is reserved for the full-blown expert, for those who eat, sleep, and drink climbing. But even for accomplished soloists the practice is a minefield full of clear and subtle dangers.

The likelihood is much overstated, but one should never get lured into soloing through peer pressure or dubious ambitions, like achieving fame. It's undeniable that many active climbers routinely solo easy, or even moderate, routes. A very few solo desperate routes (5.11 and up). But I've also known plenty of world-class climbers who never solo, no matter how easy the terrain—and if anything, their reputations have grown from their forbearance. The point is, soloing is one aspect of the sport where you cannot, or should not, emulate other climbers (save for those who never solo).

What then, is the lure? By dint of the frank jeopardy involved, soloing evokes feelings of mastery and command, plus a raw intensity that even a million-dollar-a-year ball player will never experience—not in the Super Bowl, not in the World Series, not on center court at Wimbledon. And therein lies the snare. Following a particularly rewarding solo, when everything has clicked, the climber feels like a wizard. These very feelings can foster a sham sense of invincibility. Hence, it's not unheard of that a narrow escape is followed by an eagerness to push things a little further, and so on, until the soloist is courting doom. And he'll most assuredly find it if he doesn't quickly back off. The whole insidious business is closely tied to anything that is exhilarating, deadly and fiendishly addictive. Whenever desire overrides judgment, bad things happen. If the soloing fool is fortunate, he'll have a harrowing close call, and he won't be the first to swear "Never again!"

If you do decide to solo, stay well within your limits, making sure you can downclimb if things don't feel right. And remember the soloists rule: never solo anything you are not absolutely positive you can climb without falling. The fact that you never know for sure is what makes the venture such a crap shoot.

AID CLIMBING

For a select few, aid climbing is employed only as a last resort, when free climbing is impossible and a touch of aid is required to best a dead blank or unclimbable section on a long, mostly free route. For others, aid climbing is the end-all expression of the sport, where eternity centers on the molecular purchase between a wee dollop of metal, and a gritty patch of rock, with only a long string of such placements below for security. For the complete scoop on aid climbing techniques, refer to *Big Walls,* also in the *How to Rock Climb*

Various French free techniques.

Resting in aiders.

*Using two aiders.
(below) with hand jam
assistance.*

series. Here we cover shortcut aid tactics for moving fast on stretches of straightforward aid, say A1 or A2, where the pieces are sound enough that placement testing is rarely required.

The keys to moving fast on aid are to A) minimize the number of steps required for each placement; B) maximize the distance between placements; C) move mechanically and efficiently, and free climb whenever possible.

Efficiency in aid climbing comes through rote, through vertical miles of practice. When the placements are good, shortcuts speed the process. For just a move or two of aid, consider the "French free" method, which is to simply heave up on the gear bare-handed, thus avoiding breaking out the etriers (aid slings). If the aid is unexpected, or the stretch is short, use slings for makeshift etriers. Leave them hanging on the last aided piece when you break back out into free climbing.

If the aid covers more than a few placements, it's best to have etriers, also called aiders or aid slings. To minimize weight, go with two aiders; for longer aid sections, a third etrier is worthwhile. For full-on, meat-and-potatoes aid climbing, two five-step aiders, each paired with a four-step sub-aider, are standard tackle.

Two Aiders

Say you're going light with two etriers. When it's time to break them out, clip one of them onto the first aid piece, then clip the second aider to the first and climb into the highest feasible steps, perhaps using a handjam or cling to gain that top step. Then set another piece as high as possible. If the next piece is bomber, clip the lead line in immediately. Unclip the second etrier you set, and clip it into the new piece, step into it with one leg, then clip on the other etrier for your other leg. Again climb into the highest feasible step. With the rope clipped above, you can Batman up if need be, and you can pinch the rope where it runs through the top biner with your hand, thus gaining tension on your harness while placing the next piece. A hand loop (in the form of a small loop of sling, a "hero loop") on the top of the etrier also serves well as a handhold. The whole business of daisy chains, fifi hooks, and testing is forgone in the interest of speed efficiency. The etrier resting technique of sitting on one of your legs is used widely for resting on steep aid. If the placement is bunk, bounce test the piece before relying on it, and don't clip the lead rope into the piece until your waist is level with, or above, the placement. If you're going for ultimate speed, you may not want to clip pro until it is at waist level, to avoid hoisting the rope to clip high. A third etrier makes aiding a little easier and more efficient (unless you carry the etriers a long way, and use them for only a short stretch).

CLEANING AID

Aid pitches are usually easiest to clean on ascenders. "Jumaring" may be the only choice for cleaning a pitch if the leader back-cleaned gear on the pitch—a common practice. But if it's only a short stretch of aid, the second may clip up the aid pieces, or French free climb, to avoid the need for ascenders. Jumaring may also be necessary for ascending fixed lines.

If you're right-handed, set the right-hand jumar highest on the rope, with the left-hand jumar just below (opposite if you're left-handed). Clip an etrier to each ascender with a locking biner. Girth hitch a daisy chain to your harness, and clip the daisy chain to the high ascender. Adjust the length, by clipping the appropriate loop in the daisy, so the daisy chain just goes tight on your waist when you've pushed the ascender up a full arm's length. For climbing a free-hanging rope, tether the daisy a tad shorter; for low-angle slabs, or for speed, tether it a hair longer.

I've (J.L.) jumared miles of rock over the last twenty years, and learned from the very first day that the key to efficient jumaring is to have a perfectly adjusted sling for the top hand (connecting the ascender to the harness). If the sling is tied off too short, you can't get a high enough thrust on the line, and have to jumar in short, cramped little strokes, as though you're rabbit punching the line. If the line is too long, you cannot unweight your body onto your harness, and have to hang on with the upper arm, which saps you in fifty feet. The new daisy chains enable you to adjust the length of the tie-in by inch increments. Experiment, and get the adjustment just right. And expect that you'll have to change the adjustment relative to the angle of the rock.

Another daisy chain, or two slings girth-hitched together, should be used to tether the lower ascender to the harness. The length of this tether is not as critical, since all hanging is done from the top ascender. However, beware if this lower daisy is clipped off too short, it will limit the travel of your ascender.

Safety on the Fixed Line

When jumaring up a fixed line, a provision "belay" is accomplished by periodically tying a figure eight into the fixed rope and clipping it into a locking biner on your harness. This process backs up the ascenders, and is repeated at intervals throughout the pitch. Remember, if you're not tied into the rope, your only security comes from the ascenders clamped on the line. The likelihood that both of the ascenders should at once come unclipped from the rope is highly unlikely,

Jumaring.

though not unheard of. If that happens, you fall to the ground. The reason for periodically tying off to the fixed line is to safeguard against the remote chance that your ascenders will blow off the rope. If they do, and you're tied in to the fixed line, you'll fall to your last tie-in point. It is impossible to tie into the rope when it is fixed both on the top and the bottom, but this is never the case when you are jumaring up a lead on an adventure climb. For techniques on how to safeguard yourself on fixed lines, see *Big Walls,* in the *How to Rock Climb* series.

Jug Away!

After doublechecking every buckle, sling, and biner in the system, you're ready to jug. Say you're right-handed. The right hand goes to the higher ascender, and the right foot goes into the etrier below it. Likewise, the left hand and left foot go into the lower ascender and etrier. First, slide the ascenders up the rope to take the stretch out of the line, then sit into the high ascender on your daisy chain. Start with your feet in the etrier rungs high enough so the knees bend around 60 to 90 degrees, so you can get a nice, high step.

Ascending efficiently, especially if the rope is free-hanging, takes practice. The key, as in all of climbing, is to work your legs and not your arms and to keep your arms straight when you do not need them. Keep your center in close to the rope. Stand up as far as you can extend on the lower (left) etrier, and pull both ascenders into your chest. Now lock off on the left ascender, with your left hand close to your shoulder, but most of your weight on the left foot. Slide the right ascender up as high as you comfortably can. Now you have two options. If it's not too steep, do a one-arm pullup with your right arm while pushing your weight up with your right leg, and simultaneously slide the lower (left) ascender up. Now distribute your weight between both ascenders, and repeat. Most of your weight must be supported by your right leg in this maneuver, or you'll burn out after ten feet. This is a speed technique used for very brief sections on lower-angled passages. As an

Jumaring with one etrier.

overall technique, the one arm yank is the worst option.

If the terrain is steep, the proven technique is to stand up, pull both ascenders into your chest, and slide the right ascender up as high as possible, like before. Now momentarily hang straight-armed from the high ascender and lean back until your weight is transferred to your harness, then quickly slide the left ascender up. The trick here is to limit the time hanging on the top arm and let your leg, not your arm, absorb the weight. Now you can use both arms and legs to propel your weight upward. When you need rest, slide the high ascender up, sit into the daisy chain, shake out your arm and don't cast off until you've recovered. Thirty seconds is usually enough unless you've been death-gripping the high jug with your hand/arm. If your daisy is too long, it will take extra effort to lift yourself off your harness and back onto the ascenders.

An easier, and slower, method is to sit onto the daisy chain every move. Slide the right ascender up and immediately sit onto the daisy. Then, with your weight hanging on your harness, slide the left jumar up just below the right one, stand up on both legs and arms, slide the right ascender up, and repeat. For this technique, which allows some rest between every move, it's good to have the daisy chain adjusted a little shorter.

As you ascend the rope, periodically (say, every thirty feet, or fifteen feet above every ledge) tie a new figure eight, clip into it, then unclip from the previous backup. This procedure quickly becomes automatic and takes only seconds. After you've tied off to the rope, the lower ascender may slide up reluctantly. You must understand how your brand of ascender works so you can back off the cam to slide the ascender up without causing the ascender to come off the rope.

If you have a big pack, or the rope is free-hanging, you can use the inch worm method to climb the rope. Attach the upper ascender to your harness via the daisy chain. Only the bottom ascender gets an aider, which goes to one or both feet (one usually works best). To climb the rope, stand up on your foot in the ascender and slide up the higher ascender, then immediately sit back onto your harness. Make sure your daisy chain is not adjusted too long. Slide the lower ascender up, and repeat.

Lizz Grenard jumarring up to the Great Roof on "The Nose" (VI 5.11 A2), Yosemite Valley, California.

HAULING

With few exceptions, a traditional adventure free climb is a day affair and should never require a bivouac on the wall. However the unforeseen can change the best laid plans. Your insurance is to take a minimum of extra gear, "extra" referring to anything beyond the rope and the rack, the actual climbing gear. The quantity of this extra gear determines your hauling technique. Light loads, such as the standard extra sweater, rain gear and food and water, are often carried in a day pack by the second, meaning if you're swinging leads, you will also take turns carrying the pack. If you have too much gear for this, or if the free climbing is near your limit, the leader might hoist the pack or haulbag up the haul line and up to the belay before the second follows. Usually on a day route, hand-over-hand hauling is sufficient for the low loads involved. Since most adventure climbs have at least some moderate climbing, the second follows cruiser pitches with the pack on, hauling it only on those pitches close to his limit. Make sure the haul line runs as free of obstacles as possible.

To assist hauling a heavy pack, consider using a "Wallhauler"—a pulley with a locking cam that holds the load between hauls. Without this device, run the haul rope through a high biner, and haul by pulling up on one strand of rope with one arm, and pulling down with the other arm on the downside strand of rope. The friction of the rope running over the biner makes it easier to hold the pack when resting. After you get the pack a ways above the belayer, you may want to tie off the haul line so if you drop the pack, it will not clobber the belayer.

If the next belay is to the side of the previous belay, at the beginning of the haul, the pack will

Hauling with a wall hauler.

pendulum into the plumbline beneath the upper belay. If a few feet of haul line is still at the belay, tie the pack off short and use the remaining line to lower the pack out—slowly. Rig the pack with slings and a locking carabiner so you can clip in and out of different loops on the haul line, for easy hanging of the pack, and access into the pack when it is hanging. A specialized haul pack performs this duty well.

If you have to rappel steep terrain with a heavy pack, girth hitch one or two slings into two or three stout pack loops. Clip the slings with a locking carabiner into your rappel device carabiner. Now rappel with the pack hanging between your legs. This keeps the pack from pulling you over backward like a capsized tortoise.

ALPINE CLIMBING

Alpine climbing is a dangerous game in a spectacular land. Nothing compares to a sky-high perch on a razorback ridge shooting into the clouds. There are also few things more serious than having an epic in the mountains. Alpine rock climbing requires a unique mix of backpacking, mountaineering, and rock and ice climbing skills. Alpine climbs are often long, with grueling approaches and descents, requiring all the crafts for climbing long rock routes, plus specialized alpine skills. Here we can only mention the subject; *Mountaineering: The Freedom of the Hills* is the definitive text on mountaineering and alpine topics.

Rappelling with a heavy pack.

Though this is not the venue to cover alpine climbing, those pursuing adventure climbs in the alpine milieu should observe the following considerations: Respect the alpine environment, enter it cautiously and build your experience slowly. Bring ample synthetic jackets, pants, gloves, hats, and bomber wind-and-rain gear, as well as appropriate footwear. Don't skimp on energy food and drink, or you'll freeze your ass off. Carrying a rain jacket 20 times and never using it is a cheap price to pay for having it when you need it. Preparedness, correct equipment and experience are the essentials to staying alive in the alpine world. This is a gross oversimplification of both the perils and the joys of climbing in the alpine arena. Anyone who aspires after alpine adventure on any kind of scale should approach the topic as a special study, because it is.

The majority of "climber killed" incidents involve rash tourists who grapple onto the steep and pitch off, usually while trying to downclimb. However, as the popularity of climbing grows, so does the number of "legitimate" climbing accidents.

The first years of a climber's career are traditionally considered the most dangerous; but thousands of days of climbing can also take a statistical toll on the most experienced climbers. I've (C.L.) known fourteen climbers—all experts—who have died climbing in the past six years. Ten perished in the mountains, which, sadly, is expected given the commitment and objective hazards. (Three were overcome by avalanches, two fell in crevasses, one froze to death, one got trapped by a storm and was lost, and three other expired from illness, two of which were altitude-related.) The four who died rock climbing were split on opposite extremes of risk: two died free soloing; two died toproping.

Staying healthy hinges on sound judgment, and sound judgment depends on every member of a climbing team knowing and respecting the dangers of a given venture. Most teams have a leader, stated or otherwise, but the responsibility for keeping the team safe and self-reliant concerns everyone on the rope.

On crag routes, an experienced climber will often tow a novice along, teaching him or her the ropes and showing by example how the art is performed. Most of us served an apprenticeship under a more accomplished leader, and our skills increased rapidly. This is the standard method—you tie in with someone who knows. You watch like a hawk and learn what you can. As valuable as this method is in refining your technique and gaining a feel for the work, adventure climbing, owing to the substantial commitments and the importance of experience, demands competence and iron trust from all involved. If a novice ties in with an expert and casts off on a long and arduous adventure climb, he's left to rely on the expert's judgment and prowess every step of the way. What happens if the expert gets hurt and needs the novice's aid? In a very real sense, the hazards of venturing onto a big adventure climb with unqualified partners has graver consequences than the tangible dangers of a given route. Because in the beginning you don't have experience, it's crucial to ease into the game, and to do so with a partner you can trust your life with.

Dangers

Lightning, rockfall, avalanches and sharp rock are authentic hazards beyond a climber's control. Such "objective" hazards can be minimized, however, by learning to recognize the conditions in which they are likely to occur, and knowing how to stay clear. A few considerations: Be off of high places during the afternoon thunderstorm; wear a helmet for rockfall; never

climb below other climbers unless forced into it; never travel across dangerously-loaded snow slopes; route the lead rope so it avoids sharp edges. Experience and vigilance remain our best insurance against accidents. Yet objective hazards

Watch out for loose rocks! Betsy McKitrick following "Kiss of the Spider Woman" (12b), Day Canyon, Utah.

remain, and risk is assumed every time you don the rack and cast out onto the High Lonesome. All the more reason to rope up with someone you can trust when the sky starts falling.

Subjective Hazards

Of the hundreds of people I've (J.L.) known with at least ten years' climbing experience, most have horror stories about some incident(s) that could and even should have done them in, but through luck of fate did not. Never mind zippering a string of A4 pins, or pinging off a 5.12 lieback. I'm referring to El Cap veterans rappelling off the end of their ropes, having their harness come untied because they didn't take time to double the waist loop back through the buckle, and a score of other cardinal blunders. Yes, every year wrong place, wrong time scenarios happen (accidents from "objective hazards" such as rock fall), and all the prowess in the world could not have delivered the victims. But such occurrences are rare. Every statistical report confirms that the majority of climbing injuries were to a great extent avoidable. And these avoidable injuries can and do strike even the most experienced of us. Gravity is unforgiving and does not discriminate between the hacker and the world-class ace. At the bottom of the cliff side, we all start up as equals. Overlook one thing and you just might pay the piper, no matter who you are.

Climber errors are known as "subjective" hazards: A belayer dropping a leader; a rappeller sliding off the ends of the rope; a leader zippering pro that should and could have been adequate had he not rushed the placements and settled for something less than bombproof. Minimizing hazards requires more than experience. It requires diligence with the fundamentals: Watching the leader; keeping your brake hand on the line; properly tying into the end of the rope; tying knots into the end of your rappel lines; rappelling in control and always looking for the ends of the rope to come up so you don't rappel into the void; making the effort—however time-consuming—to set plenty of solid gear; rigging directional anchors so your pro doesn"t rip if you fall or if the anchor is shock loaded from an oblique angle. Paying attention to detail, and always doublechecking your gear will save your life. A moment's lapse can end it.

Statistically, leading takes the greatest toll on rock climbers. Simple mistakes will often—but not always—cost you nothing; multiple mistakes are almost always disastrous. It cannot be overstated: Experience, good judgment, and conservative climbing will reduce your risk of getting hurt or killed.

Tape, chalk wrappers and cigarette butts littered at the base of crags have, sadly, become a common eyesore at too many areas. Nobody wants to see trash when they climb. Our climbing areas belong to America the Beautiful. They are not some trashy, toilet paper studded Euro haunt. Bolts, fixed slings, vegetation damage, cross-braided trails and noise pollution are bad enough. Worse is chipping and otherwise altering the rock.

Access problems have been caused at many areas by climber impact, and restored at other areas when climbers made a conservation plan to minimize impact. It's the responsibility of every climber to clean up trash, and follow the locally accepted rules. Given the wave of new climbers to virtually every climbing area, regard for the environment is the only thing that will keep access open. Many crags are on private land. Others are public, but once the level of pollution is deemed unreasonable in a National or State Park or Monument, the gate is closed, sometimes for good. The Access Fund, based in Boulder, Colorado, has staged many valiant battles to protect access to climbing areas, advocating climber conservation to protect the resources, and ensuring our privilege to climb. But all the lawyers in all the land cannot help us if we foul it. So respect the climbing area as you would respect your own home. And remember, it is not a right, rather a privilege, to enter a climbing area.

Tommy Caldwell on
"Renaissance Wall"
(12b) in Lumpy Ridge.

Training

CHAPTER 8

Panorama

To squeeze out your last drop of talent, to pull the frigging walls down, many skills must be learned and honed: concentration and control, focused aggression, courage, polished technique, mechanical savvy, fitness and magic, to list a few. We're all given a measure of these things at birth, and can enlarge our share through doing. More climbing means more confidence, smoother technique, greater focus. True, it is unlikely someone scared of their shadow will ever become an unchained fiend, no matter how much he or she climbs; but a comprehensive training schedule can bring startling improvements. And "training" includes more than heaving on a finger board or spanking yourself in the gym. "Training" encompasses anything that enhances your performance on the rock, be it Zazen meditation, pumping iron, eating well, forbearance of vice and license, managing injuries and, of course, strength training.

Many people find their forte and work it until they're beastly at a certain skill or exercise. In the weight room, see the buxom bench pressing; on the rock, watch those natural liebackers jump onto the nearest leaning corner crack. Every Pedro likes to shine. The problem is, once a specialist moves off his narrow turf, he's buggered. Witness the edging champ floundering on the offwidth crack, or the crack man sketching up Swan Slab. Focusing on strengths results in a long performance plateau because specific strengths add little to overall prowess. To avoid this rut, training gurus give one answer: Find your weaknesses and work them. This is universal wisdom applying equally to music, writing, personal evolution, et al. Complete the package, and reap the benefits.

While we all can use more contact and lockoff power, increased flexibility or smoother technique will often take us higher than a minuscule increase in finger might. What is limiting your climbing right now? Can't high step? Do your calves quiver every time the bolt sinks an inch below your feet? Can't slot gear fast enough on lead? Don't have the volts to crank the hard boulder problems? Lack the endurance to hang in there on sustained pitches? Do you become a regular Edward Hyde when you can't tick a move? Do you wimp out when simply hiking to the crag? Figure out the two or three things that most stifle your performance, and work on them. As you overcome weaknesses, discover other defects to improve. With time and diligence, you'll round out your skills and achieve your maximum performance.

This does not mean to neglect your strengths, which may well set you apart from other climbers, particularly if your style hinges on power, or flexibility, or whatever. But don't

Jeff Elison cranks the classic Gill problem "Right Eliminator" (V5) Horsetooth Reservoir, Colorado.

buffalo yourself. Every climber can buff technique and mental power to better utilize his/her strength(s).

Say What?

Several questions to answer: What are your weaknesses and strengths? What are your goals? How much time do you have for training, and what type of climbing is your focus? Long alpine routes, hard cracks, or steep sport climbs? Only after answering these questions can training be tailored to needs.

Unless you hire a personal trainer (which few climbers can afford), you must style a personal training regimen. If you hire a trainer, make sure they understand your goals, strengths and weaknesses. Without this knowledge you'll likely be hustled through a generic fitness program with little focus on your specific needs. A skilled climbing trainer (or guide), however, who understands your goals, can determine your technique flaws and weaknesses and devise means to improve them.

That much said, the following information is geared to touch on key factors per the training game, but is not a stand-alone treatise. The field is too broad and the material too vast for us to list anything but the basics. For a detailed study, check out *Flash Training* and *How to Climb 5.12,* also in the *How To Rock Climb* series, and *Performance Rock Climbing.*

ELEGANT TECHNIQUE

Elegant technique comes from building a diverse repertoire of efficient moves. When you encounter a particular climbing sequence, if you've been there and efficiently done that, you can motor through on cruise control, relaxed and in the flow. The ability to flow over a grim crux, to naturally move over new and yet familiar ground, depends in large part on the manner in which you first learned to negotiate similar moves.

Mental Physics

Efficient climbing hinges on optimum interaction between brain and muscle. The tricky thing to understand is that for the experienced climber, even the remotest, most bizarre climbing sequence will still be a repeat of moves he or she has already done in one fashion or another. In other words, when on-sight leading we don't tackle a "new" crux with a clean mental and physical slate, rather we crank these moves saddled with the accrued cellular history of every move we've ever done. In psychology, it's a given that no matter how long you live, your behavior will reflect patterns laid down in your formative years. For climbers, this means that when you first learn moves, a neurological pattern (an "engram") is regis- tered and stored in your bean. How does this play out? Consider the business of riding a bike. Once your body "learns" how to ride, the engram expresses itself physically— and automatically—every time you hop on a bike. You don't have to "think" about your balance or how to turn, you simply do it, automatically. If your engrams are based on bad tech- nique or freighted with negative mental pictures or thoughts, that engram will replay, like a nightmare, until you reprogram it with revised patterns.

Once a bogus engram gets laid in, it's harsh duty to revise it. Transforming these original engrams involves the same type of processing that an abused child must undertake to off load old trauma. First, he or she must recognize and experi- ence the original patterns on the feeling level. Next is to start laying in new information. Last is the conscious effort to do things differently, lest the new patterns, or engrams, will not "take". Clearly it's best to learn and practice elegant tech- nique in the first place, so you carry efficient engrams that take you forward, rather than inefficient ones that hinder you.

A vast storage of elegant technique engrams is essential to calmly and efficiently tic the many sequences found on diffi- cult climbs. With a limited encyclopedia of engrams, a new problem, outside your repertoire, can trigger a case of nerves and wasted energy, for lack of automatic response.

Bouldering, indoor or out, is a vital way to program good engrams. The relatively controlled medium allows you to fashion elegant engrams in short order—the more times they are repeated, the more automatic they become. Likewise for megapitch days, which require tens of thousands of moves and greatly enhance efficient climbing.

Mental Freeze

Fatigue and fear can short-circuit the body's fluid execution of even a perfect engram. Here, overriding factors actually short-circuit your natural response. This is where the subtler forms of mental discipline come into play. Helpful routines include instant relaxation and visualization exercises, centering, ideal performance state drills, motivation barbs, success orientation, negative thinking blocks, and all the rest. There are libraries full of books on these practices. They vary in substance from genius to dross. As the mental control/mind-body arena involves more subtle matter than bald facts, it remains fertile ground for charlatans and profiteers. Further complicating matters is that an effective ritual for Jack might prove worthless to Jill. Temperaments vary, hence the wealth of techniques. Only the individual can learn what is best for him or her.

TRAINING INGREDIENTS

Customizing a Program

How to devise a personal training schedule is beyond the scope of this manual. However, a few words on how to go about the process are worth mentioning. Understand that every sport has specific and non-specific (cross-training) exercises that have evolved to boost performance. Specific exercises are those that either replicate an aspect of the sport (for climbing, they include hang-and-finger boards, gym climbing, etc.), or work specifically on skills or muscle groups that the sport calls upon (weight exercises such as wrist and finger curls to increase forearm power, or pullups to augment pulling might). A wise and standard practice is to balance your training routine between sport specific exercises and general strength/fitness exercises. Sport-specific climbing exercises take many forms. Try and concentrate on those that are unlikely to cause injury. Circus stunts such as excessive one arm pullups and fingertip chins should be kept to a minimum, if not eliminated altogether. Learning what drills are commonly done is a matter of research, from magazines, books and from talking with other climbers. Dialing in the particulars is almost always a process of trial and error while finding out what gives you the best results in the least time and with the least injuries.

Goals, Commitment, Desire

Going to the weight room or climbing gym can take on all the aspects of hard work because it is. To remain keen, develop goals, without which all those grueling hours driving iron or heaving on plastic will lack direction and purpose; maintaining your psyche will require fanaticism; and pleasure will be lost. Everyone develops tricks to keep motivated. I (J.L.) found it easiest to have specific projects in mind, climbs I had either failed on or desperately wanted to establish or do. For example, one season in Yosemite, speed climbing caught on quickly, but by the time we had worked the bugs out of how to go about the work, I had to return to college. Determined to return the following season and rip the Valley up, I geared that winter's training toward overall fitness and spent weekends trying to polish off as many pitches as possible. The next year, we made first one-day ascents of half a dozen walls. Another year it was face climbing and bouldering, and I worked on strength through the school year. The point is, with a goal I could commit to a brutal, and otherwise tedious, workout routine. Of course, it's the intensity of the wanting that fuels the whole enterprise. A goal can invoke, but not create, desire.

Campus board training.

Components

Beginners are keen and often overdo things. And anyone with less than two seasons of training under his/her belt is a beginner. "Beginner" does not refer to the amount of weight you can heft or pullups you can crank, rather, in terms of your athletic career, the first two years are beginning stages. As your climbing life unfolds, your knowledge will increase and you'll learn ways to dial your training in, getting more results from less effort. All training routines start with an entry level program that emphasizes overall conditioning and injury prevention. In time, your training will become more focused as you discover your weaknesses, what your body can tolerate and how it best responds to the training. Whatever the level of training, every routine entails scheduling, cycling, rest days, and dealing with gym burnout. Specific training usually strives to enhance contact strength and technique training; general training often works toward increased flexibility and base strength. Advanced programs will also involve cross-training of some kind.

PLATEAU

Eventually, every conditioned athlete reaches a plateau. You'll work like hell simply to maintain a seemingly fixed level of fitness, and improvements—even small ones—will seem impossible. Everyone reaches a performance ceiling, and pushing this ceiling higher requires an intelligent approach lest you incur chronic injury and regress. Many trainers claim that cyclic periodization is the proven technique to work through plateaus and chronic injuries.

Periodization

Despite the most rigorous training, your strength and climbing ability will come and go in cycles. No one in any sport can—or should try to—maintain maximum fitness year round. Imagine if professional football or basketball players never enjoyed an offseason, if the schedule went year round. No one would last long. Yet it's remarkable how many climbers expect their performance curve to steadily and unfailingly increase without ever taking a break, or backing off. In fact, many climbers seek to improve by climbing even harder when their bodies are virtually falling apart from lack of rest and recovery time.

According to the gurus, periodic training takes advantage of the body's natural cycles to help us gradually build up to higher strength thresholds. A training cycle consists of four phases: (1) Building a foundation for the training to come, accomplished through low intensity training, slowly increasing the volume and intensity. (2) Increasing the intensity and volume of training to prepare your body for optimum performance, which arrives in (3) The peak phase, where your strengths climax at the same time. Here is when you climb your hardest routes or boulder problems, or compete your best. This peak phase is the ultimate goal of training. Don't waste your strength training through the peak. Instead, enjoy the fruits of hard training. You've earned it. The harder you push during the peak, the sooner your body will torch out. During the peak the idea is to climb very selectively. Like track athletes who, when they hit peak form, "pick their races," the peaked climber should pick his/her routes. A person only has so much mileage in peak form because you're pushing directly against your genetic ceiling, and that ceiling will inevitably drop once the body can take no more. (4) Following the peak, and you'll know when it's over, it's time to rest. Give your body the time to rebuild, for tendons and muscles to reknit, and for your brain to get re-motivated. For the dedicated climber, this fourth phase is crucial. Jumping back to phase one without proper rest and motivation is a bad idea because you're ignoring all the signs your body is telling you. A good two to four weeks of rest after every peak allows your body, psyche, and motivation to recover and rejuvenate, which amps your desire and ability to train hard through the next cycle.

Some things to remember: vary climbing and training to alternate the stresses on your body and mind; expect hard work and delayed results; understand that you'll go downhill at the beginning of your program because you're tired; know that over-training will lead to injury and a significant decrease in strength; always take time off for healing; most of all, listen to your body.

Some climbers train exclusively power, endurance, or power-endurance for six weeks or so each. Mike Caldwell, former Mr. Colorado, and trainer of his son Tommy Caldwell, who climbs a 5.14 almost every month, recommends training both fast twitch and slow twitch muscle fibers in each workout. Fast twitch fibers contract forcefully to give us power, but they also tire very quickly. They are usually the first fibers activated when we begin exercise. The fast twitch fibers benefit from brief, intense training. Slow twitch fibers, when trained, can keep working for a long time. They provide us with endurance. Staying pumped as long as possible when you're training provides good results in improving endurance.

The Caldwell's recommended workout is to warm up, but not too much or you'll bypass activation of the fast twitch muscle fibers. A bit of stretching and light bouldering should do. Then, get immediately into your heavy pulling—power routes, hard boulder problems, or campus board training. Once your power fades, move onto endurance training, keeping the pump going as long as you can stand it. Cross-training with running, hiking or cycling on your climbing rest days can further enhance your endurance.

The main advantage of this type of training, Mike Caldwell points out, is that it is fun. Every workout is a climb, and every climb is a workout. Having fun and sustaining your enthusiasm are crucial elements of any training program.

Steph Davis bouldering on the Bolt Wall, Horsetooth Reservoir, Colorado.

STRENGTH

A few critical points: Increasing power requires power training, i.e., climbing/training at your maximum for short bursts. An Olympic weight lifter does not increase his strength by doing fifty reps with baby weights, rather two or three reps with maximum weight (often getting assistance for the last two reps, if not all three). Likewise, you don't increase your strength by cruising laps on a pitch well below your limit. Improving power also improves endurance and power-endurance, because your maximum work capacity goes up. Endurance is enhanced by sustaining a moderate level of effort for a long time, by cruising laps over a pitch well below your limit. Power-endurance is the ability to maintain a near-maximum effort for a sustained length of time.

Finger Strength

Training on a campus board can give you good results in your contact, pull-down and lock-off strength. It can also wreck your fingers for life if you go into it haphazardly. Read back issues in the climbing magazines, or Eric Hörst's training books, also in this series, to devise a solid, scientifically-based program for working a campus board, and other finger strength specific exercises. Better education about training and injury prevention in the climbing elite has kept more top climbers injury-free and pulling down. Don't be left behind, training with injurious routines devised in the Dark Ages of climbing. Do your research and take a scientific approach to your training. And always start off slowly with any new program.

BOULDERING

The two most popular and efficient training modes for increasing leading performance are gym climbing and bouldering. (For the lowdown on gym climbing, see *Gym Climb,* also in the *How to Rock Climb* series.) During a good bouldering session you can crank dozens of moves at or near your limit, all without the hassles of ropes and other hardware. Just you, your shoes, your chalk bag and sweet Mother Nature. Nothing finer.

Over the years, bouldering has gotten more specific and refined. Nowadays, serious boulderers carry two or three different styles of shoes, a chalk bag, extra chalk, a toothbrush, an extended brush with a built-in blowtube for cleaning high holds, a sketch pad for nasty landings, power drinks and foods, and a blaring boom box. Some people still forgo these extras in favor of simplicity, but not many.

Besides being fun, bouldering improves your power, endurance, technique, flexibility and confidence. A seasoned boulderer acquires a vast repertoire of moves, so when he or she encounters similar moves on the crags, they become that much more familiar. And chances are, the moves won't be as hard as those on the boulder problem.

A good spotter.

Aesthetically, a beautiful day at the boulders beats an afternoon in a chalk-dusty climbing gym, hands down. Bouldering requires a refinement of the subtler points of rock climbing, something you can't replicate as well with colored grips in a climbing gym. This means the engrams you develop bouldering help you out on the sharp end of the rope more than those gained in the gym. How many indoor powerhouses have you seen who freeze up on real rock?

Another beauty of bouldering is that you can push your limits, usually with little risk of injury. By far, the hardest moves ever done on rock have been performed on boulders with their convenient access, and lure of a summit only a daunting few feet away. John Bachar, one of North America's leading free soloists, attributes his remarkable soloing ability partly to the boulder problems he does, which are much harder than the routes he solos.

Back in the 1960s, John Gill, the father of modern bouldering, pushed the bouldering standards further than anyone before or since. To rate the difficulty of his problems, Gill concocted the "B" scale. Only the hardest boulder problems of the time fit into his scale. B1 problems fall somewhere in the 5.12 range, while B2 probably checks in around 5.13. A B3 problem is so hard that it is ascended by a single climber only once—any subsequent ascent downgrades the problem to B2. The B scale served Gill and a generation of boulderers behind him; but with more people bouldering, and difficulty levels going

Remember These Things...

Remember these things once your bouldering starts to get serious:

- Practice downclimbing and reversing moves, lowering off dynos, and reversing mantels.

- On high problems, climbing up, then climbing down helps in working out the sequence. You wire the initial moves, going ever higher before reversing, familiarizing yourself with the sequence. When you are confident of your reservoir of strength and ability, you go for it. However, you can rarely reverse moves on boulder problems near or at your technical limit. It's task enough just to go up.

- Most good boulderers are also great jumpers. If you boulder alone and don't flash every problem (and you won't), you'd best learn how to fall gracefully. Know where you are in relation to both the rock and the ground, so you have an elevated chance of landing squarely on both feet. The spinning jump to the best landing spot, and the tuck-and-roll both work for emergency exits.

- Traversing offers a lot of mileage and short falls.

- Never climb any higher than where you feel comfortable jumping off from.

- If you must assume an upside down or awkward position, get a spot, or use a crash pad.

- If you fall off, you hit the ground. Always clear the ground of the problem stones or any detritus that could cause twisted or broken ankles—the most common bouldering injuries.

- Strive to develop the boulderer's mentality—that any worthwhile problem takes dozens of tries. Try the impossible. And keep trying. Some day you just might send it.

- Work on problems that simulate the type of climbing you want to train for, be it short power moves, or long, pumpy traverses.

- Alternate between days spent trying your hardest problems (power days), and days spent working on mileage/endurance. Avoid too many consecutive days of maximum cranking.

- Always listen to your body. When you feel a muscle or tendon twinge, stop before it becomes a genuine injury.

sky high, a new system was begging to be born. Bouldering guru John Sherman heard the call and devised the expanded "V" scale, which currently goes from V0 to V14 (though someone is no doubt pushing the standard higher even as this book is printed). B1 problems range from V3 to V5; B2 averages around V7 and up. While other scales exist, the V system has become the most widely adopted.

More and more we find climbers who boulder exclusive of all other types of climbing. Such specialists are generally unassuming—at first—have strong fingers and too much time on their hands. You'll know when you meet one, because they often love to sandbag other climbers. Because they've focused their energy on bouldering, they usually have the guns to do it. If you can endure the sandbag, they can be the best tour guide of an area.

Spotting

Early in my bouldering career I (C.L.) learned the value of a good spot. While pulling over the lip via a particularly awkward mantel, I asked, "got me?" After reassurance from the ground, I went for it and peeled. Neither spotter touched me as I slammed into the ground. The "spotters" looked dumbfounded at each other and said, "I thought you had him." Now I choose my spotters wisely, or don't count on the spot. The best choice is a big, experienced boulderer, who knows the value of a good spot and has the meat to give one.

When spotting, do not study the moves as the climber ascends, rather watch his/her body. Your duty is to keep the climber's head and shoulders from striking the ground. Always anticipate where they're going to fall. If the climber's plummeting bulk is too great to try and arrest in mid-air, con-

A bad spotter.

sider grabbing his/her shirt. Spotting is crucial when a boulderer is cranking upside down (or is locked into any funky, awkward attitude), or the landing is poor. A spot works fine if you're Mr. Olympia spotting an anorexic sportclimber; but if you're a hulking brute and your girlfriend weighs 98 pounds, the spot is a sketchy one. As mentioned, the realistic goal of a spot is not to catch the climber, but to simply break the fall and keep the head from smacking solid objects. A shrewd spotter stands facing the rock in a volleyball setter position. When you are working out a hard bouldering problem, you might even hand-check with your spot, keeping your hands very near the climber's back or rump, ready to ease the inevitable the second it occurs. Two— even three—people spotting is not unheard of if the situation demands. A crash pad can also soften your landing, and many boulderers never leave home without one.

The master, Ron Kauk, on "Broken Arrow" (13b), Tuolumne Meadows, California.

Tic, Tic

Many of the most classic boulders in the world have become graffiti-ridden with tic marks. Not only is it unsightly and insensitive to other climbers who have a reverence for the natural beauty of the boulder, but it portrays climbers in a bad light to non-climbers. And sometimes non-climbers have the power to shut down climbing in an area. A tick here and there is one thing, but America's boulders are not a climbing gym to be trashed with white graffiti for lack of better climbing skills. If you do use tic marks, wash them off when you're done.

MENTOR

In every sport, occupation, or art, the quickest way to excel is to study extensively under a master, or better, several masters, then use the lessons to formulate your own style and approach. Climbing is no different. Climbing with superior partners is the best way to get on the fast track. You can learn vast amounts by bouldering with hot climbers, doing hard routes with good partners, training in a gym with strong climbers, or hiring a guide or a climbing trainer.

Just make sure they have patience for your needs and progress, as opposed to using you as a belay slave. Don't get stuck in the rut of "second syndrome", where a lead dog drags you around, hogging all the leads, unless that's what you want and expect out of climbing.

With climbing partners, variety is the spice of life. Many climbers get stuck into "monogamous" climbing partnerships, which works well because you know what to expect from your partner, and what his or her limitations are. But the more good climbers you climb with and learn from, the larger your arsenal of tricks will become.

DIET

As climbing has become increasingly more specialized, folks have gained encyclopedic knowledge concerning training and technique. The same cannot be said for the diets kept by many high level climbers. Even more confusing is how certain these climbers are that they have it right, that their time-proven "diet" brings optimum performance. In fact, the majority of world-class sport climbers I know don't diet at all. They starve themselves. Understand that there are countless performance diets, and not one of them advocates starving or skipping meals as a means to acquire top efficiency. This starving routine is based on the philosophy that since Francois fasts, so should I.

Granted, diet is a sensitive issue, and everyone has their own philosophy, ideas, and needs that guide their diet, but all strenuous exercise requires good nutrition to acquire peak performance. Perhaps the two biggest myths in a typical sport climber's diet are that "good" here denotes a diet with no fat, and that said diet will spawn a lean, mean climbing machine. The lighter I am, the thinking goes, the harder I'll be able to pull down. Less freight means more power and endurance. Neither notion is true.

Without getting into the chemistry of the business, a fat-free diet is guaranteed to inhibit optimum performance, since a small amount of fat is required to metabolize your complex carbohydrates, your power food. This does not mean that you should switch over to a diet of cream horns and Jolt; rather, trying to eliminate all fat from your diet will retard your strength and endurance, dry up your connective tissues and cause unnecessary injuries. It's a little like running a car with no oil. Secondly, most climbing diets—if you could call them that—are sorely lacking in protein. It's the correct balance of protein, carbs and fat that acquires lean muscles. Weight is controlled by caloric intake.

For a comprehensive study of this field, look to the sports nutritionists. The idea that dietitians who work at Olympic training camps somehow have it wrong, that they don't know what a climber needs, is both vain and foolish. There are plenty of Olympic athletes that must keep their weight down, but none of them do so by starving. Research the topic and learn.

FINAL THOUGHTS

As mentioned, a well-rounded training schedule should include some cross-training. Just what that will be is strictly your call. The general goal of cross-training is to provide overall conditioning, build and strengthen the antagonistic muscles not taxed during climbing (otherwise you have an out-of-kilter machine), and obtain a cardiovascular pump, which can greatly increase your overall endurance. It is unlikely you can touch all three of these factors with one exercise. Most choose a speed/reaction sport (like cycling, racquetball, running, et al) for the cardio pump, and a strength routine like weight training to work on the antagonistic muscles.

Many climbers hate to stretch, myself included. To ease the tedium, I've taken to stretching between sets when lifting weights. It's a good use of my "down" time between sets.

Providing you don't expect to perform splits in two weeks, you can spend a few minutes every night doing stretching exercises and slowly increase your flexibility far more than you might think. The dividends are enormous. With so much of modern climbing requiring radical stemming and high steps, a flexible body is a requirement.

Lastly, nothing is better for a trashed body than a good, deep-tissue sports massage. Amateur, sporadic massages might feel good, but are of limited value. Massage must be performed by a professional, or skilled friend, on a regular basis, to be beneficial. The problem, of course, is cost. Many "massage therapists" want screenwriter's wages, so most of us will simply have to do without. A "Therracane," available in back rehabilitation stores allows you to apply deep pressure to your own trigger points to relax your back muscles after hard cranking.

INJURIES

Aside from the normal muscle tweaks and strains inherent in all sports, advanced climbers are particularly prone to elbow and finger injuries, most of which involve some form of tendonitis. Having suffered these impairments on several occasions, I can assure you that ignoring the injury can result in pain so intense that straightening the arm, or closing the fingers, is virtually impossible—and climbing is out of the question. Concerning treatment for these conditions, I defer to climber/orthopedist Dr. Mark Robinson, who has conducted several studies involving climbing injuries. Writes Dr. Robinson:

Do the following to self-cure tendonitis:

- Decrease activity until the pain is gone, and all swelling and tenderness disappear.
- Wait two weeks more.
- Start back with easy strength exercises (putty, gum, rubber squeezers) for two to three weeks.
- Do low-angle, big-hold climbing for one month.
- Move to high-angle, big-hold climbing for one month.
- Get back to full bore.

Anti-inflammatory medicines (aspirin, Advil, Aleve, Nuprin, etc.) can be used to control symptoms and speed the recovery process. They should not be used to suppress pain to allow even more use, since this eventually will lead to more problems and a longer recovery period.

"Therracane" in use.

What the doctor is telling us is that time and patience are

the key ingredients to full recovery, and that returning prematurely to high-stress climbing is as foolish as ignoring the injury in the first place. "The tissues of the musculo-skeletal system are capable of remarkable feats of repair and restoration," Dr. Robinson assures us, "but these processes are slow." Furthermore, there is absolutely no proof that anything in legitimate medicine can accelerate these processes, save the use of anti-inflammatory drugs, which simply eliminate the restrictions and allow the natural healing to proceed. Understand that if you have good insurance, you probably will be referred to a sports medicine clinic. Such establishments are not in business to refuse your money. I've gone through the whole routine at a famous clinic, and after several months was no better off than if I'd simply bought a bottle of Aleve, and spent two months in the library reading crime fiction. In extreme or very specific cases, an injection of time-release cortisone can work wonders. But it can also do more damage than good. Each injury is a little different, and there is no generic verdict on the long-term effectiveness of cortisone. My father (J.L.), a surgeon, told me that whenever you try to rush nature, you invariably run into problems. The safest bet is to go the conservative route, and simply wait out the injury.

Injury Prevention

We know the medical experts have told us that certain exercises virtually assure injuries, and that we should avoid these if we're in for the long haul. But aside from that, what can we do? Some support of critical tendons can be achieved by taping. Trouble spots: around the fingers on either side of the main (second) joint; around the wrist; and around the forearm, just shy of the elbow. And use the open grip when possible. But professional athletes are relying more and more on two things to avoid injuries: stretching and warming up. Aerobics and yoga might not make you stronger, but they may keep you from getting injured. And a very important practice is to do a little stretching and some easy climbing before jumping onto the main event. Warming up is part of any sport, and should be essential for climbers, whose movements so stress the elbows and fingers. This is particularly true for bouldering. Get limbered up and try and crack a light sweat, then max yourself. And if you tweak something, stop before you make it worse.

This warm-up ritual is vital for those returning from an injury, or nursing a chronic problem. For instance, I have always loved dynamic bouldering, but years of wrenching latches have left me with small bone chips in my left elbow. Specialists have said orthoscopic surgery might help things, but have advised me to just deal with the stiffness until the problem becomes unbearable. If I warm up, the pain usually subsides. If not, it's torturous.

LIFESTYLE

Christian Griffith at home in Boulder, Colorado.

Beth Wald photo

You don't see many Gold Medal winners, rocket scientists, or 5.14 climbers closing out the bars or huddled over a crack pipe. Greatness requires discipline and focus. On the other hand, keep things in perspective. You could spend your life training and never doing anything else. Know when enough is enough. It's fun to put passion and energy into climbing, to achieve your dreams; and nothing beats sending a route you once thought impossible. But once the whole business becomes an obsession, you're putting too much pressure on yourself. Remember, we're talking about climbing rocks, after all.

Don't count on a helicopter rescue. Here, the Coast Guard rescues an injured climber on El Gran Trono Blanco, Cañon Tajo, Mexico.

Greg Epperson photo.

Self-Rescue

Self rescue means getting your climbing team out of any jams you might get into, from the routine rope climb to free a stuck rappel line, to the desperate rescue of a broken leader. Most climbers have little or no knowledge of self rescue or first aid. This is unfortunate, since anyone who climbs enough is bound to encounter some manner of mishap—either their own, or someone else's. Self-rescue techniques can save precious time in a desperate situation; combined with rudimentary first aid skills, they may save a life, possibly your own.

As a rescuer, you must always remember the first priority of rescue: keep yourself safe. You don't want to create a bigger tragedy by blundering a self rescue beyond your capabilities. If you get hurt, who's going to help the victim?

> **Rule #1 of Self-Rescue:**
>
> **Keep Yourself Safe.**

Prevention Is the Best Cure

Climb soberly and in control and you've a good chance to avoid epics in the first place. It's much easier to prevent a bad situation than deal with one. Never take shortcuts on your anchors; stay focused on lead; and bail off if the climb doesn't feel right. Double check belay and rappel riggings. Remain keenly alert to potential hazards, especially loose rock and bad weather. Wear a helmet if the rock is suspect. Choose your partners wisely. Read *Accidents in North American Mountaineering,* published every year by the American Alpine Club, to see where others went wrong. These are the basics.

Despite all precautions, accidents happen. Ideally, every climbing party should be self-sufficient, knowledgeable and capable of dealing with any situation that arises. Never count on outside rescue as a "safety net." Responsible climbers prepare themselves to deal with emergencies before they occur. Anyone who calls themselves a "guide" should have these self-rescue techniques down.

A knowledge of first aid is useful for sport climbers and essential for anyone heading onto adventure climbs or expeditions. If possible, take a Wilderness First Responder or Emergency Medical Technician course, and keep your certification current. Get the low down (ask experts) on courses before spending your time and money. For wilderness situations, a Wilderness First Responder course is more valuable than an ambulance-based EMT course. A Wilderness EMT is the foremost certification for a serious climber/rescuer.

COMPLICATED AND CONFUSING

This following material can be as intimidating and confounding as Quantum Mechanics. The surest way to learn self-rescue techniques is to take a seminar from a veteran guide. Bring your partner or partners so they can learn how to save your arse as well. After the course, study this chapter, and practice different scenarios until you're comfortable with the techniques. Then review the techniques once or twice a year, so you can bring them to swift use when it counts. Be extremely careful when practicing these techniques. Use backup ropes to keep everyone safe. It is tragically ironic (but understandable, given the complex systems) that a few climbers have died while practicing rescue techniques.

Each rescue is different. Learning the various knots and techniques is like acquiring a box full of tools. For each situation, you'll apply those tools differently to effect the rescue. Realistic scenarios include ascending the rope to free a jammed rappel line; escaping the belay to rescue an injured partner; hauling your second up a crux; passing a knot to lower an injured climber two rope lengths; rappelling past a knot; or counter-balance rappelling with an injured climber. One of the best arguments against going with a skeleton rack is that a serious and involved self-rescue requires not only a working understanding of compound techniques, but also a spectrum of gear, particularly biners, slings and cordelettes. More on this later.

> #1 Self-Rescue Technique:
>
> Prevention. Don't get in trouble.

Exceptions to Self Rescue

In some situations it may be best to wait for the rescue team (if there is one)—for example, if you suspect a spinal or head injury, or if the rescue is beyond your level of competence or manpower. If your partner has a life-threatening injury, alert others in the area (if anyone else is in the area) to notify emergency medical services, and choose the quickest rescue.

Most proficient climbers strive to avoid outside rescue if possible. It puts others in jeopardy, and there's typically a long wait involved, which is critically detrimental if a climber is badly injured. And if you're climbing outside Yosemite or Rocky Mountain National Park (which have crack rescue units), there's no guarantee that the local rescue team are highly experienced professionals. Plus, getting rescued is not good for your reputation as a climber, although some of the best have been rescued. I've (J.L.) participated in many rescues, and have worked with "official" personnel ranging from crackerjack rangers who have climbed twenty big walls, to swaggering, jackass S.W.A.T. team operatives with jowls full of Red Man and pistols on their hips. If you and your climbing mates learn and practice the techniques in this chapter, you should be able to deal with most situations. The best action in almost all rescue situations is to take responsibility, use good judgment, and solve problems yourself.

The following serves only as an introduction to self-rescue techniques. Many variations exist but we've tried to spare you the headaches of covering every alternative (which is a book in itself). Instead, we've provided just enough information to perform each self-rescue technique with abundant slings, cord, and carabiners, and also with minimal spare gear, which is what you'll most likely have at hand.

Once again, avoiding bad situations always beats dealing with them. Stay on your toes, because gravity never sleeps.

KNOTS AND EQUIPMENT

With a handful of carabiners, slings, and cord, and knowledge of several specialized knots, you can improvise all the self-rescue techniques covered here. A cordelette—a 16- to 18-foot piece of 6 or 7mm perlon or 5.5mm Spectra—is an invaluable addition to your self-rescue arsenal. On a long traditional route, a party of two will ideally carry four cordelettes—one for each belay, and one for each partner for self rescue. However, unless you routinely carry four cordelettes, focus on the minimal gear self-rescue techniques. It is a good idea to periodically loosen the Grapevine knots on your cordelettes so you can quickly untie them in a rescue.

The essential self-rescue knots include four friction knots that "grab" a rope when weighted, but can be slid up the rope when unweighted; three knots for tying off a load that are releasable under load; and a knot formed through two carabiners that serves as a ratchet for hauling.

The friction knots - the Prusik, Klemheist, Bachman, and Autoblock - utilize a smaller diameter cord or narrow sling, wrapped three to five times around the rope, to "grab" the rope when weighted. The smaller the diameter of the cord or sling relative to the rope, the fewer wraps you'll need. The newer, and more slick the cord and rope you have, the more wraps you'll need. Make certain you have enough wraps, and keep them tidy, so the friction knot does not slip. Slippage can partially melt and glaze the nylon or Spectra, which decreases the friction created by the knot, and can cause further slippage. Never trust your life, or the life of a victim you are rescuing, to a single friction knot. Always keep friction knots backed up.

Normally you'll use a sewn or tied loop of webbing or cord to create a friction knot. Adjust the knot or stitching on the cord or webbing so it is not at the bottom of the loop—the clip-in point—or inside the friction knot. Ideally, the knot or stitching will be equidistant between the bottom of the friction knot, and the bottom of the loop.

Prusik Knot

The Prusik is the standard knot learned by most climbers for climbing a rope, though the Bachman knot is superior for the task. The ideal Prusik cordage is of smaller diameter than the rope you wish to climb. Five millimeter or six millimeter diameter cord works best for ascending a standard ten to eleven millimeter climbing rope, or double nine millimeter ropes. After weighting the Prusik, it may be difficult to slide it up the rope. The trick is to loosen the "tongue," or center loop, before sliding the knot.

"Dress" the Prusik cleanly to ensure maximum bite on the climbing rope. If the Prusik slips when weighted, add another wrap around the climbing rope, and make sure the cord isn't twisted.

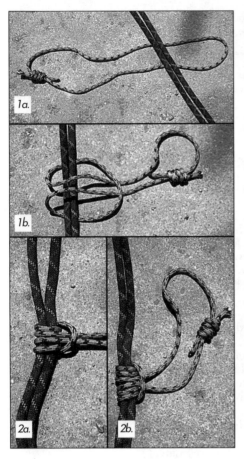

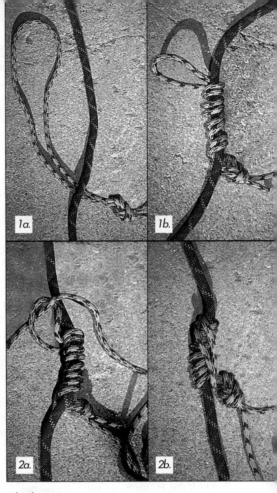

Prusik Knot

1) Girth Hitch the cord or sling around the rope to be ascended.

2) Pass the loop of the sling around the rope and back through the center of the Girth Hitch two more times. Load the loop coming out of the Prusik to see if it "bites." If the Prusik slips, add more wraps.

Klemheist Knot

1) Wrap a loop of cord or webbing sling four or five times around the rope, toward the load.

2) Pass the other end of the sling through the loop. Clip into the sling where it comes out of the loop. Add more wraps if the Klemheist slips.

Klemheist

The Klemheist bights the rope well, is easy to tie, and works well with cord or webbing (9/16" to 11/16" web is best). When unweighted, the Klemheist also releases and slides more easily than a Prusik. Keep the sling or cord well-dressed and tidy for maximal bite.

Mule Knot

The Mule Knot allows you to tie-off a hanging climber on your belay device to free your hands, and it unties under load, making it ideal for self-rescue applications. To be fail-safe, the Mule knot must be secured by an Overhand or Fisherman's knot.

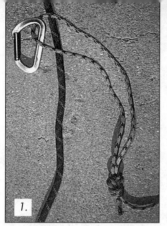

Bachman Knot

1) Clip a carabiner into a sling.

2) Wrap the sling three or four times around the rope and through the carabiner.

3) Load the loop coming out of the Bachman Knot. If it slips when weighted, add more wraps.

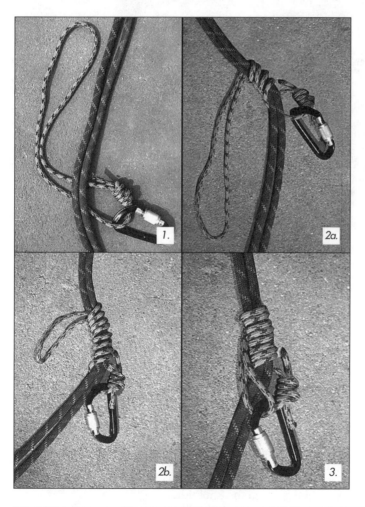

Autoblock

1) Clip a loop of cord or short webbing sling into a carabiner.

2) Wrap the cord four or five times around the rope. The remaining loop should be relatively short.

3) Clip the final loop back into the carabiner. Add more loops if the Autoblock slips.

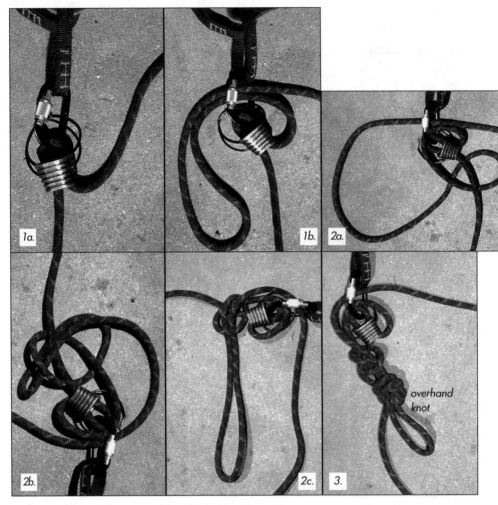

Mule Knot

1) Pull a bight of rope from your brake hand through your belay device carabiner.

2) Tie a Mule Knot by twisting a coil into the non-load strand, then passing a loop around the load strand and back through the coil to create a "slip" knot.

3) Back up the Mule Knot with an Overhand or Fisherman's Knot.

Bachman Knot

The Bachman is my (C.L.) preferred knot for improvised rope ascending. Incorporating a carabiner into the friction knot gives a handle for sliding the knot up the rope, which makes the Bachman the easiest friction knot to slide. The Bachman also creates a friction knot for load hauling that cannot get sucked into a pulley.

With the Bachman, be sure to weight the sling and not the carabiner, lest the Bachman slide down the rope, possibly scorching the cord. The Bachman knot works well with cord or webbing. Keep the knot tidy.

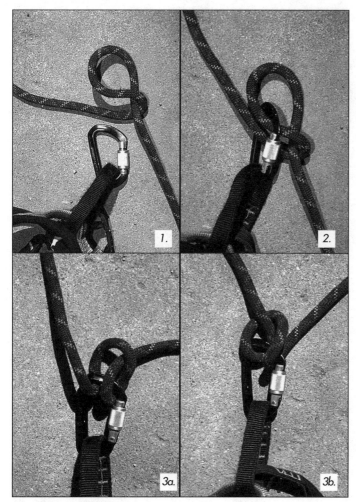

Munter Hitch

1) Fold the rope around itself as shown in the photo.

2) Clip both strands of the folded rope into a locking carabiner.

3) The Munter inverts through the carabiner when you switch from feeding rope out to taking rope in.

Autoblock

The Autoblock is the quickest rappel backup to rig. Some climbers always carry a piece of perlon cord tied into a loop—about the size of a shoulder length sling, or slightly shorter—the perfect size for tying an Autoblock onto their rappel lines.

Munter Mule

The Munter Mule works well for tying an injured climber off to the anchors. It can be released under load, and used to lower the climber. To achieve maximum safety, the Munter Mule must be secured with an Overhand or Fisherman's knot. Never load the back side of a Munter Mule.

Mariner's Knot

Securing a long webbing sling (or double slings girth-hitched together) to the climbing rope with a Klemheist, and to the anchors with a Mariner's knot, allows you to get the weight of

4a. 4b.

4c. 5.

Munter Mule

Rig a Munter Hitch on a locking carabiner (steps 1 to 3).

4) Tie a Mule Knot as described on page 186.

5) Back the Mule Knot up with an Overhand or a Fisherman's Backup Knot.

a fallen climber off your belay device. The Mariner's knot can be released under load, and works best with ⅜" to ¹¹⁄₁₆" webbing.

Garda Knot

The Garda knot serves as a pulley and ratchet, allowing the rope to pass one way only, with no back-sliding. Used in a Z-rig for hauling, the Garda conveniently holds your partner between heaves—should you have to haul them. The Garda adds substantial drag to the system, so the 3:1 mechanical advantage hauling system is realistically more like 2:1,

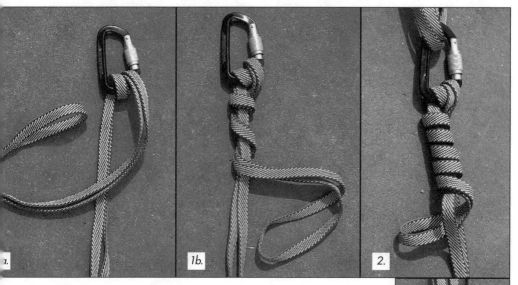

Mariner's Knot

1) Wrap a loop of webbing twice around a carabiner that is connected to the anchors, then four times around itself.

2) Pass the loop between the two strands of the webbing. Tension on the sling holds the Mariner's Knot in place.

3) Clip this loop off with a carabiner to ensure that the Mariner's Knot cannot unweave.

nonetheless doubling your strength. The Garda can also be used with a foot sling for ascending a rope, in conjunction with a friction knot on the rope attached to the harness.

The carabiners used in the Garda should have the same shape. Locking carabiners, while desirable for their security, may not pinch against each other hard enough to secure the rope, owing to the locking sleeve. With asymmetrical D-shaped carabiners, the gates should open downward. Otherwise, having the gates opening upward adds a little security to the knot, but is a bit more difficult to rig.

Some climber/rescuers disdain the Garda knot because it behaves squirrelly. Make sure you keep everyone well-backed up, and keep an eye on the Garda to ensure that the rope and carabiners stay properly oriented, with the main loop of the Garda passing around the spine of the biner, away from the gate. You can use a Bachman knot to back up the load strand of the line to be hauled, or tie backup figure eights periodically in the line and clip them to the anchors. Never use the Garda knot if the possibility of impact loading exists, because the pinching effect of the Garda can seriously damage the rope. Another limitation of the Garda is that it is difficult to release under load.

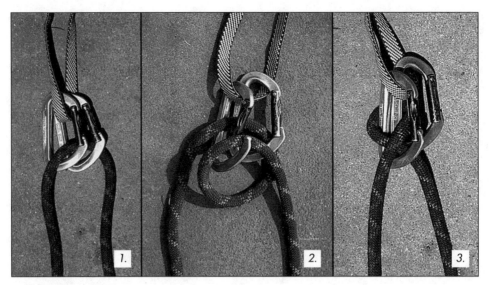

Garda Knot

1) Clip two carabiners parallel to each other onto a sling, then clip the rope through both caribiners.

2) Run the rope around the back of both carabiners, and clip it to the closest biner, outside to inside.

3) Slide the loop up onto the spines of the two carabiners. Be careful to keep the rope from riding up on the gates of the carabiners, lest the Garda come unclipped.

RETREATING FROM A ROUTE

Retreats happen for various reasons: bad weather, bad psyche, moving too slow, the climbing is too hard, or too dangerous—or worse: someone gets injured. Most retreats are routine: you just rappel and leave anchors—your own hard-earned gear if the route's not fixed—until you reach the ground.

If you climb long routes, you're bound to suffer a few epic storms. Always be prepared for weather. (Again, a lightweight wind/rain jacket is a critical asset in heavy weather.) When retreating, it's usually best to go down the route you came up, belay station to belay station, or natural anchor to natural anchor. Hopefully you have sufficient slings and hardware to reach the ground. Running out of gear during a long descent is serious business. One time when Richard Harrison and I (J.L.) had just completed a new route up the North Face of Mt. Wilson, Red Rocks, we took the wrong descent and ended up in a labyrinthine canyon requiring over twenty rappels, many free-hanging. By the time we gained the deck, we had one knifeblade left.

You can also cut up rope to make slings in an emergency, though this makes your line shorter for subsequent rappels. For this reason, and to free an impossibly stuck rope, it's important to carry a small knife on multi-pitch routes, and some spare cord or webbing.

First Down

The first climber down should carry the rack and slings to set the next anchors. If you're unsure of the descent, he or she should be equipped for ascending back up the rope in case no anchors are available below. If anchors do not appear, hopefully you can go back up or traverse and try another descent line. Otherwise, you're stranded.

ASCENDING A ROPE

An improvised rope ascent can save the day in many situations: if your rope gets stuck on a rappel; if you fall under an overhang and can't get back to the rock; if you drop your jumars on a big wall; if the leader is incapacitated high on a pitch and cannot be lowered back to the belay; or if you make a deadend rappel.

Many variations exist for ascending the rope. Some climbers always carry two pieces of perlon pre-tied to the correct lengths for ascending the rope. It's not a bad idea, but you'll rarely, if ever, need to climb the rope. For overall climbing efficiency, some climbers leave the perlon loops at home and substitute a standard piece of gear, like webbing or a cordelette, if they have to climb the rope. The key point is to have the gear available when you need it. Nylon webbing, ⁹⁄₁₆" and ⅝", and Perlon cord, 5 to 6mm, work best. Nylon grips better than Spectra, and has a higher melting temperature, so it's the first choice for the slings that wrap the rope. Spectra webbing can work, though it's not recommended. The middle of a rescue is no place to learn about Spectra's low friction and low melting temperature. Spectra cord is generally sheathed in nylon, so it works fine for friction knots. For ascending a rope, the Bachman knot is the friction knot of choice. All the following descriptions call for its use. You can also substitute a Klemheist, or Prusik, but they don't slide up the rope as well as a Bachman knot.

STUCK LINE

Say you've just finished a great route, then you prerigged your inexperienced partner to rappel last. On the way down, she laid the rope deep inside a one-inch crack. Now the knot is jammed, the rope will not pull, and you have five rappels to go. It's starting to drizzle, and darkness is one hour away. Bummer.

If you're lucky you have both rappel strands to ascend, with the rope still running through the top anchors. In this case, wrap the friction knot around both strands of rope. If one of the ends is out of reach, hopefully you have enough rope at the belay to lead up to the rope jam—and hopefully, some protection exists. I (C.L.) recently had to jumar a stuck rappel line, trusting whatever the rope was jammed on to keep holding.

Fortunately, I was belayed on a second rope, with occasional lead pro to calm my nerves. At the top, I discovered the rope was scarcely held by a simple twist jammed in the crack. The worst scenario would be ascending a stuck rope, trusting your life to whatever the rope is stuck on, with no pro available for a belay. What else could you do, though, if you're stranded high on a remote climb? Pray it never happens to you.

You can minimize the number of times you have to deal with stuck ropes by taking special care when setting and pulling your rappel ropes (see Rappelling).

When practicing improvised rope ascending, start on a vertical or slightly less-than-vertical wall. After you've mastered that, practice on a free-hanging rope, which is much more difficult. Rigging and climbing a rope quickly and efficiently requires practice—don't wait until you're dangling in space to learn!

Stuck Line With Ample Gear

Gear required:
    1 cordelette
    1 double-length or 2 shoulder-length slings
    2 carabiners
    2 locking carabiners

Rigging the system:
1. Attach the double sling (or two shoulder-length slings girth-hitched together) and cordelette to the rope with Bachman knots. If you're ascending double rap lines, wrap the Bachman knots around both ropes. Set the cordelette below the sling.

2. The sling attaches to your waist, and the cordelette to your feet and waist. Adjust the length of the sling so that it goes tight on your harness when you've pushed the Bachman knot up a full arm's reach. Having the proper length here is critical —make sure the Bachman isn't out of reach when you sit back. You can shorten a sewn sling by tying overhand or figure-eight knots in it. Tie off the cordelette into a waist loop and foot loop. The foot loop should be as high as you can reasonably stand up on, to allow big moves. The waist loop should be just long enough to slide the lower Bachman knot up to the higher one.

3. Clip the sling and cordelette into your harness with a locking carabiner. Back up the Bachman knots, to prevent decking if they fail: tie a figure-eight knot in the rope(s) you're about to climb, below the Bachman knots, and clip it to your harness with a locking biner (or two carabiners, gates opposed). If you're starting on flat ground, wait until you get up a few feet before tying this backup.

Double check everything. Now work the stretch out of the rope. Slide the upper Bachman knot as far up as you can reach, sit into it, and relax. While hanging from your harness, slide the lower Bachman knot up just below the upper one.

2.

Bachman knots

waist loops

backup
figure eight
knot

foot loop

3.

4. Grasp the rope for balance and step up in the foot loop. Some people use both feet in this loop, but one usually works best. Quickly slide up the higher Bachman as far as you can reach,

5. sit into it, and relax. Now slide up the lower Bachman.

6. Stand up in the foot loop and again slide the upper Bachman knot as high as possible.

7. Sit into it. Slide the lower Bachman up. Repeat steps six and seven to ascend the rope.

8. Every fifteen to thirty feet, accounting for the ground and ledges, tie a new backup knot in the rope(s) and clip into it so you cannot fall far if the ascending system fails. Unclip and untie the original backup knot. Make sure you are always clipped to at least one backup knot during the transition.

4.

5.

6.

7.

8.

9. Option A: Three or four shoulder-length slings or a long piece of webbing can substitute for the cordelette. Make sure you have a foot loop (1 sling will work - 2 slings girth-hitched together will provide a better length) and waist loop (1 sling), both clipped or girth-hitched to the lower Bachman knot (1 sling).

Option B: If you have to climb the rope a long ways, especially if the line is free hanging, a chest harness (commercial or improvised) with a carabiner (or better yet, a pulley) attached to the rope between the Bachman knots, can make the effort less strenuous. You'll need to shorten the foot loop because the Bachmans cannot slide tight against each other with a pulley between them. Test this thoroughly before casting off. This is probably more effort than it's worth if you can climb the rope proficiently without it.

Stuck Line With Minimal Gear

Eight pitches up, you're following a hard traverse. Your partner forgot to set pro after the crux, and now you're looking at

9a.

9b.

Ascending a rope with ample gear.

1. 2. 3.

a twenty-foot swing into space. Because you're scared, it's hard to relax, then suddenly you're off. A huge pendulum leaves you dangling mid-air beneath a roof, unhurt, but also unable to reach the rock. You have two slings, a carabiner, and a belay device with a locking carabiner. The buzzards are starting to circle above.

Stuck line with minimal gear.

This one's tough. Hopefully you've practiced.

Gear required:
1 carabiner
2 shoulder-length slings (3 is better, or 1 single and 1 double)
1 belay device with a locking carabiner.

If you have extra slings or cord available, two friction knots (as described above) work best for climbing the rope. If you're short on cord and webbing and have to use a belay device, a self-locking Gri-Gri, GiGi, or New Alp Plaquette works best for locking off your weight. A standard belay plate or tube can be difficult to lock off while hanging, especially if the rope is thin, or new and slick. If you can't lock your belay device, try a Garda knot.

Rigging The System
1. What now?

2. Wrap a Bachman knot on the rope and girth-hitch a second sling, or better yet, a double length sling, to the Bachman sling to extend it. This will serve as your foot loop. If you're short on slings but have spare rope, like a haul line, use the rope to extend your Bachman knot to your feet. A gear sling can also work. Option: A Klemheist or Prusik can substitute for the Bachman if you're shy a carabiner.

3. Slide the Bachman up as high as possible, then a little further.

4. Reach your foot up into the foot sling,

5. then stand up on it.

6. This is the crux. "Sit" on your foot. You may have to hook one arm around the rope to hold your torso up - few will be able to balance as poised as the model in the photo. Hopefully, you now have enough slack between the Bachman knot and

4.

5.

6.

Stuck line with minimal gear.

your tie-in knot to rig your belay device on the rope. If so, rig the device. If you don't have enough slack, you need to start over and figure out how to slide the Bachman knot higher. Can you push it up with a nut tool?

7. Stand up on the foot sling while pulling slack through the belay device.

8. Lock off the belay device and sit into it.

9. Hold the belay device locked off with one hand and slide the Bachman up as high as possible.

10. Stand up straight in the foot sling, while pulling rope through the belay device. Lock off the belay device, and sit into it. Repeat steps 9 and 10 to ascend the rope.

11) Back the system up by periodically tying figure-eight loops in the rope and clipping them to your harness.

7.

8.

9.

Option A:

Another method exists that is quicker, but less safe, because you rely on a single Bachman knot attached to the waist. This system only works for climbing a single strand of rope. It is possible to rig a Prusik, Klemheist, or second Bachman knot to back up the primary Bachman - if you have enough gear.

Gear required:
3 carabiners
2 locking carabiners
1 double and 1 shoulder-length sling (or 3 shoulder-length slings)

Rigging The System

12. Wrap a Bachman knot around the rope with a double-length sling (or two slings girth-hitched together) and clip the lowest loop into your harness with a locking carabiner. Tie a figure-eight loop in the rope and clip it to your harness to back up the Bachman. Double check everything. Work the stretch out of the rope (already done if you're hanging on the end of the rope), sit onto the Bachman knot, and relax.

Clip two carabiners into a sling and rig a Garda knot on the rope you plan to climb, well below the Bachman. Set the Garda so it can slide up the rope, but not down. The sling will be your foot loop. Tie it short so your foot sits close to the Garda. Slide the Garda up the rope with your foot as high as you can.

13. High step in the foot sling and quickly slide the Bachman knot up.

Sit into the Bachman and relax. Slide the Garda up the rope as high as you can. Repeat to climb the rope. Frequently retie backup knots in the rope, since you are relying on only one Bachman knot attached to the harness.

10.

Stuck line with minimal gear.

11.

Bachman knot

Garda knot

12.

13.

ESCAPING THE BELAY

So you went against your better judgment and climbed with the guy everyone said was dangerous. He just took a huge whipper on the third pitch, ripped four nuts, and now he's hanging on the rope, helpless, 120 feet above you. You can't lower him to the ground or back to the belay, and you're pinned to the belay. You think about your soon-to-be ex-sweet-ie, eating a candlelight dinner alone, again.

Good thing you took that self-rescue clinic last spring. What was it they said about choosing careful, competent partners? To escape the belay and effect a rescue, you must get the victim's weight off your belay device and onto the anchors. First free your hands, then free your belay device, then transfer the weight of the fallen climber onto your anchors. Also, in any rescue, it's good to communicate to the victim and let him know what's going on. Make sure your voice sounds calm and collected, even if you're completely freaked, to help relax the victim.

Gear required:

1 carabiner

1 locking carabiner

1 cordelette or 1 double-length sling or 2 girth-hitched shoulder-length slings.

Escaping the Belay with a Cordelette

1. Free your hands by tying the victim off to your belay device. Pass a bight of rope through the belay device carabiner and tie a Mule Knot around the strand of rope running to the fallen climber. Back the Mule knot up with an Overhand or Grapevine knot. Now the victim is tied off to your belay device. (You can also wrap the belay rope several times around your leg to lock off the climber and free your hands. This is quicker, but less bomber).

2. Tie a loop into one end of a cordelette and rig a Klemheist on the victim's rope.

3. Tie the cordelette to the anchor with a load-releasable Munter Mule. You may need to adjust the anchors, especially if the pull is upward.

4. Untie the Mule knot securing the climbing rope to the belay device and ease the victim's weight onto the Klemheist, making sure it doesn't slip. Keep your brake hand on the rope to backup the Klemheist.

5. Rig the brake side of the rope directly to the anchors with a Munter hitch.

6. The Munter hitch is now your backup. Dismantle your belay device, while keeping a brake hand on the Munter hitch. Pull slack through the Munter hitch and secure it with a Mule knot and Overhand backup.

7. Slowly release the Munter-Mule on the cordelette and ease the victim's weight directly onto the anchors.

Mule knot

Klemheist

Munter mule

8. Retrieve the cordelette. Now you can escape the belay.

At this point you can ascend or descend the rope, and render first aid (see Leader Rescue). Then you can either descend with the victim, or go for help. Never rappel on the back side of the Munter Mule. Instead, tie a figure eight and clip it to the anchors.

Escaping the belay with a cordelette.

Escaping the Belay with Slings

1. Belaying the leader while anchored with a string of clove hitches.

2. Free your hands by tying the victim off to your belay device with a Mule Knot, backed up by an Overhand or Grapevine knot. Now the victim is tied off to your belay device.

Or, wrap the belay rope four or five times around your thigh to lock off the climber and free your hands.

Munter hitch

Munter Mule

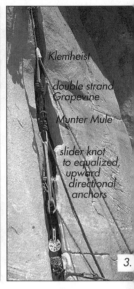

1.

2.

3.

Escaping the belay with slings.

Klemheist

double strand Grapevine

Munter Mule

slider knot to equalized, upward directional anchors

Mule knot

3. Rearrange at least two anchors to be bomber against an upward pull. Rig a Klemheist on the victim's rope with webbing and attach it to the newly arranged upward anchor with a Mariner's knot if you have enough webbing.

If you're shy on webbing, use the back side of the rope from the belay to tie off the Klemheist sling, as shown, by tying a double strand Grapevine through the sling, then a Munter Mule to the equalized anchors.

4. Untie the Mule knot on the belay device and ease the victim's weight onto the Klemheist, making sure it doesn't slip.

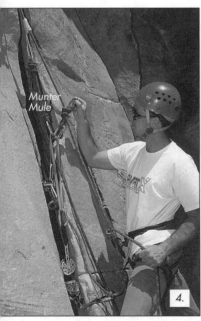

Munter Mule

4.

5.

6.

Keep your brake hand on the rope to backup the Klemheist, and tie the climber off to the anchors with a Munter Mule. Clip the Munter Mule in with a locking carabiner, or two carabiners with gates opposed. Double check everything.

5. Slowly release the Munter Mule (or Mariner's knot) securing the Klemheist to the anchors and ease the victim's weight onto the new Munter Mule. Now they are tied off directly to the anchors. Dismantle the Klemheist and belay device.

6. At this point you can escape the belay. If you need to rappel on the extra rope at the belay, don't rappel on the back side of the Munter Mule. Instead, tie the rappel line off to the anchors with a figure eight or clove hitches as shown.

HAULING YOUR PARTNER

Your second just fell off the easy roof, and is hanging in space five pitches up. He doesn't have gear or knowledge to climb the rope, so you have to haul him up, or you're spending the night on this alpine wall, and both of your jackets are in the second's pack! You feel stupid for not placing enough gear to check his swing as you led out the roof, and for not keeping your jacket with you.

Or perhaps the second is simply unable to follow your huge lead because he's in over his head, or maybe he's injured. If the second is light, and you're burly, you can often get him up a pitch just by yarding on the rope. With enough tension, a 5.5 climber can bicycle up a 5.12d face climb. If the second is portly, or hanging in space, or if the rope drag is considerable, hand-over-hand hauling is impossible. Here you need mechanical advantage to multiply your strength.

Hauling Your Partner the Hard Way

A prepared leader can haul a second through the difficulties.

1. Perform steps 1. through 4. in escaping the belay (page 198). Tie a figure eight knot in the rope and clip it into your harness to back up the Klemheist, and later, the Garda knot.

2a. Attach a Garda knot on the brake side of the rope to the anchors, rigged so the rope moves in the hauling direction, but cannot backslide and lower the climber. Dismantle the belay device.

2b. Option: Some climbers and guides avoid using the Garda knot, because it is somewhat fickle and you must keep an eye on it. To replace the Garda, clip the rope through a locking carabiner attached to the anchors that will serve as a pulley. Rig a Bachman knot on the climber's side of the rope, and clip the Bachman next to the pulley carabiner, so the rope cannot backslide. This method adds less friction to the hauling system than a Garda knot. A Gri-Gri also makes an excellent ratchet, but we'll get to that soon.

3. Remove any slack in the rope between the Klemheist and the Garda or Bachman ratchet. Untie the Munter Mule on the cordelette and ease the climber's weight onto the ratchet,

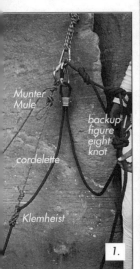

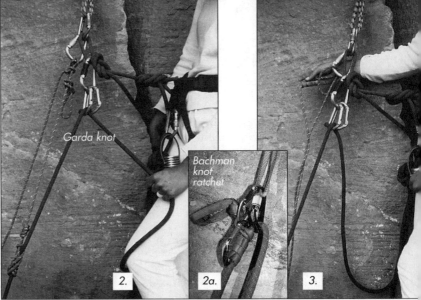

1.

2.

2a.

3.

Hauling your partner the hard way.

making sure it holds. Keep the climber backed up!

4. Clip a carabiner on the cordelette next to the Klemheist. Run the rope through this carabiner, and shazaam! You have a 3:1 Z rig, although the actual advantage, after frictional losses, is probably closer to 2:1. Now haul until the Klemheist reaches the Garda or Bachman knot, then reset the Klemheist a full arm's reach down the rope, haul again, and repeat. If you have to haul very far, periodically tie new backup knots for the climber - and keep an eye on the Garda knot. It's also possible to back up the Garda with a Bachman knot.

With this rigging, you must pull up to haul. You can also redirect the hoisting rope through a high biner, allowing you to pull down. This lets you use your body weight, but you'll pay a high price of increased friction from the extra bend in the line.

5. You can also redirect the rope and gain 5:1 mechanical advantage. Add a second Klemheist where the haul line exits the ratchet, and clip the hauling end of the rope to the new Klemheist. If you're short on slings, you can use a trucker's hitch, as shown, to substitute for the second Klemheist. To create the trucker's hitch, tie a slip knot in the rope just below the ratchet, and clip the rope to it.

Rope travel is painfully slow with this rig, but it provides good mechanical advantage and a downward pull.

6. Another option is to piggy back a 2:1 C rig onto the 3:1 Z rig, which gives a 6:1 advantage. Put a second Klemheist on the hauling rope where it emerges from the first Klemheist. Clip the rope from the back side of your tie-in to this Klemheist and pull up.

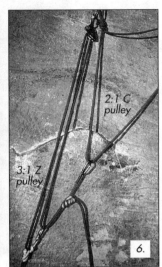

No Cordelette?

Two shoulder-length slings will serve. From the beginning:

1. Tie the hanging climber off to your belay device with a Mule knot and Overhand backup.

2. Set a Klemheist on the climber's side of the rope below the belay device. Girth-hitch another sling to this one (or start with a double-length sling in the first place) and tie a Mariner's knot to the anchors.

3. Tie a backup figure eight in the rope and clip it to the anchors. Double check everything.

4. Untie the Mule knot on your belay device and ease the climber's weight onto the Mariner's knot and Klemheist. Rig a Bachman or Garda ratchet on the anchors. Dismantle your belay device. Release the Mariner's knot so the climber is hanging on the ratchet. Tie the Klemheist sling off so you can clip a carabiner close to the Klemheist to maximize the length of your strokes. Now clip the hauling end of the rope to this carabiner to create the 3:1 Z hauling rig. Modify the system to create a 5:1 or 6:1 advantage if necessary.

Hauling Your Partner Made Easy

If you're belaying with a Gri-Gri directly off the anchors, hauling your second is greatly simplified. This is a great technique for guides, or those dragging partners up routes. When your partner needs hauling, he or she is probably already hanging on the rope, the Gri-Gri is locked off, and your hands are free. A little advance planning has paid off. To give them a hoist:

1. Belaying the second directly off the anchors with a Gri-Gri.

2. To haul, set a Klemheist on the climbing rope below the belay device. Tie an Overhand knot in the sling close to the Klemheist, to shorten the free loop of sling, and clip a biner

Substituting slings for the cordelette.

to the sling. Run the free rope from the exit of the Gri-Gri down through this carabiner and back up to create a Z rig with a 3:1 mechanical advantage (neglecting friction).

3. Yard on the free rope to haul your partner. You can change the hauling direction so you pull down, if the situation dictates—at a cost of increased friction—by running the free rope through a high carabiner.

Quick and Dirty

If you're belaying with a standard belay device directly off the anchors, you can easily haul your partner a short distance using the belay device and your brake hand as the ratchet.

1. Wrap the rope around your leg four times, or tie a Mule knot and Overhand backup on the belay device (not shown) to lock off the climber.

2. Set a Klemheist and hauling carabiner on the climber's rope, clip the brake side of the rope to the Klemheist, unwrap the rope from your leg, and haul. Pay special care to maintain your brake hand duties.

3. You could also incorporate a Bachman knot into this setup to free your brake hand. This only works well if the rope is skinny relative to the slots in your belay device. A fat rope will cause too much friction in the belay device.

RESCUING A FALLEN LEADER

Your best friend just ripped off a handhold, two pieces pulled, and now he's hanging limp on the end of the rope, too high up to be lowered back to the belay. Add to this the fact that you're a dozen pitches up a new route in the Canadian Arctic, and you've got a situation on your hands. You never thought it could happen to you, but now your worst nightmare is reality. How much of your eighth grade first aid class do you remember now? Wish you'd studied this chapter a little more closely, eh?

The difficulty of this self rescue depends on the victim's

1.

GriGri

Klemheist

2.

3.

disability, the experience of the rescuer, the availability of extra slings and biners, and the other complexities of the situation. Fortunately, this risky rescue is rarely performed. Again, a conservative partner and route selection may have avoided this situation. Was the leader aware of the rock quality and actively testing the holds? Were better gear placements available? Was the rack ample for the job? Was the pitch beyond the leader?

If you find yourself facing such a serious rescue, you'll need good judgment, along with most of the tools in the self-rescue toolbox, to pull it off. Hopefully you've rehearsed this scenario; otherwise, buen suerte, amigo. If you have this one down, you can pull off almost any rescue.

The key is to stay calm. If you can, lower the leader to previously placed pro and have them clip in. If lowering the leader isn't possible, have them build a back-up anchor. In any case, take a couple of minutes to plan the rescue, ensuring

Hauling your partner made easy.

Quick and dirty partner hauling.

Bachman knot ratchet

Klemheist

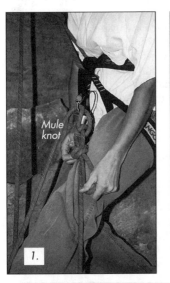

Mule knot

1.

2.

3.

your own safety every step of the way. In order to do this, you must A) Escape the belay; B) Ascend the rope to the victim; C) Shore up the high anchors; D) Stabilize the victim and perform first aid; E) Descend the rope to free it from the belay anchors; F) Reascend the rope to the victim; and F) Descend with the victim. Make sure you communicate with the victim throughout the process to let him know you've got things under control.

You must have absolute faith in the top anchors to pull this one off. If the high pro pulls while you're ascending to the rescue, the result could be disastrous for you and the victim. At least you know the top anchor held the fall (unless your leader is laying on a ledge). If the leader is capable of setting backup anchors, have him do so. You may also choose to lower the leader as far as possible before initiating the rescue, to minimize the distance you have to ascend to reach him.

Remember, this is a very involved rescue. You will have to deviate from this recipe and improvise as your situation demands. Also, you can't simply browse through these pages and fully understand the techniques involved. You have to work it out, with ropes, cordelettes, slings, carabiners, and a great deal of patience. Better yet, work through it with a qualified guide, then teach your friends so you have it down.

If you have decided the top anchors are reasonable, and that you have the technical skills to pull off the rescue, and that no safer form of rescue is available, you must do the following:

A: Escape the Belay

1. This leader has seen better days.

2. First, free your hands by tying a Mule knot on your belay device.

3. Adjust the anchors so they will withstand both an upward and downward pull. Tie a loop in one end of your cordelette and rig a Klemheist on the climbing rope above the belay device. Secure the cordelette to the anchors with a Munter Mule.

4. Release the Mule knot on your belay device, and ease the victim's weight onto the cordelette, making sure the Klemheist bites.

5. Keep your brake hand on the rope to back up the Klemheist, or wrap the break side of the rope four times around your leg to backup the victim. Attach the rope to the upward anchors with a Munter hitch on a locking carabiner, or two carabiners with gates opposed.

6. Remove the rope from your leg, cinch the Munter hitch tight, and tie it off with a Mule knot backed up by an Overhand. Dismantle the belay device. Untie the Mule knot in the cordelette, and ease the victim's weight onto the Munter Mule you just tied to the anchors.

B: Ascend the Rope

7. Collect all the slings, cord, and carabiners you can. Rig two friction knots for ascending the rope, and attach them to your harness.

8. Tie a foot loop in the lower cordelette and ascend the rope to the victim.

C: Shore Up the Anchors.

9. Now you face a crucial decision: Should you first back up the top anchors, or attend to the victim. In this case you choose to back up the anchors first.

The situation dictates where to set the backup anchors. If possible, set the new anchors near the victim. If backup anchors are not available near the victim, you must set them above. If the top anchor is close, shore it up. Otherwise, set the backups wherever you can.

D: Stabilize Victim and Perform First Aid

10. To the best of your ability, assess and stabilize the victim's injuries. Improvise a chest harness for him, and attach it with a Klemheist to the climbing rope, adjusted so it holds his torso upright.

11. Anchor the victim with a Klemheist on his rope, and a Munter Mule to the backup anchors. If you're shy on web-

Escaping the belay.

4.

Munter hitch

5.

Munter Mule

6.

7.

8.

Ascending the rope.

bing and cord, you can cut the cordelette you just used to tie the victim's chest harness to the climbing rope.

12. Backup your rope with a Klemheist on a sling clipped to the anchors. In this picture, it would be better if the rope were also clipped through the backup anchor, either directly through the locking carabiner, or with a quickdraw.

E: Descend to the Belay

13. Now you need to descend back to the original belay anchors to free the rope. If the rope is still weighted tight against the belay anchors by the victim, you may have to descend by reversing the Bachman knots down the rope.

14. Or: if you can get some slack in the line by jockeying the victim's weight around, you may be able to rappel back to the belay. Keep the upper Bachman knot (from ascending the rope) rigged as your rappel backup.

Shore up the anchors.

new backup anchors

9.

15. At the belay, rerig your friction knots to ascend the rope, and hang from them. Retie into your original end of the rope. Tie a backup figure eight in the rope a couple of feet below the Bachman knots and clip it to your harness with a locking carabiner. Now untie the Munter-Mule from the belay anchors to free the climbing rope.

16. Reascend the rope to the backup anchors.

OPTION: You can avoid steps 13 through 16, descending to the belay and reascending to the victim, and save time, by untying the Munter-Mule from the original belay anchors after you begin to ascend the rope the first time (step 8). This completely frees the rope from the belay anchors, increasing the danger of the rescue by forcing you to rely completely on the anchors above the fallen leader. After step 10, where you administer first aid and rig a chest harness for the victim, reascend to the backup anchors (if they are above the victim).

OPTION: If the leader is climbing with double ropes, and both ropes are clipped to the key lead protection, you could leave one rope tied off at the belay, and free the other rope for descending with the victim. This way you can avoid descending to the belay and reascending to the victim.

F: Descending with the Victim

If the backup anchor matrix is below the top anchor that the leader fell on:

17. Clip yourself to the anchor matrix. Backup the victim and dismantle your ascending system.

18. Untie from your side of the rope and pull the rope down through the high anchor. You'll have to abandon this anchor. Get used to it, because this rescue is going to cost you gear.

19. Tie the end of the rope into the victim.

If the backup anchor matrix is at the top anchor, you can skip steps 17 through 19.

20. Set the rope so it runs from the victim's tie-in, up to the

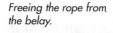

Freeing the rope from the belay.

16. 17. *sling to anchor the rescuer* *sling to back up victim to rescuer* 18. 19. *figure eight tie-in*

Descending with the victim.

backup anchor matrix, then down to your rappel device. Rig an Autoblock on the rope below the rappel device and clip it to your leg loop, to increase friction, and so you can free your hands at will.

To counterbalance the victim, tighten the rope between your rappel device and the victim, unclip your tie-in sling from the anchors, and let the Autoblock lock onto the rope to hold your weight. If you have a Gri-Gri, use it to rappel, negating the need for the Autoblock. Double check everything.

21. Slowly release the Munter-Mule connecting the victim to the anchors, and disconnect the cordelette from the backup anchors.

22. Tie this same cordelette into your harness with a Munter Mule to pull the victim down with you as you rappel. Triple check everything.

Now the rope between you runs through the anchor matrix, with the victim tied into one end of the rope, and you hanging from your rappel device, counterbalancing the victim. Rappel. With this system, you cannot rappel more than half a rope length at a time. You can only reach the original belay if you gained enough slack by pulling the rope down from the top anchors to lower backup anchors. If you can't reach the original belay, establish a new rappel anchor while you still have at least six feet of free rope remaining. (In step 19, you tied the free end of the rope to the victim, eliminating the possibility of rappelling off the end of the rope. If you haven't done this, do it now.)

rappel device

Autoblock rappel backup

20.

23. If the victim is incapacitated, flop him on your back, piggyback style. You may have to adjust the Klemheist to the victim to position him properly.

24. At the next rappel anchors (which you may have to establish), you may continue down counterbalance rappelling, but if you have far to go, and especially if you have two ropes, you should switch to the Spider rappel. To continue counterbalance rappelling:

Lock off the Autoblock or Klemheist rappel backup to free

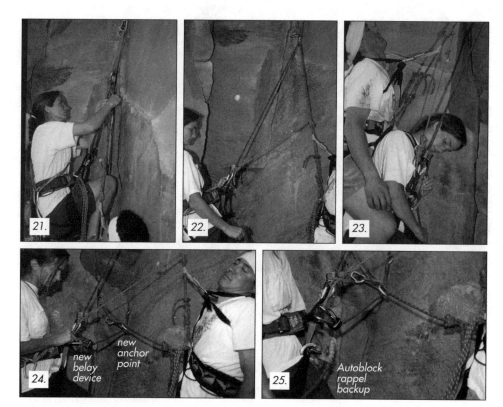

21.

22.

23.

24. *new belay device* *new anchor point*

25. *Autoblock rappel backup*

your hands. Clip the fresh end of rope, pre-tied into the victim's harness, through the new anchors. Take the victim's rappel device, rig the new rope through the device, and connect it to your harness to counter balance the victim on the new anchors.

More descending with the victim.

25. Rig an Autoblock or Klemheist below the new rappel device to backup your brake hand, and clip it to your leg loop.

26. Double check the new rigging. Untie the Klemheists above the victim on the original rope end, and reset them on the new rope.

27. Ease your weight from the original rappel device to the one you just rigged, allowing the Autoblock to hold your weight. Now dismantle the original rappel device, untie the victim's original tie-in knot, and pull the rope down through the top anchors.

28. Tie the new free end of rope into the victim, and rappel again.

Repeat steps 24 to 28 to reach the ground, or until you transfer to a Spider rappel. You'll have to abandon all the gear in each of your anchor clusters, so hopefully you have enough equipment to get down.

OPTION: If the second is injured below the belay, and hanging on the rope, proceed as if you're rescuing the leader, but use the friction knots to descend the rope to your victim. This

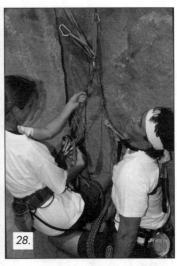

Klemheists

26. 27. 28.

More descending with the victim.

situation is actually simpler than a leader rescue, and safer, because you have a toprope. If you have mastered the leader rescue, you should be able to figure this one out.

It would be a good exercise to work it out, too, because self rescue requires thinking on your feet, not memorizing step-by-step rope tricks.

SPIDER RAPPEL

You want to make full-length rappels with a victim, or novice partner, and keep them by your side. The spider rappel was made for you. Ideally the victim is opposite the rescuer's brake hand.

1. Rig a rappel device on the rope(s). Fold a cordelette in half and tie it off double-stranded as shown, with and a short tail and long tail coming down from a loop clipped to the rappel device. Tie a figure-eight loop at the bottom of each tail. Slings can also be rigged for the same effect—the idea is to have one short tail and one long tail coming off the belay device.

2. Clip the shorter tail to your harness, and the longer tail to the victim's (or novice's) harness, with locking biners. The stagger allows you and the victim to hang at different levels, so you're not in each other's lap during the descent. Rig a backup Autoblock or Klemheist on the rope(s) below your belay device for safety and to increase the friction in your rappel system.

Now you're ready to rappel. You must control the rappel for both you and the victim. You may need to rig a disabled victim to ride on your back. Be very careful not to let the rappel line(s) run across the cordelette, lest you burn through it.

Transition from Leader Rescue to Spider Rappel

You just rescued your fallen, incapacitated leader with a counterbalance rappel. You have twelve rappels to go, so a Spider rappel will be much faster (though hardly fast) than counterbalance rappelling, and require less abandoned hardware, because you can make full length rappels with two ropes.

Beginning after step 23 of rescuing the leader, page 211:

3. Arriving at the next rappel anchor point in counterbalance rappel mode, lock off the Autoblock or Klemheist backup to free your hands. Arrange the anchors to suit your needs, and rig a cordelette or slings for a Spider rappel (step 1 above). Clip yourself and the victim to the legs of the cordelette, and secure the upper loop of the cordelette to the new anchors with a Munter Mule or Mariner's knot on a separate cord or sling.

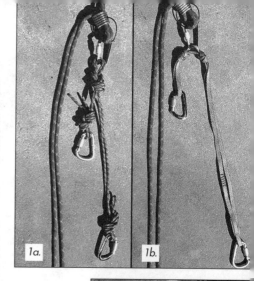

1a.   1b.

4. Clip a backup sling from your harness to the anchors. Because the victim is tied to you through the cordelette, this sling backs them up as well. Remove the Klemheists from the the victim's rope, and clip his chest harness to the upper loop of the cordelette to support his torso. Double check everything.

5. Loosen the Autoblock and ease your weight onto the new anchors. Untie the victim from the rope and pull the rope down through the top anchors.

6. If you have an extra rope, tie both ropes together, and rig them through the anchors you're hanging on for the next rappel. If you only have one rope, set the middle of your rope at the new anchors for the next rappel.

Put your rappel device on the newly rigged rappel rope(s) and clip it to the upper loop of the cordellette. Add an Autoblock or Klemheist backup, and double check every-

rappel device

double strand figure eight knots

Autoblock rappel backup

2.

Munter Mule

3.

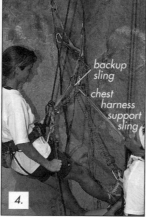

backup sling

chest harness support sling

4.

5.

rappel device

Autoblock rappel backup

6.

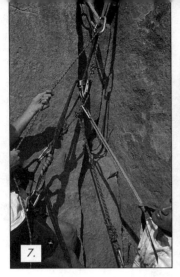

thing.

7. Carefully release the Munter Mule or Mariner's knot attaching you to the anchors, and ease your weight onto the new rappel line until the Autoblock grabs the rope to hold your weight.

8. Now rappel.

PASSING A KNOT

You're two pitches up, time is of the essence for your victim, and the quickest way down now is to lower her two rope lengths to the ground, in one shot. To do this, tie the ropes together, stack them neatly, lower the victim down a rope length, pass the knot around the belay device, and then lower her down a second rope length.

You better be sure the ropes reach the ground. Otherwise, you've seriously compounded your difficulties, as your victim dangles mid-air, three-hundred-thirty feet below you. Also, make sure it's a clean lower, without sharp edges and obstacles to snag the knot and jam or damage the rope. If not, stick to the Spider rappel.

When Lowering

Before beginning, tie the victim into one end of the ropes, tie the ropes together, and tie the other free end of the rope into the anchors. Carefully stack the ropes, with the victim's end on top. Rig the victim's rope in the belay device, attached directly to the anchors.

1. Tie a loop in one end of the cordelette and set a Klemheist on the rope between the device and the victim. Tie the cordelette off tight to the anchors with a Munter Mule backed up by an Overhand knot. Double check everything, then lower the victim.

The Klemheist serves as a backup to the belay device, and adds friction, but you must manage it as you lower the victim or it will lock the rope up, so set the Klemheist within easy reach.

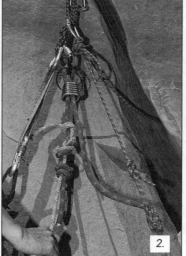

1.

2.

3.

Option: if a cordelette isn't available, attach a long sling to the rope with a Klemheist, and to the anchors with a Mariner's knot.

Passing a knot when lowering.

2. When the knot joining the ropes is about twelve inches from jamming in the belay device, allow the Klemheist back-up to lock up and hold the victim.

3. Rig a second belay device (your partner's) or a Munter hitch on the top side of the knot.

4. Add a Klemheist backup on the brake side of this new device, and clip the backup to your waist. Pull slack through the belay device and Klemheist so the belay device is next to the knot. Double check everything again.

5. Dismantle the first belay device, then untie the Munter Mule on the cordelette, and carefully lower the climber on the cordelette until the new belay device, on the top side of the knot, grabs her weight.

6. Untie the original Klemheist and retrieve the cordelette.

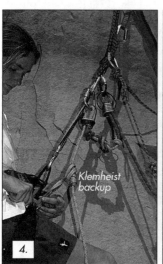

4.

5.

6.

Finish lowering the victim to the ground.

Double check each step of the way. If you bungle a single step in this process, the victim's weight will jam the knot into the belay device. If this happens (and it does), you can use a Block and Tackle (described shortly) to reverse the problem.

Once the victim reaches the ground, if she can untie from the ropes, you can make standard rappels and retrieve your ropes. A quicker way down, if you can abandon the ropes, is to make a double-length, single-strand rappel, passing the knot on the way down. A cordelette is a boon here.

Another situation where you might need to rappel past a knot is if your rope has been damaged, say by rockfall, or a leader fall. In this case you can isolate the damaged spot inside a figure eight or butterfly knot. Now you'll have to rappel past the knot, but it beats the terror of rappelling on a rope cut halfway through.

Passing a Knot on Rappel

Passing a knot on rappel is similar to passing a knot when lowering. Always make sure there's a knot in the lower end of the bottom rope, eliminating the chance of rappelling off the lower end after you pass the knot.

With Ample Gear

1. Rig your rappel device on the rope. Tie a loop into one end of a cordelette and set a Klemheist on the rope six inches above your rappel device. Fasten the cordelette to your harness by tying it into a locking carabiner with a Munter-Mule knot, backed up by an Overhand knot. This will be your rappel backup on the way down. Make sure the Klemheist is tied close enough so it could never extend beyond your reach. Double check everything, and rappel, managing the Klemheist with your guide hand so it will slide down the rope.

2. When the knot you have to pass is about a foot below your rappel device, let the Klemheist backup lock onto the rope, holding your weight. Pull a little slack through your rappel device to make sure the Klemheist grips well.

Klemheist

Munter Mule

1.

3. Set a second rappel device or Munter hitch on the new rope to be rappelled, just below the knot. Rig an Autoblock just below the new belay device.

4. Double check everything, then dismantle the original rappel device. Release the Mule knot on the cordelette and slowly ease your weight onto the new rappel device, until the Autoblock locks to hold your weight. Make sure the Autoblock is locked firmly onto the lower rope so you cannot slip.

5. Dismantle the Klemheist on the upper rope, and retrieve the cordelette. Proceed rappelling.

With Minimal Gear

1. Attach a double length sling or two slings girth-hitched together to the rope just above your rappel device. Attach the slings to your harness with a Mariner's knot on a locking carabiner. Rappel.

2. Let the Klemheist lock onto the rope so it holds your weight

3.

new rappel device

Autoblock backup

4.

5.

when your rappel device is about a foot above the knot.

3. Tie a figure eight in the new rope two feet below the knot, and clip it into your harness. This is your backup. Double check it.

4. Dismantle your rappel device and reset it just below the knot. Double check everything.

5. Untie the backup figure eight, and tie a Mule knot, backed up by an Overhand, on your rappel device. Make sure the rappel device is set close to the knot joining the ropes.

6. Release the Mariner's knot and ease your weight onto the tied-off rappel device. If your sling is short, you may have to drop onto the rappel device, or grab the rope and lower yourself until the belay device catches you.

7. Remove the Klemheist from above the knot (if you can). Reset it below the knot if you have another knot to pass, or if you want to continue backing up the rappel. Untie the Mule knot on your rappel device,

8. and continue rappelling.

Passing a knot on rappel with ample gear.

Passing a knot on rappel with minimal gear.

Klemheist

Mariner's knot

1.

2.

backup figure eight knot

3.

4.

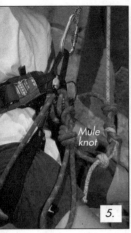

BLOCK AND TACKLE

Everyone makes mistakes, and the day's just not going your way. You were trying to lower the victim two rope lengths, but the knot jammed in the belay device before you saw it coming. The victim is hanging in space, and cannot unweight the rope for you. Clearly, this is a job for the block and tackle. More attentiveness could have prevented this extra step, though.

For short hauls, and fixing mistakes by the rescuer, such as unweighting a jammed Garda knot, a block and tackle can be a lifesaver. You need a cordelette (or a long piece of unsewn webbing) for this rope trick, which breaks down like this:

1. The knot fastening two ropes is jammed in the belay device.

2. Tie a loop in one end of the cordelette, and wrap a Klemheist on the climbing rope below the belay device.

3. Wind the free end of the cordelette back and forth (several times) between a carabiner on the Klemheist and a carabiner on the anchors. Each wrap secures more mechanical advantage.

4. Pull on the free end of the cordelette to make a short haul and free the jammed rope. Tie the cordelette off with a Mule knot backed up by an Overhand to hold the load.

5. Now, if you want to pass the knot, tie a backup figure eight in the rope three feet up from the knot and clip it into the anchors.

6. Take the rope out of the belay device, and rerig the device on the other side of the knot. Tie the belay device off with a Mule knot backed up by an Overhand.

7. Release the Mule knot on the cordelette, and ease slack into the block and tackle until the tied-off belay device holds the victim's weight.

8. Remove the cordelette from the rope.

9. Release the Mule knot on the rope and resume lowering.

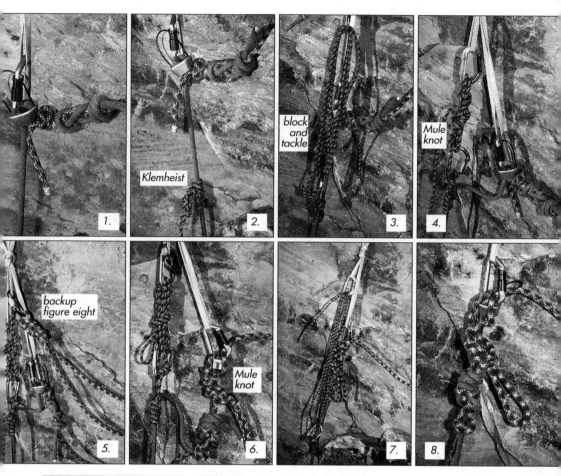

EVACUATING THE VICTIM

You've got your victim to the ground, but it's two rugged miles to the trailhead. If the victim is critically injured, try to summon a rescue team or helicopter to carry the victim.

If the injuries are not critical, or if no other option exists, a single rescuer can carry a victim (on the ground) "piggyback" style by converting the rope into a Tragsitz, which creates shoulder straps for the rescuer and leg loops for the victim. Hopefully the victim is not a former linebacker.

To make a Tragsitz:

1. Coil the rope in a large mountaineer's coil, and tie it off with twenty feet (or so) of free rope coming out of the coil. Note: Practice to find the right coil diameter for your physical size.

2. Twist the coil into an "eight," then put one arm though each loop of the eight, with the cross on your back.

3. Place the victim's legs through the loops. The last twenty feet of rope lashes the victim to your back.

In a slightly better world, you're at a popular crag and a bunch of climbers have gathered to help you evacuate the vic-

tim. You redress and resplint the victim's wounds, improving the job you did on the wall. Now improvise a litter using a climbing rope, packs, and jackets. Six rescuers at a time can share the load of carrying the victim down the trail. Ideally you'll send a runner (or better, two) down the trail to call 911 and summon an ambulance to meet you at the trailhead. A rope litter is not rigid like a backboard or Stoke's litter. Do not use it if you suspect spinal injuries.

1. Lay the rope back and forth on the ground as shown.

2. Run the remaining rope (as shown) in the shape of an enlarged body.

3. Pad the rope strands with foam from a pack, with clothes, or whatever you can find.

4. Lay the victim on the pad. Starting from her feet, daisy chain the rope back and forth across the top of the victim, up to the shoulders, and tie the rope off.

5. Ideally, you'll have six people to carry this litter, using the rope for handles. Frequently check the victim to be sure the litter does not impede circulation to her arms or feet.

As a final note, before launching any rescue, take a few moments to calm yourself, and plan the entire operation from beginning to end, to avoid missteps and maximize efficiency. Pre-planning is everything. Once you commit to a plan of action, changing systems is extremely time-consuming and often dangerous.

By taking that extra minute to consider likely options, you're apt to choose the best one.

CONCLUSION

There are various manuals on rescue techniques, some credible, some rather outdated. Few are shorter than War and Peace, or less confounding than Einstein's Theory of Relativity. The best of the books, and the most current for modern rock climbers, is *Self-Rescue*, a book also in this *How to Rock Climb* series, and written by David Fasulo. A common error in many rescues, and one I have seen demonstrated countless times, is the tendency of some rescue personnel to

Making a Tragsitz.

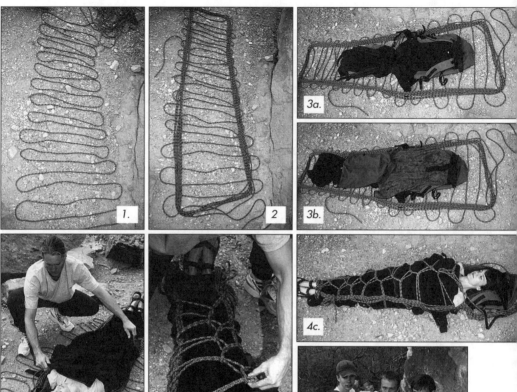

needlessly complicate the systems involved. This is a critical mistake, since all rescues should be measured by efficiency, and efficiency results from doing things the easiest, most straightforward way. While the preceding information on self rescue is by no means a stand-alone treatise on the subject, the key elements have been covered and explained with efficiency in mind. In short, the preceding techniques are the simplest ways of dealing with very complex situations, where lives might hang in the balance, and every minute counts.

But while these systems have been simplified to essentials, they are nonetheless complicated. Even a twenty-year veteran needs ample practice to proficiently execute the methods when the rain is drilling down and her partner's femur is sticking out of his britches. No matter how thoroughly you understand the theory of these systems, you must practice them to have any chance of efficiently pulling them off when it counts. Be prepared in advance, and always keep your guard up to avoid accidents.

Rope litter

Index